Jan Saunders'
WARDROBE QUICK-FIXES

Jan Saunders'

WARDROBE QUICK-FIXES

Krause Publications

Iola, Wisconsin

Published in Iola, Wisconsin 54990, by Krause Publications

Designed by Ayers/Johanek Publication Design, Inc.
Illustrations by Annette Cable
Technical Drawings by Pamela Poole

Manufactured in the United States of America

Library of Congress Cataloging in Publication Data

Saunders, Janice S.
    [Wardrobe quick-fixes]
    Jan Saunders' wardrobe quick-fixes.
        p.   cm. — (Star Wear)
    Includes index.
    ISBN 0-8019-8391-6 (pbk.)
    1. Clothing and dress—Alteration.   2. Clothing and dress—
Repairing.   3. Machine sewing.   4. Serging.   I. Title.   II Title:
Wardrobe quick-fixes.   III. Series: Star Wear series.
TT550.S28 1995
646.4—dc20   94-23786
                                                      CIP

    4 5 6 7 8 9 0   4 3 2 1 0 9 8

OTHER BOOKS AVAILABLE FROM KRAUSE

Contemporary Quilting

Appliqué the Ann Boyce Way

Barbara Johannah's Crystal Piecing

The Complete Book of Machine Quilting, second edition, by Robbie and Tony Fanning

Contemporary Quilting Techniques, by Pat Cairns

Fast Patch, by Anita Hallock

Fourteen Easy Baby Quilts, by Margaret Dittman

Machine-Quilted Jackets, Vests, and Coats, by Nancy Moore

Pictorial Quilts, by Carolyn Vosburg Hall

Precision Pieced Quilts Using the Foundation Method, by Jane Hall and Dixie Haywood

Quick-Quilted Home Decor with Your Bernina, by Jackie Dodson

Quick-Quilted Home Decor with Your Sewing Machine, by Jackie Dodson

The Quilter's Guide to Rotary Cutting, by Donna Poster

Quilts by the Slice, by Beckie Olson

Scrap Quilts Using Fast Patch, by Anita Hallock

Speed-Cut Quilts, by Donna Poster

Stitch 'n' Quilt, by Kathleen Eaton

Super Simple Quilts, by Kathleen Eaton

Teach Yourself Machine Piecing and Quilting, by Debra Wagner

Three-Dimensional Appliqué, by Jodie Davis

Three-Dimensional Pieced Quilts, by Jodie Davis

Craft Kaleidoscope

Creating and Crafting Dolls, by Eloise Piper and Mary Dilligan

Fabric Painting Made Easy, by Nancy Ward

How to Make Cloth Books for Children, by Anne Pellowski

Jane Asher's Costume Book

Quick and Easy Ways with Ribbon, by Ceci Johnson

Learn Bearmaking, by Judi Maddigan

Shirley Botsford's Daddy's Ties

Soft Toys for Babies, by Judi Maddigan

Stamping Made Easy, by Nancy Ward

Too Hot To Handle? Potholders and How to Make Them, by Doris L. Hoover

Creative Machine Arts

ABCs of Serging, by Tammy Young and Lori Bottom

The Button Lover's Book, by Marilyn Green

Claire Shaeffer's Fabric Sewing Guide

The Complete Book of Machine Embroidery, by Robbie and Tony Fanning

Creative Nurseries Illustrated, by Debra Terry and Juli Plooster

Distinctive Serger Gifts and Crafts, by Naomi Baker and Tammy Young

The Fabric Lover's Scrapbook, by Margaret Dittman

Friendship Quilts by Hand and Machine, by Carolyn Vosburg Hall

Gail Brown's All-New Instant Interiors

Gifts Galore, by Jane Warnick and Jackie Dodson

Hold It! How to Sew Bags, Totes, Duffels, Pouches, and More, by Nancy Restuccia

How to Make Soft Jewelry, by Jackie Dodson

Innovative Serging, by Gail Brown and Tammy Young

Innovative Sewing, by Gail Brown and Tammy Young

The New Creative Serging Illustrated, by Pati Palmer, Gail Brown, and Sue Green

Owner's Guide to Sewing Machines, Sergers, and Knitting Machines, by Gale Grigg Hazen

Petite Pizzazz, by Barb Griffin

Putting on the Glitz, by Sandra L. Hatch and Ann Boyce

Quick Napkin Creations, by Gail Brown

Second Stitches: Recycle as You Sew, by Susan Parker

Serge a Simple Project, by Tammy Young and Naomi Baker

Sew Any Patch Pocket, by Claire Shaeffer

Sew Any Set-In Pocket, by Claire Shaeffer

Sew Sensational Gifts, by Naomi Baker and Tammy Young

Sew, Serge, Press, by Jan Saunders

Sewing and Collecting Vintage Fashions, by Eileen MacIntosh

Simply Serge Any Fabric, by Naomi Baker and Tammy Young

Singer Instructions for Art Embroidery and Lace Work

Soft Gardens: Make Flowers with Your Sewing Machine, by Yvonne Perez-Collins

The Stretch & Sew Guide to Sewing on Knits, by Ann Person

Twenty Easy Machine-Made Rugs, by Jackie Dodson

Know Your Sewing Machine Series, by Jackie Dodson

Know Your Bernina, second edition

Know Your Brother, with Jane Warnick

Know Your Elna, with Carol Ahles

Know Your New Home, with Judi Cull and Vicki Lyn Hastings

Know Your Pfaff, with Audrey Griese

Know Your Sewing Machine

Know Your Singer

Know Your Viking, with Jan Saunders

Know Your White, with Jan Saunders

Know Your Serger Series, by Tammy Young and Naomi Baker

Know Your baby lock

Know Your Pfaff Hobbylock

Know Your Serger

Know Your White Superlock

Star Wear

Embellishments, by Linda Fry Kenzle

Make It Your Own, by Lori Bottom and Ronda Chaney

Sweatshirts with Style, by Mary Mulari

Teach Yourself to Sew Better, by Jan Saunders

A Step-by-Step Guide to Your Bernina

A Step-by-Step Guide to Your New Home Sewing Machine

A Step-by-Step Guide to Your Sewing Machine

Contents

Acknowledgments

Many heartfelt thanks to:

- my wonderfully supportive husband, Ted Maresh, and my son, Todd Moser, for their understanding and resourcefulness around my deadlines—I promise no more pizza for at least another month;

- Robbie Fanning for coming up with this idea and having the confidence in me to carry it out;

- Gail Brown for her continuous input, interest, constructive assistance, and belief in this project;

- Jackie Dodson for her honest opinions, encouragement, and patience as I finish this book;

- the talented artists in this book, Annette Cable and Pamela Poole;

- all those friends and colleagues who contributed ideas which helped me to shape and organize this book; and

- the home sewing industry at large for giving me the inspiration and a forum in which I love to make my living.

The following trademark terms and brand names appear in this book:

Aleene's OK-to-Wash-It	Fly Front Zipper Guide	Rit Fabric Whitener & Brightener
Aleene's Tack-It Over & Over	Fray Check	Scotchgard
Axion	French Fuse	Stainguard
Band-Aid	Fusi-Knit	Stainmaster
Beacon Chemical Company's Fabri Tak	HeatnBond	Stitch 'n Stretch
	Hem-N-Trim	Stitch 'n Tear
Biz	Hump Jumper	Stitch Witchery
Bond's 527	It Stays!	Stop Fraying
Clo-Chalk	Ivory	Straight-Tape
Clotilde's Sticky Stuff	Jean-A-Ma-Jig	Sulky Iron-on Transfer Pens
Collin's Unique Stitch	Jones Tones	Tear-Away
Color It Gone Stain Remover Kit	Jurgen's Jewel & Fabric Glue	Teflon
Create-A-Zipper	K2r	Thermo-Web
Disappearing Ink Marking Pen	Knit Fixer	Top Job
Do-Sew pattern tracing material	Knit Fuze	Trans-Web
Drawstring Restringer	Liquid Fabric Mender	Transparent Nylon Mono-filament thread
Dritz Insta Tack	Lux	
Dritz Liquid Stitch	Magic American Chemical's Fabric Mender Magic	Tulip Fabric Paint
Dritz Transfer Crayons		Ultraleather
Dylon Double Duty	No-Fray	Washington Millinery's Bridal Glue
Dylon Run Away	Plaid's Glu-N-Wash	Wink
Easy-Knit	Plaid's Stickit Again & Again	Wisk
Easy-Stitch	Plexi 400 Stretch Adhesive	Wonder-Under
Emergency Shirt Buttons	Polident	Woolite
Era Plus	Quilter's Cut 'n Press	Woolly Nylon
EZ Fabric Glue	Rainbow Thread Braid	Zipper Pull Repair Kit
EZY hem gauge	Res-Q Tabs	Zipper Rescue Kit
Fabric Fading Kit	Res-Q Tape	Zipper Safety Hook
Faultless' Bead Easy Re-Apply Adhesive	Rit Color Remover	Zippers By The Yard

Foreword

Somehow, way back when, I became passive about modern life. My store-bought pants were too tight? My sewing machine was at an inconvenient height? Oh, I wish it weren't so. These shoulder pads make me look like a linebacker? Sigh.

Once the computer in our office froze up. Several of us gathered around it, whining, fussing. "It's broken, it's broken. What shall we do?" Another woman came over, sat in front of the machine, and began banging all the keys like a nine year old. The computer unfroze. We all burst out laughing.

I am laboriously trying to cultivate the habit of banging keys when my brain freezes. Jan Saunders' new book is helping. No longer do I have to put up with inconvenience or discomfort. Too tight? Loosen it, silly. Too plain? Decorate it. Broken? Fix it.

While Jan gives in-depth details for sew-ers and non-sew-ers alike, what she really conveys is something more valuable—an attitude of taking charge. This applies to computers and clothes and sewing machines and everything else.

Robbie Fanning
Series Editor

Preface

Do you have a closet full of "bloopers" and "misfits"? You know—those clothes you made or bought, then later realized just weren't right?

- Do you have a skirt that you bought at a "super-steal" price that doesn't go with anything else in your closet?

- If you knew a goof-proof method of replacing the zipper on your favorite pair of jeans, wouldn't you be wearing them instead of shopping for new?

- If you could get a little more room in the waistband, wouldn't you wear those stylish wool gabardine trousers more often?

- How about that 100% cotton shirt that goes to the bottom of your laundry basket every week because you hate to iron?

- Have your clothing needs changed from corporate power suits to comfy sweats (or vice versa)?

- Is there a dress in the back of your closet that you aren't wearing because of those awful buttons?

If any of these questions sound familiar, then your wardrobe may be in need of some Quick-Fixing. I offer this book in the hope that it will spark your imagination and motivate you to restyle, alter, repair, and embellish your misfits, thereby transforming them into active members of your working wardrobe. You may even have fun in the process. Then, once your existing wardrobe is refurbished, you can learn tips on caring for your clothes and shopping with savvy to help you avoid future bloopers.

If you are an occasional sew-er or are trying sewing for the first time, I hope these Quick-Fix ideas produce immediate results and help you to gain the confidence to go on and try something else. Each chapter contains no-sew, easy-to-sew, and speed-sewing shortcuts for professional results, as well as quick and practical serging applications. Use the handy Skill-Level Index on page 159 to locate techniques you'll feel comfortable with.

When I began the project, I sent every Tom, Dick, and Sherry I know a questionnaire asking what, if anything, they had done to improve items in their wardrobes. Rather than write a comprehensive "How-To" book on altering and repairing clothing, I wanted to provide a fun conversation among people who actually sew (some more, some less) or at least wear the clothing in question. The results are the shortcuts, questions, project ideas, pet peeves, and alteration suggestions that appear throughout the book, like this one:

"I have changed a jacket from double- to single-breasted so it fit my hips!"

Linda Turner Griepentrog
Editor, *Sew News* magazine
Peoria, IL

The original title of this book was *Improving Ready-to-Wear,* so many of the ideas people offered were based on this concept.

> *"Improving ready-to-wear means two things to me:*
> *1) making off-the-rack clothes fit like custom-made and*
> *2) embellishing ready-mades to look like designer wear."*

Ruth Holt
District Manager, Dannemann Fabrics
Wilmington, DE

> *"I'm sure you remember that the only way I was ever*
> *able to improve ready-to-wear was to remove the price tag*
> *and put it on! Maybe take it to the dressmaker for minor*
> *adjustments to the hem or sleeves."*

Bertha Gold
College Professor
Cleveland, OH

Of course, all of the ideas in this book will work on clothes you've made yourself as well as those you've bought "off the rack." In Part I, Quick-Fix Alterations, Improvements, and Goof-Proof Repairs, you'll learn how to modify a garment that's too short, too long, too tight, too loose, doesn't wear well, or isn't quite flattering, as well as how to do basic mending and repair work. Part II covers how to upgrade your wardrobe by buying smart in the first place, caring for what you've bought or made, and embellishing your basics for a designer touch. Part III, Jan's Quick-Fix Sewing and Serging Guide, along with the reference charts and glossary in the back of the book, should give you the information you need to put the many ideas in this book into practice.

The next time you sit down to the dreaded repair pile, go shopping for yourself or your family, or need something new when your budget won't allow it, look in the Table of Contents to see if there's a better, more efficient, or creative way to tackle the project. Think of *Wardrobe Quick-Fixes* as a quick reference and an idea book—a helpful gift for kids living away from home for the first time and an important addition to any sew-er's library.

I think all of us would like to see better quality in the clothes we wear—even if we have to do it ourselves. I'm hoping that the techniques in this book will make your *Wardrobe Quick-Fixes* a snap.

Part I

Quick-Fix Alterations, Improvements, and Goof-Proof Repairs

With a few basic tools and my time-saving sewing techniques (found in Part III, Jan's Quick-Fix Sewing and Serging Guide), just about anyone can alter, improve, and repair their clothing with dramatic results.

In Part I, see how to fix almost anything. Learn, for example, what do if it's too long (chapter 1)...too short (chapter 2)...too tight (with some suggestions for how to dress thinner without dieting; chapter 3)...or too loose (chapter 4). Read how to add durability, warmth, and figure-flattering comfort in chapter 5 in less time than it takes to shop for new.

Has your repair pile surpassed the dirty laundry pile? Chapter 6, "Quick-Fix Repairs," describes basic sewing, speed-sewing, and goof-proof no-sewing techniques to cut it down to size, and many of these repairs can be done while you're watching TV. Now, let's turn those rejects relegated to the back of your closet into working members of your wardrobe.

If it's too long...

Shorten Slacks and Shorts

Hemming or rehemming a garment is probably the quickest fix and the most common way to improve the look and fit of a garment. Master the following hemming basics for shorts and slacks; then go beyond the basics to improve the fit, look, and proportion of anything from a too-long sleeve to a skirt with a kick-back pleat.

...by Tapering the Hem Allowance Before You Hem

If the pant leg you are hemming is tapered in or belled, the hem needs to conform to the shape it is being turned up into. To make it work:

1 Let down the existing hem, noting the old hem allowance (it should be 1½–2" [4–5cm]).

2 Measure and mark the new hem as described on page 130.

3 For tapered pants, rip out the inseam and outseam up to the new hem fold. Then restitch the seams, tapering from the new hem fold *out* to what will be the new finished edge, as shown in Figure 1.2. This is an important step, especially if the hem is lower at the heel, because you need more fabric in the hem allowance to go the extra distance. For belled pants, taper the stitching in so that when the hem allowance is folded, it will fit neatly into the bell of the pants.

Figure 1.1 Cut off pants to a cropped length and rehem them.

"I have improved ready-to-wear pants by cutting them to a cropped length and rehemming them (Fig. 1.1)."

Linda Turner Griepentrog
Editor, *Sew News* magazine
Peoria, IL

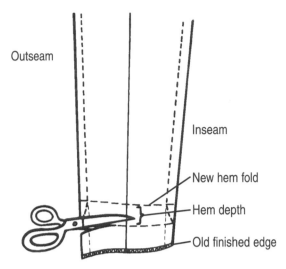

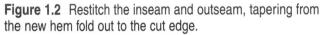

Outseam

Inseam

New hem fold

Hem depth

Old finished edge

Figure 1.2 Restitch the inseam and outseam, tapering from the new hem fold out to the cut edge.

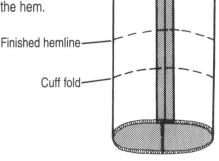

Stitch in-the-ditch to secure cuffs

Figure 1.3 Stitch cuffs vertically in-the-ditch at the seamlines to keep them from falling down.

4 Finish the raw edge (see Reference Chart A) and hem.

...by Adding Straight Turn-Back Cuffs

Turn-back cuffs can be added to a pair of slacks or be used to shorten a sleeve. Cuffs can also be used to shorten children's clothing because they can be let down without much difficulty and without an obvious old hemline showing. If you buy a garment intending to let the cuffs down eventually, choose a pant or sleeve style that is fairly straight, not tapered or belled. This way the cuff will not have to be cut and shaped to fit the taper (see Fig. 1.2).

For the quickest cuff, simply fold up most of the hem allowance on a sleeve or pant leg to create the cuff. Then stitch the cuffs vertically in-the-ditch at the seamlines to keep them from falling down (Fig. 1.3).

If you need to take up more fabric than the existing allowance provides, you will need to create a hem allowance that is double the width of the desired cuff plus 1¼" (3cm).

1 To finish the cuff, overcast the raw edge as shown in Fig. 1.4a (see Reference Chart A).

2 Fuse, blindhem, or topstitch the hem as explained on pages 131-134 (Fig. 1.4b).

3 Press the cuff up in place. To prevent it from drooping, stitch in-the-ditch at the inseam and out-seam (see Fig. 1.3). On a sleeve, stitch in-the-ditch at the underarm seam and stitch a couple of hand catch-stitches just under the cuff edge, attaching the cuff to the sleeve (Fig. 1.4c).

Figure 1.4 You will need double the width of the cuff plus 1¼" (3cm) for the hem allowance. Overcast or serge-finish the raw edge. Fuse, blindhem, or topstitch the hem.

Finished hemline

Cuff fold

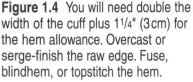

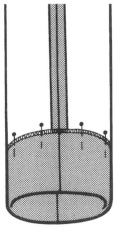

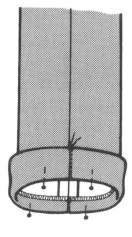

a

b

c

...by Shortening the Crotch Depth

If your slacks or shorts are too long in the crotch, rather than shortening them from the waistband, try this.

NOTE — *Comfortable-fitting slacks or shorts have a crotch that is ½-1" (1.3-2.5cm) lower than the body.*

Unless you have thin thighs, your goal here is to shorten the crotch, leaving the leg size intact. To do this, turn your slacks or shorts inside out and sew the inner leg seams deeper into the crotch area. Start 7" (18cm) down the inseam, then gradually taper the seam up into the crotch, taking out ⅛" (3mm) from the inner leg seam to the crotch intersect. Repeat for the other side. Try the slacks on and sit in them to be sure they are comfortable before trimming out the excess (Fig. 1.5). If you need to take up the crotch even more, take another ⅛" (3mm), and so on, until you have removed enough for the slacks to be comfortable; then trim out the excess seam allowance.

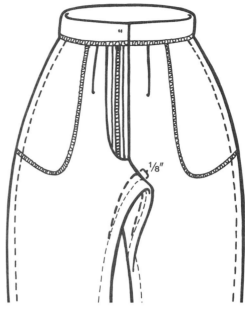

Figure 1.5 Stitch a deeper inner-leg seam to shorten the crotch. Start 7" below the crotch intersection, then taper the seam up to a comfortable depth. Repeat for the other side.

Shorten Shirt and Jacket Sleeves

The following ideas are Quick-Fix solutions for overlong jacket and shirt sleeves. For more traditional and time-consuming solutions, you may prefer working with a dressmaker (see pages 116-117). Or, review the Slacks and Shorts section earlier in this chapter. Most of the techniques explained there can also be used on sleeves.

"I nearly always have to shorten the sleeves on long-sleeved tops and jackets. What are some innovative ways to do this?"

Susan Wisinski
Owner, WisinCulin Design
LaHonda, CA

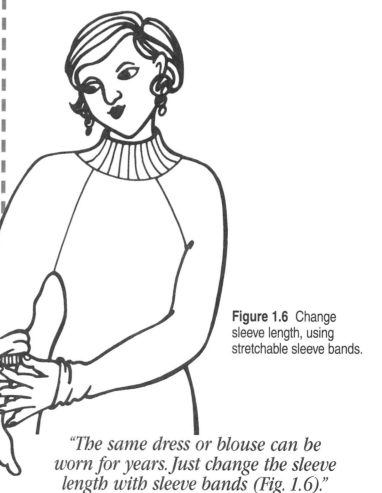

Figure 1.6 Change sleeve length, using stretchable sleeve bands.

...by Adding Sleeve Bands

Sleeve bands are metal springlike circles that fit snugly around your forearm without strangling. If your sleeves are too long, simply put your hand and forearm through the band, then pull it over the sleeve. Position them about 4" (10cm) above the hem of the sleeve; then using your other hand, pull your sleeve up from above the band. The band keeps your sleeves up out of the way.

"The same dress or blouse can be worn for years. Just change the sleeve length with sleeve bands (Fig. 1.6)."

Jan Ward Healzer
Repcon International
Nixa, MO

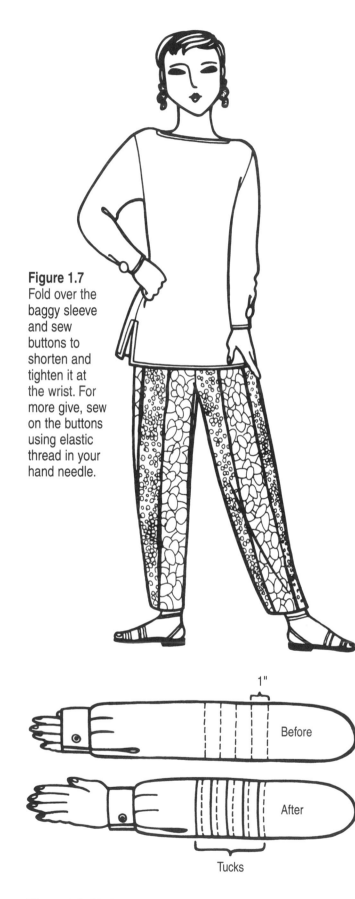

Figure 1.7
Fold over the baggy sleeve and sew buttons to shorten and tighten it at the wrist. For more give, sew on the buttons using elastic thread in your hand needle.

Figure 1.8 Mark straight lines at 1" (2.5cm) intervals, and stitch 1/4" (6mm) tucks to shorten a sleeve.

...by Making Quick-Fix Button-Over Sleeves

A quick and effective way I have tapered and shortened a sleeve was simply to fold over the fullness and stitch a button or two to hold the fold in place (Fig. 1.7). The opening is usually small enough to get your hand through yet secure enough to drape neatly at your wrist. However, if you need more give, stitch the buttons on by hand using elastic thread.

...by Taking It Up with Tucks

"I recently picked up a man's silk shirt on sale. The size was right but the sleeves were too long. I carefully marked straight lines at 1" (2.5cm) intervals above the sleeve placket (Fig. 1.8). I folded 1/4" (6mm) tucks on the lines marked, and stitched. It took about five rows to shorten the sleeve enough, but it looks very feminine now, and it fits."

Cheryl Sparks
Artist
Indianapolis, IN

Adding tucks is an innovative way of taking up excess sleeve length that is fast, easy, and decorative. For the straightest tucks:

Machine Readiness Checklist
> **stitch:** straight
> **foot:** standard zigzag, blindhem, or edgestitch
> **stitch length:** 2.5-3 (10-12 stitches per inch)
> **stitch width:** 0
> **needle:** appropriate for the fabric (see Reference Charts B and C)
> **thread:** multipurpose and matching color to the fabric
> **accessories:** quilting bar

Measure, mark, pin, and press the width of the tuck desired. Remember when figuring a tuck width that the fabric taken up by a tuck is double the width of the tuck. For example, a 1/2" (1.3cm) tuck will take up 1" (2.5cm). On heavier fabrics, tucks take up slightly more than double because the fabric must bend and fold over a wider distance.

For narrow tucks, use your blindhem or edgestitch foot and near or far left needle position. Fold the fabric, place the fold against the guide in the foot, and edgestitch (Fig. 1.9). For deeper tucks, adjust your quilting bar out to the right the distance needed, and stitch, guiding the quilting bar along the fold of the tuck (Fig. 1.10).

NOTE FROM JAN— *Throughout the book you will see steps in many techniques that can be done either on a sewing machine or a serger. To help you make the choice, read the Sew-Easy Tips (instructions for the sewing machine) or Serge-Easy Tips (instructions for the serger), then decide.*

...by Making Cuff "Dickies"

Don't want to shorten jacket sleeves with a vent, placket, and buttons? Fold the sleeve up to a comfortable length; then, to disguise the hem and lining that is turned up, make interchangeable solid or print "dickies" that stick to coat or jacket sleeves, creating colorful turn-back cuffs.

Machine Readiness Checklist

stitch: straight
foot: standard zigzag (if using a synthetic suede or leather, use a Teflon foot)
stitch length: 2.5-3 (10-12 stitches per inch)
stitch width: 0
accessories: Velcro dots or pressure-sensitive adhesive

1 Measure for cuff circumference:

Circumference of the jacket sleeve: _____
Add 1/2"-11/4" (1.3-3cm) for seam allowances
[2 × 1/4" (6mm) = 1/2" (1.3cm);
2 × 5/8" (1.5cm) = 11/4" (3cm)]:   +_____
The result equals cuff circumference: =_____

2 Measure for cuff depth (Fig. 1.12):

Turn up the sleeve (lining side out) the desired amount and measure this depth: _____
Add 21/2" (6.5cm) for cuff extension and hem fold: +_____
The result equals cuff depth: =_____

Cuff circumference plus seam allowances

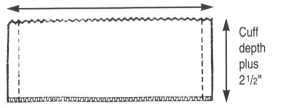
Cuff depth plus 21/2"

Figure 1.12 Measure for cuff dickie circumference and depth.

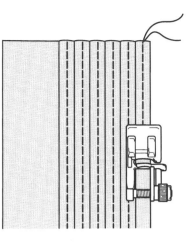

Figure 1.9 Stitch narrow tucks using the blindhem or edgestitch foot and the center or far left needle position. (Reprinted with permission from *A Step-by-Step Guide to Your New Home Sewing Machine* by Jan Saunders [Radnor, PA: Chilton, 1992].)

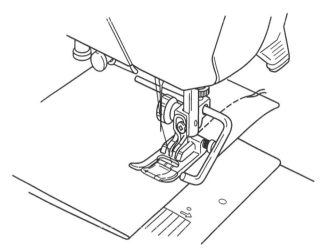

Figure 1.10 Stitch deeper tucks, guiding the fold along the quilting bar.

Serge-Easy Tip

For a decorative tuck, use pearl cotton, pearl rayon, ribbon floss, or other decorative thread in your upper looper. Set your stitch for a wide balanced 3-thread overlock and a short stitch length (see Reference Chart A). Tucks will take double the width of the stitch (Fig. 1.11).

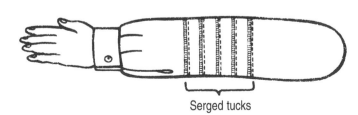
Serged tucks

Figure 1.11 Serge tucks, using decorative thread in the upper looper, a wide width, and a short stitch length.

Figure 1.13 For interchangeable cuff dickies, stitch the hook-side Velcro dots equidistant around the top of the cuffs, and the loop side dots equidistant around the inside of the jacket sleeves.

Cuff dickie

Figure 1.14 The hint of color adds a fashion detail as the sleeve is shortened in the process.

Hook-and-loop fastener

3 Cut two lengths of fabric the appropriate dimensions.

4 Serge-finish (see the following tip) or overcast (see Reference Chart A) one long side of each cuff dickie. Pink the other long sides of the strips. If you have not rolled the hem or decorated it with a serging stitch, press under a ⅝" (1.5cm) hem along the overcast edge; topstitch ½" (1.3cm) from the fold.

Serge-Easy Tip: *Instead of turning a hem, finish the dickie edge that will show by serging a rolled hem or use a decorative thread in the upper looper and a short stitch length for a decorative edge finish.*

5 To make interchangeable dickies, follow steps 6 and 7. For permanent dickies, skip ahead to step 8.

6 Attach two to four of the hook-side Velcro dots equidistant along the pinked edge (Fig. 1.13). If you haven't serged the other edge, topstitch or blind-hem it.

Quick-Fix Tip: *An even faster way to attach your cuff dickies is to use liquid pressure-sensitive adhesive. This adhesive is the type used on "sticky notes," so the cuffs stick temporarily and peel off for storage. Store with waxed paper against the adhesive side of the cuffs (see page 77).*

7 Attach the loop side of the Velcro to the inside of the sleeve so the hook and loop sides of the dickies match. Stick on the cuff dickie and turn up the jacket sleeve. The hint of color adds a fashion detail, and the sleeve is shortened in the process (Fig. 1.14).

8 If you want only one set of cuff dickies, rather than attaching them to the sleeve with hook and loop fasteners, stitch in-the-ditch at the undersleeve seam using clear nylon monofilament as the top and bobbin threads (see Fig. 1.3).

Sew How: *For more ideas on synthetic suede cuffs and matching interchangeable accessories, see pages 80-81.*

...by Adding Elastic Shirring

For a narrow sleeve, shorten and add an elegant treatment with a little bit of elastic thread shirring.

1 Wind a bobbin with elastic thread by putting the bobbin on your bobbin winder, stepping on the foot pedal, letting the bobbin winder turn, and guiding the elastic thread by hand. Do not stretch it. If you have a self-winding bobbin, wind the elastic thread on the bobbin by hand without stretching it.

2 From the hem edge, measure up the sleeve about 5-6" (12.5-15cm) and mark that point with a pin.

3 Using all-purpose thread as your top thread and elastic thread in your bobbin, sew a row of straight stitches on the right side of the sleeve, up to the pin and back (Fig. 1.15). (You may need to open the sleeve seam a bit to get up into the sleeve.) Pull threads to the wrong side and securely tie them off. For added security, put a drop of liquid seam sealant (Fray Check, Stop Fraying, or No-Fray) on the knots.

...by Moving the Cuffs

Here's how to shorten a sleeve from the cuff.

1 Decide how much you need to shorten the sleeve. With a seam ripper, carefully rip out the stitches that hold the cuff to the shirt sleeve (Fig. 1.16a and b). Pin the cuff back onto the sleeve so the finished edge of the cuff is in the desired position. Mark along the top of the cuff to establish the new cuff position.

2 Unpin the cuff and cut off the excess sleeve fabric, leaving a 1/2-5/8" (1.3-1.5cm) seam allowance below the cuff placement marks (Fig. 1.16c).

3 Regather or take a deeper pleat in the sleeve so the fullness fits back into the cuff. Pin the cuff into position. (The placket will end up a bit shorter, but there should still be enough room for your hand to fit through the cuff before buttoning it.)

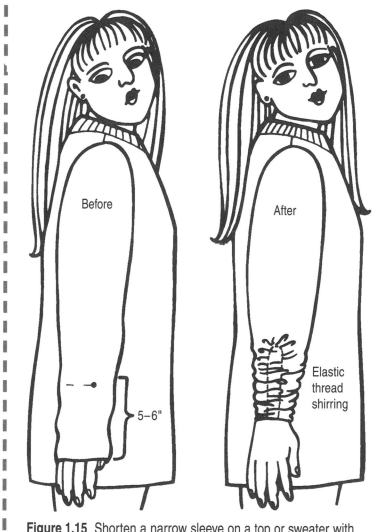

Figure 1.15 Shorten a narrow sleeve on a top or sweater with elastic thread shirring.

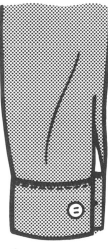

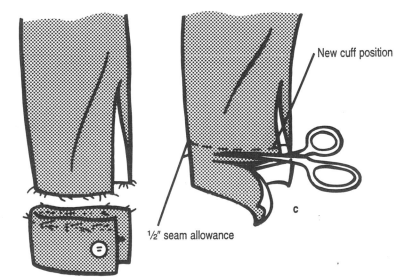

Figure 1.16 Mark along the top of the cuff to establish the new cuff position, using a water-erasable or disappearing marker.

Figure 1.17 Trim away excess, leaving a $1/2$–$5/8$" (1.3cm–1.5cm) seam allowance. Fit sleeve fullness back into cuff. Restitch, using the same thread color and stitch length as before.

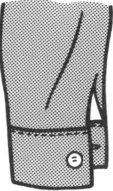

Restitch

Figure 1.18 Pull up and stitch a tuck inside the sleeve above the cuff.

Quick-Fix Tuck
If a sleeve needs to be shortened $3/4$" (2cm) or less and does not have a lot of fullness at the cuff, pull up and stitch in a tuck on the inside of the sleeve just above the cuff (Fig.1.18).

Tuck

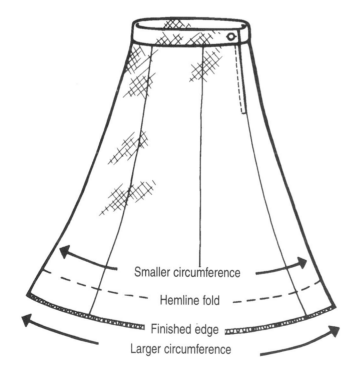

Smaller circumference

Hemline fold

Finished edge

Larger circumference

Figure 1.19 On a flared skirt, the circumference at the hemline fold is smaller than at the finished hem edge, so the hem allowance must be eased into shape before stitching.

4 Using the same thread color and stitch length as was originally used on the cuff, topstitch the cuff back into place (Fig. 1.17).

Shorten Skirts

To shorten a dirndl, flared, or straight skirt (without a kick pleat), review the hemming information on pages 129-132. Then follow these easy instructions.

...by Hemming a Flared Skirt

On a skirt with a lot of flare (4- or 8-gore, for example), the circumference at the hemline fold is smaller than the circumference at the finished edge before the skirt is hemmed (Fig. 1.19). For a smooth, professional hem, the hem allowance must be eased in and shaped before stitching. This technique is called "ease-plusing."

For a narrow flair, overcast or serge-finish the hem edge; then press it up the desired amount by steaming the hem into shape.

Machine Readiness Checklist

stitch: straight
foot: standard zigzag (lightweight fabrics); transparent embroidery (midweight to heavy fabrics)
stitch length: 2-3 (10-12 stitches per inch)
stitch width: 0
upper tension: tighten slightly

1 Finish the raw hem edge (see Reference Chart A).

Sew-Easy Tip: Overcast the hem edge with a 3-step zigzag stitch (see Reference Chart A). Then, reset your machine for a straight stitch and slightly tighten the upper tension.

Serge-Easy Tip: Serge-finish the hem edge with a 3-thread overlock and a slightly tightened needle tension (see Reference Chart A). If you have a differential feed, increase it to 1.75 to 2 and stitch. The increased needle tension and differential feed both ease in the hem edge automatically. If you don't have differential feed, complete steps 2 and 3.

2 On your sewing machine, position the presser foot so the needle stitches $1/4$" (6mm) from the edge. On the serger, overcast the edge so the knife is barely

trimming and the stitches form over the raw edge. Place your index finger firmly on the fabric behind the foot and sew.

3 While sewing or serging, let the fabric bunch and pile up behind the foot, holding it as long as you can. Release it, reposition your finger, and continue in this way (stitch, hold, release) around the hem edge (Fig. 1.20). This eases the hem edge so it will shape easily into the body of the skirt.

4 Pin up the hem, placing pins perpendicular to and ¼" (3mm) from the finished edge. On the wrong side of the fabric, steam press the hem allowance, shaping it into the body of the garment without pressing over the pins. Finish your hem by using one of the techniques found on pages 131-132.

Time Saver: A great tool for hem shaping is the EZY hem gauge—just fold the hem up, and steam press to shape it (Fig. 1.21). After shaping the hem, pin it by placing pins perpendicular to and ¼" (6mm) from the finished edge.

...by Taking Up a Flared Skirt from the Waistline

"Can I shorten a flared skirt that is too long and too tight in the waistline and hips?"

Bernice Saunders
Retired (and my mom)
Columbus, OH

"I bought a beautiful gored skirt on sale for $10 that was quite long but narrow in the hips. So I shortened it from the waistband instead of from the bottom. I cut off the amount I wanted to shorten, leaving room for the elastic. I serged on the elastic, folded it over, stitched it down, and was done in about a half hour. By shortening this skirt from the top, I got the extra room in the hips I needed. If you don't have enough fabric to turn down for a casing, add a facing using bias hem tape (Figs. 1.22-1.26)."

Diana Bade
Executive secretary, Kwik-Sew Pattern Company
Minneapolis, MN

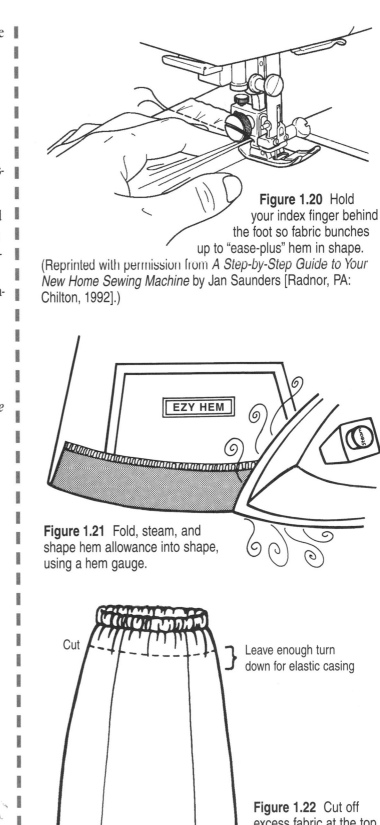

Figure 1.20 Hold your index finger behind the foot so fabric bunches up to "ease-plus" hem in shape.
(Reprinted with permission from *A Step-by-Step Guide to Your New Home Sewing Machine* by Jan Saunders [Radnor, PA: Chilton, 1992].)

Figure 1.21 Fold, steam, and shape hem allowance into shape, using a hem gauge.

Cut

Leave enough turn down for elastic casing

Figure 1.22 Cut off excess fabric at the top of the skirt, leaving the width of the elastic plus ⅝" (1.5cm) to turn down for the casing.

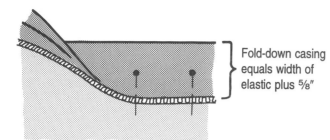

Figure 1.23 Serge-finish the raw edge. To sew in a new piece of elastic, first fold down the casing the width of the elastic plus ⁵/₈" (1.5cm), pin, and press.

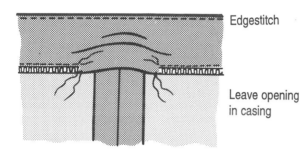

Figure 1.24 Edgestitch ¹/₈" (3mm) from the fold, and stitch around the bottom of the casing, leaving room to pull elastic through.

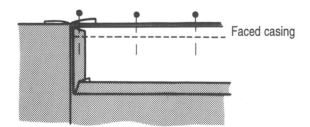

Figure 1.25 For a faced casing put right sides together and stitch on wide bias tape using ¹/₄" (6mm) seam allowances.

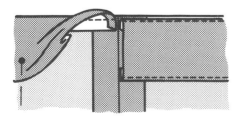

Figure 1.26 Turn facing to wrong side and press. Stitch lower edge of facing to the skirt to create the casing. Leave room to pull elastic through.

...by Hemming a Pleated Skirt

To hem a pleated skirt, prepare and use the appropriate hemming techniques for the fabric found on pages 131-132. Then, after the hem is stitched, edgestitch the inside of the seamed pleat the width of the hem (Fig. 1.27; see also Fig. 1.9) (see also pages 134-135). This makes the pleat crisper and gives it more "staying power."

...by Hemming a Skirt with a Kick Pleat

"I would like instructions for shortening skirts with a back kick pleat."

Karen Bennett
Director of consumer affairs, Big Bear Stores Co.
Columbus, OH

1 Let down the hem, removing the original stitching on both the skirt and lining. Remember to notice how the hem at the kick pleat was originally folded and stitched (I often draw a sketch and take notes). You may have to rip some stitches that hold the lining in place so that both the lining and skirt are hanging free of each other.

2 Measure, mark, and pin up the hem of the fashion fabric. Measure, mark, and pin up the lining hem so it hangs 1" (2.5cm) shorter than the hem fold of the fashion fabric. Trim off the excess of both the fashion fabric and lining so that you have a finished hem depth of 2" (5cm). Do not trim away any bulk from inside the kick pleat.

3 Blindhem (see page 132) the skirt and skirt lining hems separately. Refold the kick pleat as before and topstitch (Fig. 1.28).

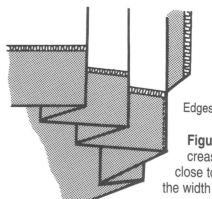

Figure 1.27 Keep a pleat creased by edgestitching close to the fold or seamline the width of the hem allowance.

Serge-Easy Tip: *If after you have loosened the lining, you cannot get it back into the kick pleat, rip enough stitches so the lining is hanging free. Then, measure, mark, and cut the lining off so that when the skirt hem is turned up, the lining hangs 1" (2.5cm) shorter than the skirt hem. Trim the lining in a curve as shown so the top of the curve ends up just above the top of the kick pleat (Fig. 1.29). Then serge-finish the raw edge and curve.*

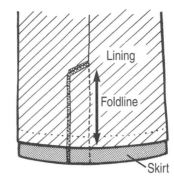 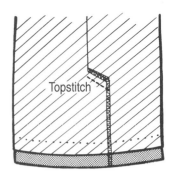

Figure 1.28 Fold the pleat and hem over themselves, incorporating the lining in the pleat.

Shorten Kids' Clothes

All of the techniques discussed in this chapter can be used on kids' clothes, but here are some ideas that make these smaller projects even easier.

...by Making a Quick-Fix Hem

"Children's pants or sleeves have such a small circumference that temporary stitching is sufficient and easy to rip out when things need to be lengthened. Thread your sewing machine with nylon monofilament thread, top and bobbin (I like the fine-as-hair size .04 type best). Fold up the hem the desired amount and stitch in-the-ditch at each seamline."

Gail Brown
Author; Sewing and serging expert
Hoquiam, WA

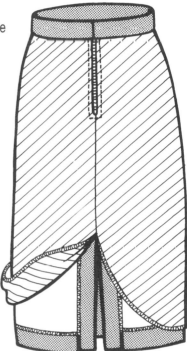

Figure 1.29 Trim the lining so the top of the curve ends just above the kick pleat.

Figure 1.30 Turn hem up and stitch in-the-ditch at inseams and outseams; roll up a too-long serged hem; add tucks above the hem; or knot spaghetti straps to shorten children's clothing.

Shortened straps

Shortening tucks

Stitch in-the-ditch

Serged and turned up

...by Using Other "Short" Cuts

If Gail's Quick-Fix hem will not work for whatever you are shortening because the circumference is too large or the clothing is worn a lot and needs to be secured better, try one of these "short" cuts (Fig. 1.30).

DOUBLE-ROLL THE HEM

On most lightweight fabrics, double-roll the hem, then carefully hand hem as described on page 132. If double-rolling makes the garment too short, first let down the original hem; then double-roll and hand hem.

TAKE A TUCK ABOVE THE HEM

If you need somewhat less than a doubled hem, stitch large tucks above the hem (see Figs. 1.8–1.11).

SERGE-FINISH IT AND ROLL A CUFF

For pants and overalls without a stitched-and-turned hem (such as a jeans hem), let the hem down, serge-finish the edge (if it hasn't been done already), then roll up a cuff the required amount.

KNOT A SPAGHETTI STRAP

To shorten spaghetti straps without sewing, tie a knot on the top of each strap.

> **Sew How:** *For more innovative ideas from Gail Brown, see the listing of her sewing, serging, and home-dec titles listed in the front of this book.*

If it's too 2 short...

"What is the best way to remove the line when hems are lowered?"

Carol McGuire
Publisher, *American Fastener Journal*
Columbus, OH

In most cases, lengthening a garment involves letting down the hem. Use my Quick-Fix "Solution" to get rid of the mark left by the hemline, or consider decorating over the line (see "Decorate It" later in this chapter).

Quick-Fix "Solution"—*Mix equal parts of white vinegar and water and spray it on a press cloth. Place the dampened cloth on the wrong side of the fabric over the crease and press. Remove the iron, let the steam escape, then press until the area is dry. On some fabrics I have had better results using the white vinegar at full strength. Always test the solution on a seam allowance to be sure the fabric will not spot or discolor.*

Lengthen It

...by Letting Down a Cuff

If you shortened children's clothing by making a cuff, lengthen pant legs or sleeves by letting down the cuffs.

1 Remove hemming stitches and press out the hems and cuffs (Fig. 2.1).

2 Straighten out the side seams. Then rehem using one of the methods on pages 131-133. For even more length, face or rib the hem as described later in this chapter.

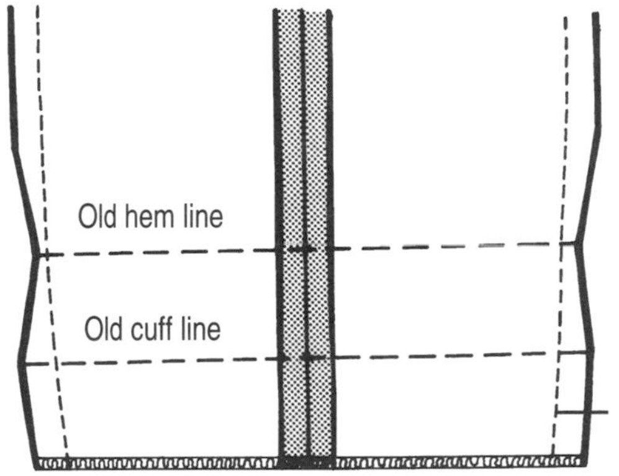

Figure 2.1
Let down the cuff, straighten out side seams, and hem for extra length.

Old hem line

Old cuff line

Restitch to straighten out the seam

Quick-Fix Lengthening
In chapter 1 we stitched a temporary hem in children's clothing using monofilament thread and stitching in-the-ditch at the inseams and outseams. To lengthen this clothing, simply rip out these stitches and let the hem down.

Bias hem tape or facing

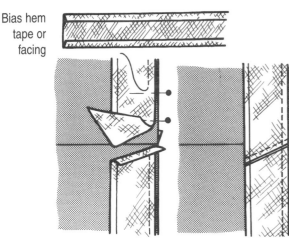

Figure 2.2 Place hem tape and fashion fabric right sides together. Stitch tape around the circumference of the hem. After steaming tape into place around the hem, cut it off and join the ends by hand or machine.

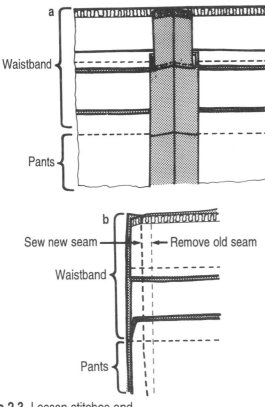

Waistband

Pants

Sew new seam → | ← Remove old seam

Waistband

Pants

Figure 2.3 Loosen stitches and flip up the waistband. Pinch the seam allowance together. Starting about 5" (12.5 cm) below the waistline seam, pin or machine baste, then restitch the center-back seam, tapering up and out to the waistline seam and straight up through the waistband. Fold the waistband down and secure it by stitching in-the-ditch at the waistline seam.

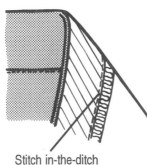

Stitch in-the-ditch

...by Adding Facing

One of the most common methods of lengthening is letting down the existing hem and facing it, adding a band of lightweight fabric to the length that is then turned under as the hem allowance.

1 Remove hemming stitches and press over the hem allowance. If there is hem tape or lace on the hem edge, either rip out the stitches that secure it to the fabric or cut it off.

2 Unfold one edge of prefolded hem facing (often called hem tape, available in your local fabric store). Place the hem tape and fashion fabric right sides together and stitch tape around the circumference of the hem so that the stitches are in the fold (Fig. 2.2).

NOTE—*Before cutting it to length, fold the faced hem up, and shape it into the garment with a steam iron. This way you don't inadvertently cut the tape too short.*

Cut the tape off as shown and join it either by hand or machine.

3 Finish the hem as described on pages 131–133.

...by Letting Out the Waistband (for an Over-40 Posterior)

"I like to lengthen my crotch seam on pants to make room for my over-40 posterior. Do you have any suggestions or shortcuts?"

Robbie Fanning
Author; Series editor, Chilton Books;
Publisher, *The Creative Machine* newsletter
Menlo Park, CA

Try this on slacks that have a center-back seam in the waistband—women's and men's tailored trousers are generally made this way. This method of letting out the waistband also lowers the crotch curve. You may also want to try this before cutting a deeper crotch curve (instructions later in this chapter).

1 Remove the center-back belt loop.

2 Remove stitches that hold the waistband in place about 3" (7.5cm) on either side of the center-back seam. Flip up the waistband, then pinch the two sides of the seam allowance together.

3 Starting about 5" (12.5cm) below the waistline seam, pin-baste the center-back seam, tapering up and out to the waistline seam, then straight up through the waistband (Fig. 2.3). Remove the original seaming and try the pants on. Has this alteration lengthened the crotch enough? Is the waistline comfortable? If the waistline is comfortable, stitch the center-back seam. If the crotch is still too short and you can't let out any more of the seam, you may have to cut a longer crotch curve (as explained below).

4 Press the seam open, fold the waistband down, and stitch in-the-ditch at the waistline seam. Restitch the belt loop in place.

...by Cutting a Longer Crotch Curve

If you have a closetful of pants that are uncomfortable because they pull up in the front or back, take 10 minutes and lower the crotch. For a comfortable fit, the crotch should fall between ¹/2–1" (1.3-2.5cm) below your body. Here's how to make this simple alteration.

1 Turn the pants inside out and put one leg inside the other.

2 Slip the pants over the narrow end of your ironing board for easy marking. At the crotch point (where all the seams come together), make a mark ¹/4" (6mm) lower than the original seamline on the leg (Fig. 2.4).

3 Measure 3-4" (7.5 - 10cm) up from either side of the new crotch point as shown in Figure 2.4. Pin-mark or use a fabric marker to draw the new crotch curve.

4 With a basting-length stitch, restitch the crotch curve on the altered line, trim the seam allowance to about ⁵/8" (1.5cm), and try them on. Do they feel better? If the pants are still not as comfortable as you would like, restitch the crotch curve down another ¹/4" (6mm), making the seamline lower than before (see Fig. 2.4). Trim the seam again and try them on. Repeat this step, measuring down ¹/4" (6mm) at a time until the pants are comfortable.

5 Restitch the new crotch curve, using a short stitch length. Most important, for fit and comfort trim the seam allowance to ¹/4" (6mm) and overcast it together using the 3-step zigzag or by serge-finishing (see Reference Chart A).

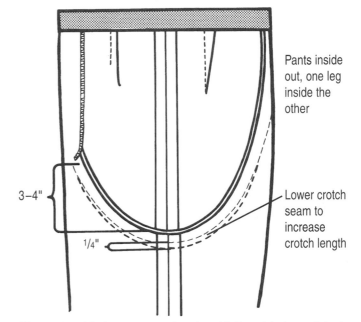

Pants inside out, one leg inside the other

3–4"

¹/4"

Lower crotch seam to increase crotch length

Figure 2.4 Mark a new crotch point ¹/4" (6mm) below original crotch point. Taper new crotch seam from 3–4" (7.5 cm–10cm) above and on either side of the crotch point.

"To get more room in the seat of my favorite jeans, I sew one of the back pockets closed and cut out the fabric behind the pocket. Then, I cut the crotch seam open in both directions and insert a gusset made from the pocket fabric by stitching over the original topstitching."

Mary Carollo
New Home sewing machines
Elmhurst, IL

Figure 2.5 Lower the waistline by sewing rows of elastic-thread shirring below the original waistline.

Add elastic shirring

"I have 'lengthened' elastic waistbands by sewing rows of elastic below the purchased one, thus making the waistline lower (Fig. 2.5). I have also solved this problem by buying separates."

Betty Farrell
Author; Executive, Brewer Sewing Supplies
Chicago, IL

Quick-Fix Marking Method

"To duplicate the crotch curve on my favorite pair of slacks to a too-short-in-the-crotch pair, I turn the pair to be altered inside out and slip one leg into the other. Next, I turn my comfy pants inside out the same way, and slide the pair to be altered inside the comfy pair, carefully matching the waistline seams. Then I slide both pairs over the ironing board so the crotch intersections are on top of each other and are positioned on top of the board for easy marking (the crotch curves won't match). Mark the comfy crotch curve onto the pair to be altered, pushing pins through the seamline, then marking with chalk. I baste the new crotch seam and try the pants on, walk around, and sit in them before trimming out the excess seam allowance. This doesn't work every time, but it's a good starting point and I have a closetful of comfortable pants this way."

Jan Nunn
Sewing instructor; Professional dressmaker
Portland, OR

...by Adding Elastic (to "Lower" a Too-High Waistline)

"I must be long-waisted because one-piece dresses hit me above my waist. Any ideas?"

Cathie Moore
Administrative assistant (and mother of two)
Louisville, KY

Quick-Fix Cover-up—*I have the same problem and have used a wide elastic belt to cover up the too-short waistline.*

Try Betty Farrell's idea (sewing in rows of elastic), or, rather than sewing additional casings below the original line of elastic, try sewing rows of elastic thread shirring.

Machine Readiness Checklist

stitch: straight
stitch length: 3-4 (6-9 stitches per inch)
stitch width: 0
foot: embroidery
upper tension: tighten slightly, then test the shirring on a fabric similar to your garment

1 Decide how much lower the waistline needs to be by trying on the dress and tying a strip of ¼" (6mm) elastic around your waist. Move around and let the elastic settle around your natural waistline. This will be where the center row of shirring will be.

2 Have a friend or spouse mark the waistline along the top edge of the secured elastic using a water-erasable or disappearing marker. Wind a bobbin of elastic thread (see pages 8-9) and place it in your machine through normal bobbin tension.

Sew-Easy Tip: I have the best luck with elastic thread with a high cotton fiber content, available through your local sewing machine dealer.

3 Use all-purpose thread as your top thread and elastic thread in your bobbin and start at a side seam on the right side of the fabric. Center the presser foot over the line marked in step 2 and slowly sew around the waistline. As you sew, the fabric will shirr. When you get around to where you started, pull enough thread and elastic thread out of the machine to tie it off securely.

4 Try on the dress: Does it need an additional row of shirring? If so, repeat step 3, sewing a presser-foot's width away from and just below the first row of shirring.

...by Letting Down the Waistline Seam

Sometimes you need the waistline lowered an inch (2.5cm) or less. If the waistline seam is also the elastic casing, then:

1 Remove the stitches at the waistline seam to release the elastic. Chances are the seam allowance is serged together, too. *Do not rip out these stitches.*

2 Restitch the waistline at the edge of the serged seam allowance (Fig. 2.6). Press the seam smooth and flat.

3 Reattach elastic either by:

• Adding elastic thread shirring (instructions earlier in this chapter)

• Stitching a casing over the seamline with bias tape

• Attaching Stitch 'n Stretch elastic treatment (instructions in "Quick-Fix Elastic Shirring" in chapter 4)

• Stitching elastic at the waistline seam, if your machine or serger is able to attach elastic with an elasticator accessory (Fig. 2.7)

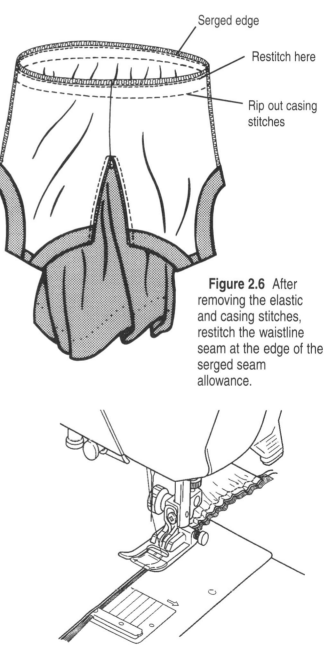

Serged edge

Restitch here

Rip out casing stitches

Figure 2.6 After removing the elastic and casing stitches, restitch the waistline seam at the edge of the serged seam allowance.

Figure 2.7 If your machine or serger has an elasticator accessory, use it to restitch the elastic at the waistline seam.

Add fagoting for
extra length

Figure 2.8 For extra length,
use fagoting trim to attach
sleeve and hem bands.

Figure 2.9 Starting
at the side seam,
thread yarn through
the guide in the foot
and stitch over the
hemline crease,
using nylon monofil-
ament thread, top
and bobbin, and a
straight or zigzag
stitch.

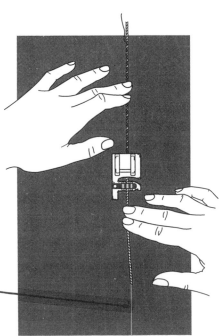

Old hem crease

Decorate It

When lengthening a garment, trims can be used as decoration to cover the crease that's left once a hem is let down or
as stylish (and lengthening) additions to the bottom edge of
the garment.

...with Fagoting

Every seven to ten years, I purge my scrap box (scrap
pile, scrap collection) and donate to the local daycare center,
my church, or the Goodwill. The following project is the reason I don't do this more often.

In the early '70s, I made a gauze dress that was too short
later on in the decade. I loved the dress and wasn't ready to
get rid of it, so I improved it by stitching fagoting trim to a
hem band made with fabric leftover from the original project.
(Fagoting joins two pieces of fabric together with stitches
that look like a ladder.) I was lucky the fabric hadn't faded.
After adding the band, it looked like I was trying to get more
wear out of the dress (which I was) but I didn't want it to
look that way, so I fagoted on sleeve bands. This dramatic
improvement resulted in several more years of stylish wear
(Fig. 2.8).

> **Sew How:** *To learn more about fagoting, read* Know
> Your Sewing Machine *by Jackie Dodson (Chilton, 1988).*

...with Decorative Stitching and Yarn Tracing

Run a row of decorative stitching over a noticeable hemline crease. Then repeat the motif somewhere else on the garment. Another easy way to disguise the hemline is to
yarn-trace over it.

Machine Readiness Checklist
stitch: straight
foot: braiding or cording
stitch length: 2.5-3 (10-12 stitches per inch)
stitch width: 0
thread: nylon monofilament, threaded top and bobbin
accessories: yarn to match or contrast with the fabric

1   Starting at the side seam, thread the yarn through
    the guide in the foot and stitch over the yarn at
the hemline crease (Fig. 2.9).

2   For more interest above the new hem edge, add
    another line of yarn, this time creating a passe-
menterie design. I saw this done on a child's dress; the

dress's suspenders were also decorated the same way (Fig. 2.10).

3 After yarn-tracing, face the hem with hem facing and blindstitch it (see page 16).

...with Ribbon, Trim, Rickrack, or Bias Tape

"Heat'n Bond iron-on adhesives allow you to improve ready-to-wear by personalizing it with appliqués, ribbon, lace, trim, plus much more."

Amy Kuypers
Daisy Kingdom
Portland, OR

1 Buy grosgrain ribbon or trim 1/4" (6mm) wide or wider.

2 Measure the length of ribbon you need and fuse a strip of paper-backed fusible web (web comes in 1/4 – 3/4" [6mm–2cm] widths) to one side of the ribbon following manufacturer's instructions.

3 Let the fused ribbon cool and remove the paper backing. Snip a few threads and open one of the side seams the width of the ribbon. Lay the ribbon, fusible side down, so that one end is through the side seam.

4 Fuse the ribbon over the hemline, moving along the length of the ribbon with your iron. At the end, slip the other free end into the side seam. Fuse, then restitch the seam, catching the ribbon ends in the seam (Fig. 2.11).

Sew-Easy Tip: *Embroider a ribbon with decorative stitching, then fuse it onto a wider ribbon for a colorful effect (Fig. 2.12).*

Sew-Easy Tip
If you plan to disguise the hemline crease after letting down a hem, remember to add the decorative "band-aid" to another part of the garment for balance and style.

Yarn tracing to disguise an old hemline crease

Figure 2.10 A passementerie design above the new hem edge is repeated on the suspenders of the dress.

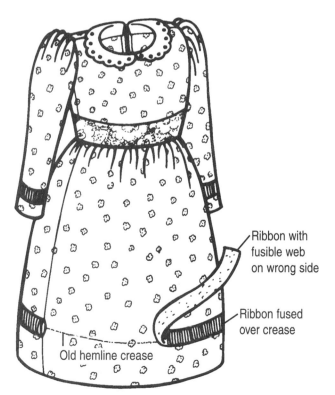

Ribbon with fusible web on wrong side

Ribbon fused over crease

Old hemline crease

Figure 2.11 Fuse ribbon over the old hemline crease, catching the free ends in the side seam.

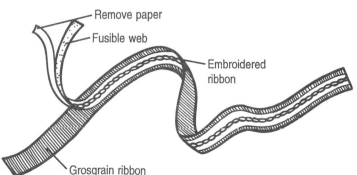

Remove paper

Fusible web

Embroidered ribbon

Grosgrain ribbon

Figure 2.12 Embroider a narrow ribbon and fuse it to a wider ribbon for more interest.

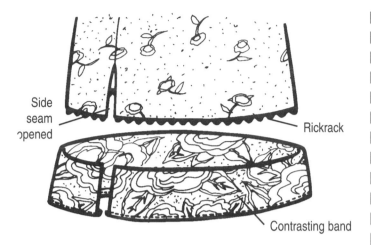

Side seam opened

Rickrack

Contrasting band

Figure 2.13 Place piping or rickrack on the fashion fabric, right sides together, and attach it around the circumference of the hem.

Penny-Saver Tip

For an ethnic look, make bands and trims from your fabric scrap collection, using scraps with the same color palate as the clothing you are improving.

Contrasting band

...with a Piped or Rickrack Band

Add piping or rickrack at the noticeable hem crease; then add a hem band for even more length.

1 Let down the existing hem and press over the crease.

2 Cut off the hem at the crease. Release a few stitches at one side seam. This is where you will start and end the piping or rickrack.

3 Place piping or rickrack on the fashion fabric, right sides together, and attach it around the circumference of the hem. (Attach rickrack by sewing down the middle of it.) The ends will be stitched into the open side seam (Fig. 2.13).

Sew-Easy Tip: When applying piping, use a piping foot (Fig. 2.14). The groove(s) on the underside guide the piping on straight for best results.

Serge-Easy Tip: For fast, accurate serged piping, use the piping or cording foot available for your serger (Fig. 2.15).

4 With right sides together, attach a matching or contrasting band the width needed for extra length plus hem allowance (Fig. 2.16). Sew the band to the piped edge so the stitched side is up and the second row of stitching is to the inside of the first. This way the first row of stitching, which attached the rickrack or piping to the hem edge, will not show on the right side of the garment.

5 Stitch up the side seam and complete the hem as described on pages 131-133.

...with a Ruffle

A quick and easy way to add length is to add a ruffle.

Machine Readiness Checklist
stitch: zigzag
foot: transparent embroidery, cording or braiding
stitch length: 1.5-2 (12-15 stitches per inch)
stitch width: 1.5 (wide enough to clear the cord)
accessories: length of pearl cotton, carpet thread, or nylon fishing line

1 Measure the hem circumference. The length of a gathered ruffle made out of a light to mid-weight fabric should be 2½ times the circumference. Cut the ruffle the appropriate length and

Top   Underside

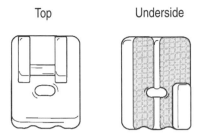

Figure 2.14 The groove(s) on the underside of the piping foot guides piping straight. (Reprinted with permission from *A Step-by-Step Guide to Your New Home Sewing Machine* by Jan Saunders [Radnor, PA: Chilton, 1992].)

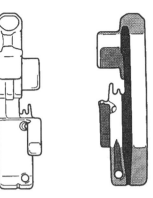

Figure 2.15 The groove on the underside of the serger piping foot guides the piping and zipper coil straight.

width desired. Open the side seam at the hem edge about 1" (2.5cm).

2 Finish one edge of the ruffle as described on page 141 (see Reference Chart A).

3 Gather the ruffle.

4 Place the cord under the foot (and through a groove or hole where appropriate) so the cord extends 2" (5cm) behind the foot.

5 Guiding ¹/₂" (1.3cm) from the unfinished edge and on the wrong side of the fabric, zigzag over the cord, being careful not to catch the cord in the stitches (Fig. 2.17).

6 Pull up gathers, adjusting fullness from both ends. Once the fabric has been gathered to the desired length, knot the cord to anchor it and prevent the gathers from pulling out.

7 Starting at the opened side seam and with right sides together, stitch the ruffle to the garment's hem edge with a row of short straight stitches. Stitch just under the zigzags made to gather the ruffle so they won't show from the right side of the fabric. Close the side seam at the hem edge through the ruffle. Machine overcast or serge-finish the seam allowances together where the ruffle was attached.

Sew How: For even faster gathering and attaching information, read Teach Yourself to Sew Better — A Step-by-Step Guide to Your Sewing Machine, *by Jan Saunders (Chilton, 1990) and* ABCs of Serging, *by Tammy Young and Lori Bottom (Chilton, 1992).*

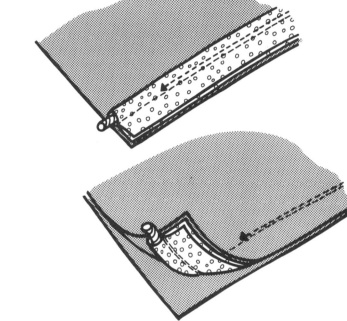

Figure 2.16 Sew the piped edge with the stitched side up and to the inside of the first row of stitching. This way the first row of stitches that attach the piping to the band won't show on the right side of the garment.

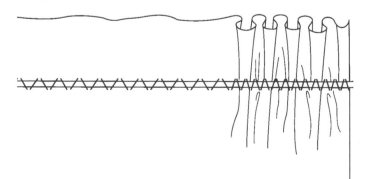

Figure 2.17 Zigzag over a cord for fast, easy, and durable gathering. (Reprinted with permission from *A Step-by-Step Guide to Your New Home Sewing Machine* by Jan Saunders [Radnor, PA: Chilton, 1992].)

Figure 2.18 Zip-on a band, extension, or ruffle.

Zip-on a ruffle

Sew How

To learn lots more about sewing with knits, read The Stretch & Sew Guide to Sewing on Knits, *by Ann Person (Chilton, 1994). You will also enjoy the great-fitting, easy-to-make Stretch & Sew patterns, available through your local fabric store. If you can't find them in your neighborhood, call this toll-free number to find out who carries them: 1-800-547-7717.*

...with a Zip-on Length

To add length to a skirt or sleeve, zip on a band, extension, or ruffle with this innovative exposed zipper application (Fig. 2.18).

1 Buy a zipper at least 2" (5cm) longer than the circumference of the piece to be lengthened. Loosen the side seam where the zipper will begin and end.

Quick-Fix Tip— Sometimes it is difficult to find a zipper long enough for this technique, so look for Zippers By The Yard or Create-A-Zipper at your local fabric retailer or order them through one of the mail-order sources listed in the back of the book.

2 Place the zipped zipper along one edge of the fashion fabric, right sides together. Align the edge of the zipper tape with the cut edge of the fabric, leaving an even amount of zipper at each end. This gets the zipper pull out of your way.

3 Using your zipper or piping foot, adjust the needle position on your sewing machine and stitch next to the coil as you would piping or cording (Fig. 2.19).

Sew-Easy Tip: Although you can use your zipper foot, the coil rides under the ridges in the piping foot for the most accurate stitching.

Serge-Easy Tip: To attach the zipper with your serger, the zipper must be at least 4" (10cm) longer than needed. Using the piping or cording foot available for your serger, apply this exposed zipper by serging on and off, slightly trimming the zipper tape and avoiding the pull and stop. The ridge in the foot rides over the zipper coil for accurate application (see Fig. 2.15).

4 Stitch the other side of the zipper to the band, extension, or ruffle, being sure the cut edge is aligned with the edge of the zipper tape and even with the first side of the zipper application.

5 Unzip the zipper slightly so that the pull is beyond the seamline. Stitch the side seam, catching the zipper tape and coil in the seam. Cut off the excess zipper tape so that it is even with the edge of the fabric. The side seam acts as the zipper stop, and the zipper coil looks like a piece of textured piping.

NOTE— *Make the zippered extension removable by using a separating zipper (Fig 2.20).*

Rib It

Ribbing can be used on both woven and knit garments, and can add extra wear to areas that have stretched out or to sleeves and pant legs that have become too short. You can even add ribbing to a turned-under neckline that you want to be higher or a cardigan that you wish were wider. Here are some simple guidelines for a trouble-free ribbing application.

"Pants are never long enough in my size. How would you correct this? Do you have any way of lengthening a sleeve?"

Jeanne Moser
Family friend; Mother of four
East Kingston, NH

...with a Single Ribbing Band

Machine Readiness Checklist

stitch: zigzag
foot: embroidery
stitch length: 4-5 (5-6 stitches per inch)
stitch width: 4
upper tension: loosen almost to 0
thread: color contrasting to garment for top thread and bobbin

1 You'll need to determine how wide and how long to cut your ribbing band before applying it. First, decide how long the band should be. Measure the circumference of the sleeve, leg, or neck opening to which the ribbing will be applied. For a cardigan, measure the length of the opening, starting at the bottom edge of the front, up and across the back neck, and then down to the other bottom front edge (remember to include the length of any ribbing you plan to add to the bottom edge of the cardigan). Once you've determined the circumference of the opening, use the Band Length Cutting Chart to measure and cut the band to the appropriate length.

Table 2.1

Band Length Cutting Chart

Opening to Measure	Band Length
Crewneck, turtleneck, sleeve cuff, leg band	2/3 the circumference of the opening
V-neck, U-neck, cardigan band	3/4 the circumference of the opening

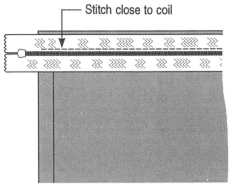

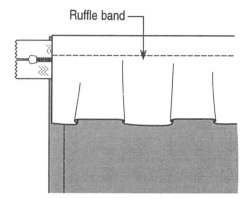

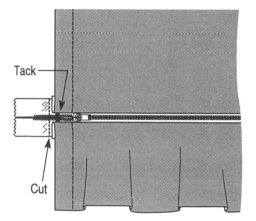

Figure 2.19 Using your zipper or piping foot, adjust your needle position and stitch next to the coil.

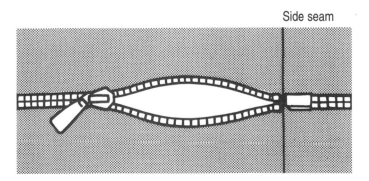

Figure 2.20 Make the zippered extension removable by using a separating zipper.

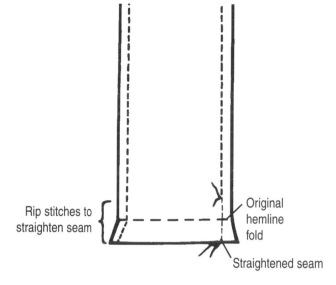

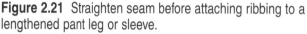

Rip stitches to straighten seam

Original hemline fold

Straightened seam

Figure 2.21 Straighten seam before attaching ribbing to a lengthened pant leg or sleeve.

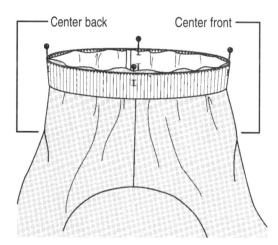

Center back · Center front

Figure 2.22 Quarter-mark band and opening, then seam. (Reprinted with permission from *A Step-by-Step Guide to Your New Home Sewing Machine* by Jan Saunders [Radnor, PA: Chilton, 1992].)

Figure 2.23 With band side up, pull band with your right hand while guiding the seamline with your left for a smooth application. (Reprinted with permission from *A Step-by-Step Guide to Your New Home Sewing Machine* by Jan Saunders [Radnor, PA: Chilton, 1992].)

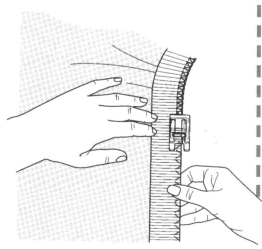

2 Next, decide how wide you want the finished band to be (from the folded edge to the seamline). The ribbing band should be double the finished width plus 1/2" (1.3cm) for the seam allowances. So, for a ribbing that will be 1" (2.5cm) wide when finished, cut the ribbing 2 1/2" (6.5cm) wide.

3 Pin the band into a circle so the narrow ends are right sides together. Stitch a 1/4" (6mm) seam using a tiny zigzag stitch (1 width, 1 length, see Reference Chart A). Gently steam press the seam open.

4 Fold the band in half the long way so the seam is on the inside of the band. If the ribbing is difficult to handle, speed-baste the long raw edges together, using a long, wide zigzag.

5 For a crewneck, turtleneck, cuff, or leg band, quarter and mark the band and opening. Pin the band into the opening, matching the marks (Fig. 2.22). For a V-neck, U-neck, or cardigan, quarters won't work, so use the chart that follows to determine the ribbing needed to hug the back neck from the center back to the shoulder seams. Once the ribbing has been pinned into position from shoulder seam to shoulder seam, evenly distribute the rest of the ribbing around the neckline.

Table 2.2

Ribbing Needed for Back Neck

General Garment Sizing	Distance from Shoulder Seam to Shoulder Seam
extra small	4 1/2" (11.5cm)
small	4 3/4" (12cm)
medium	5 1/4" (13cm)
large	6" (15cm)
extra large	7" (18cm)

*These measurements are general guidelines that you may have to fine-tune for each project.

6 With the band side up, stitch or serge on the ribbing band using a 1/4" (6mm) seam finish (see Reference Chart A) by stretching the ribbing to fit the opening (Fig. 2.23).

Quick-Fix One-Seam Ribbing Band— *To seam a
band fast without the bulk of two seam allowances
lying on top of each other, try this trick Sue
Hausmann (host of* The Art of Sewing *PBS television
show) showed me.*

1 Fold the band in
half the long way.

2 Then fold the band up so a V-shaped fold is
created on the ends.

3 Stitch or serge a ¹/₄" (6mm) seam, seaming from
the folded end to the cut edges (see Reference
Chart A).

4 Turn the band so that the seam is on the inside, as if
you were putting a pair of socks together and turning the top of one over the other (Fig. 2.25). Although
you still have four layers of fabric in the seam allowance,
the one line of stitching cuts down on the bulk and is a
lot faster than the traditional seaming method.

...with a Double Ribbing Band

Add extra length to sleeves or pant legs by adding a single ribbing band (see pages 25-27). For additional length add
a double band.

1 Let down the hems of
both pant legs or sleeves.

2 Press out the
hemlines.

3 Measure, mark, and stitch the
ribbing as described on pages 25-27.

4 For a double band, cut one band ⁵/₈-³/₄"
(1.5-2cm) wider than the other, and seam each
into a circle (unless for a cardigan, then seam band ends
[Fig. 2.26]).

5 Place the narrow band and wide band together,
with the raw edges even. Baste the bands together
using a long and wide zigzag and a loosened upper tension (Fig. 2.27; see *Speed Basting* in the Quick-Fix
Glossary on page 147).

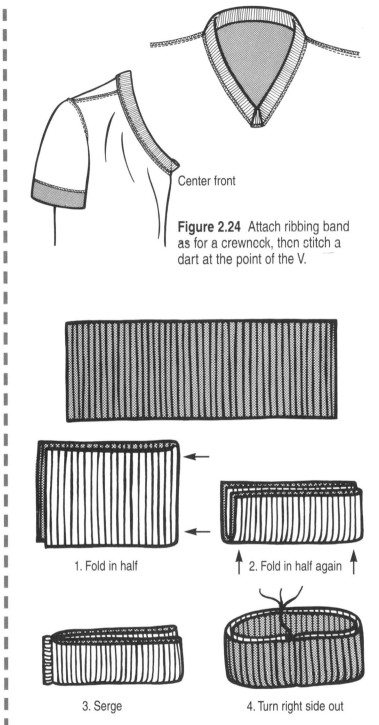

Figure 2.24 Attach ribbing band
as for a crewneck, then stitch a
dart at the point of the V.

1. Fold in half   2. Fold in half again

3. Serge   4. Turn right side out

Figure 2.25 Quick one-seam band: fold band in half the long
way. Then fold band up so it creates a V-shaped fold on both
ends. Seam narrow cut ends and turn right side out.

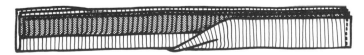

Figure 2.26 Seam cardigan bands at each end, using a ¹/₄"
(6mm) seam allowance.

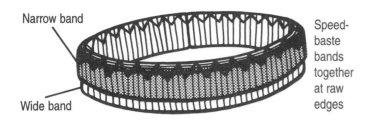

Figure 2.27 Place the narrow and wide bands together with raw edges even. Baste bands together at the seam allowance, using a long, wide zigzag and a loosened upper tension.

Figure 2.28 Add a ribbing band between the dress bodice and skirt for extra length. Then add ribbing accents to other parts of the dress so the band at the waistline looks like it was part of the original design.

Figure 2.29 Cut ribbing with the most stretch going around the body, across the grain, and parallel to the ribs.

6 Stitch bands into the opening as described on page 26. Not only does double ribbing give you more length, it also adds color and style.

...with a Ribbed Waist Inset

For a comfortable extended accent, add a ribbing band between the bodice and the skirt of the dress. For best wear and recovery, use a ribbing that is a cotton and Lycra blend. Can't find a matching color? Use a neutral contrasting color. If you plan to wear your improved dress without a belt, add ribbing to a sleeve cuff or pocket top so the band in the middle of the dress looks as if it is part of the original design (Fig. 2.28).

1 Remove elastic and any stitching that joins the bodice to the skirt of the dress.

2 Press everything flat and steam the seamlines to remove needle holes.

3 Cut across the ribs of the ribbing, creating a band that is the width you want to add to the waistline plus 1/2" (1.3cm) for seam allowances. If the seamlines will not press out, the band must be wide enough to cover the old seamlines, too, so cut the bands accordingly.

4 Measure the ribbing to the desired length and add 1/2" (1.3cm) for seam allowances. Remember, ribbing stretches the most across the grain, so bands must be cut perpendicular to the ribs as shown (Fig. 2.29). A good starting point is to cut the ribbing to measure three-quarters of your waistline measurement. Before cutting, stretch the ribbing around your waist to check that it fits comfortably. Seam the ribbing into a circle using a 1/4" (6mm) seam allowance.

5 Mark off the ribbing into eight equal parts; mark both the bodice and skirt into eighths. Match marks, and pin, so the ribbing is sandwiched between the bodice and skirt, matching center front, center back, side seams, and points in between.

6 With the ribbing on top, serge or stitch ribbing in place on the bodice, stretching it from pin to pin as necessary to attach it to the bodice. Remember to remove the pins as you go (see Reference Chart A). Repeat to attach the ribbing to the skirt.

NOTE—*You may have to stretch the ribbing to fit the skirt, or slightly gather the skirt to fit the ribbing before stitching.*

If it's too **3** tight...

The following improvements can be done in two hours or less and are designed to give you needed room in a jacket, shirt, dress, or waistline. Since clothing that is too tight is already cut to size, simple choices for getting more room are somewhat limited to letting out seams and moving buttons, snaps, or hooks. In some areas it is possible to add an extension or gusset (a triangular- or diamond-shaped piece of fabric cut on the bias and inserted at the underarm, crotch, or waistline for more ease and comfort (Fig. 3.1), but this alteration can be time-consuming and complicated. If you are a non- or occasional sew-er and cannot find a suggestion that will help solve a problem for you in this chapter, seek out the services of a professional dressmaker (see chapter 9).

Move the Buttons

If you need just a little room, move the buttons, hooks and eyes, or other closures (see how to do this by hand on pages 125–126). Move the button over just far enough so it won't throw off the fit. I frequently move buttons over as much as 3/4" (2cm).

Quick-Fix Button Extension — This idea came from a recent issue of Sew News *magazine (November 1993, p. 92; see the source list in the back of the book). Add a strip of contrasting fabric, ribbon, or woven trim as a button extension. Remove buttons from, and add button-holes to, the left side of the jacket front. Make button-holes the same size and even with those on the right side of the jacket. Stitch buttons to both sides of the extension, then button it on the inside of the jacket (Fig. 3.2).*

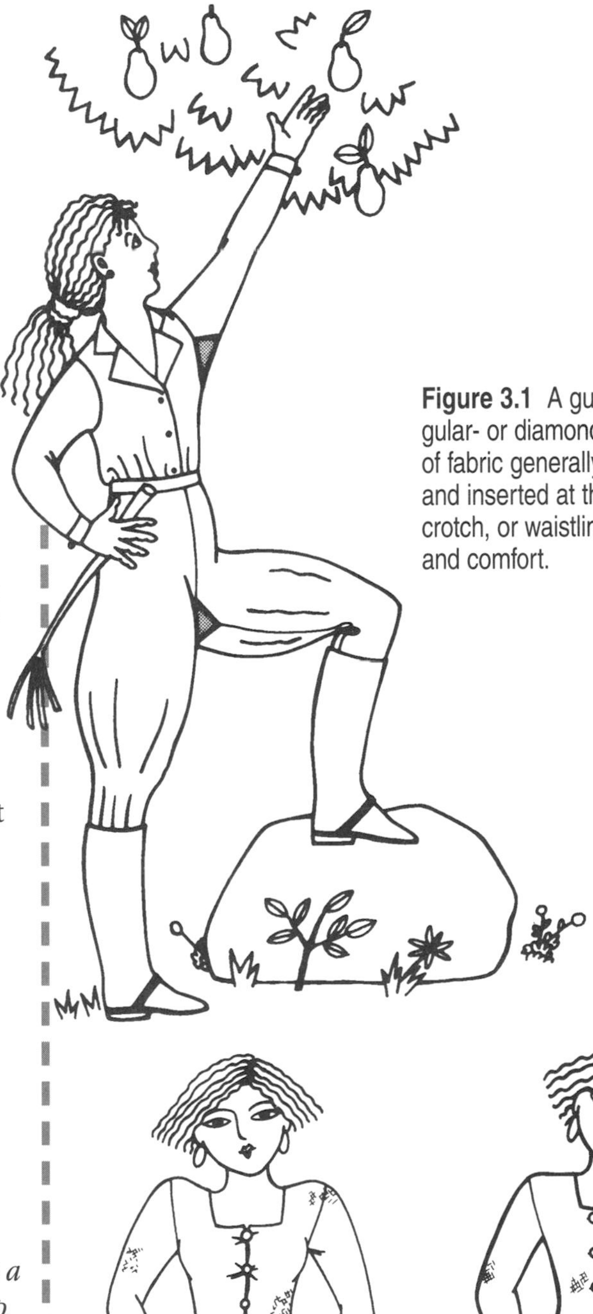

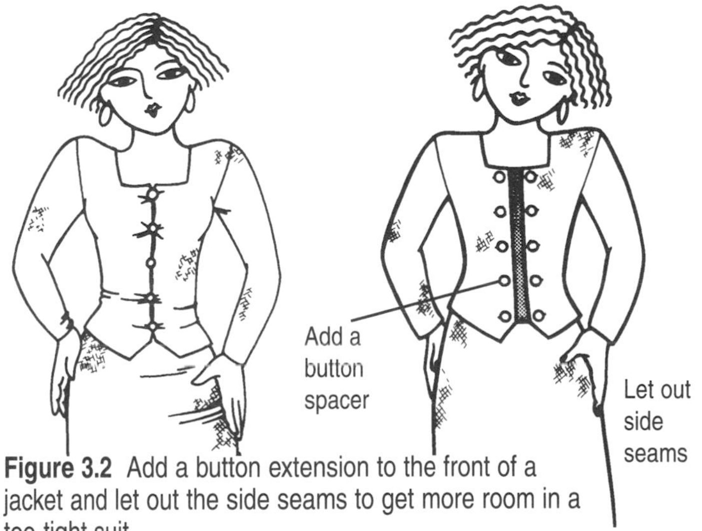

Figure 3.1 A gusset is a trian-gular- or diamond-shaped piece of fabric generally cut on the bias and inserted at the underarm, crotch, or waistline for more ease and comfort.

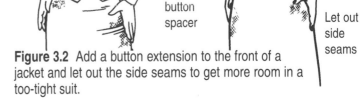

Add a button spacer

Let out side seams

Figure 3.2 Add a button extension to the front of a jacket and let out the side seams to get more room in a too-tight suit.

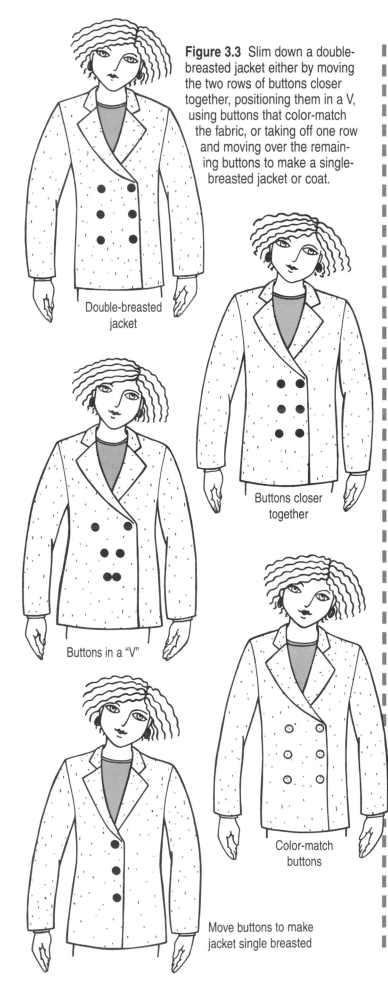

Figure 3.3 Slim down a double-breasted jacket either by moving the two rows of buttons closer together, positioning them in a V, using buttons that color-match the fabric, or taking off one row and moving over the remaining buttons to make a single-breasted jacket or coat.

Double-breasted jacket

Buttons closer together

Buttons in a "V"

Color-match buttons

Move buttons to make jacket single breasted

Make a Double-Breasted Jacket Single Breasted

"I have changed a jacket from double- to single-breasted so it fit my hips!"

Linda Turner Griepentrog
Editor, *Sew News* magazine
Peoria, IL

Double-breasted jackets add pounds visually because the two rows of buttons add width across the torso. To slim down the jacket, either move the two rows of buttons closer together, position them in a V, use buttons that color-match the fabric, or take off one row and move over the remaining buttons to make a single-breasted jacket or coat (Fig. 3.3).

Let Out the Side Seams

"You would be surprised how much can be added to the width of a blouse by letting out all the seams."

Sue Hausmann
Vice-President of education and merchandising,
Viking White Sewing Machines;
Host of *The Art of Sewing*, PBS television show
Cleveland, OH

1 Turn the shirt or top inside out and look at the side seams. Usually, a row of straight stitching runs about 1/2" (1.3cm) inside the serged edge of the seams. Thread your machine with a color that matches the fabric and use a stitch length appropriate for the fabric (see Reference Chart A). If necessary, loosen the hem 2-4" (5-10cm) on either side of the side seams.

2 Stitch just next to the overcast edges (Fig. 3.4). Remove the stitches from the original seamline (see page 127 for instructions on "un-sewing"). Rehem at the side seams. If you are able to get an extra 3/8" (1cm) from two seams, you have added another 1 1/4" (3cm) (3/8" × 4 cut edges = 1 1/4"; 1cm × 4 cut edges = 4cm) to the circumference.

Stitch Down and Cut Out In-Seam Pockets

"To cut down on bulk at the side seams, I sew in-seam pockets shut and trim away the pocket lining underneath."

Denice Williams
Sales representative, Bureau of National Affairs
Columbus, OH

How many times have you been told not to put things in your pockets? For a slimmer look with less bulk, sew the pockets closed.

1 Place skirt or slacks over the ironing board so that the pocket is centered over the board and the right side of the garment faces you.

2 With one hand, lift up the waistband and smooth the pocket underneath; then pin the pocket closed, placing pins perpendicular to the pocket opening and pinning through the skirt lining, if applicable (Fig. 3.5).

3 Use matching thread and hand or machine stitch parallel to the seamline, stitching through all fabric layers, and where possible, sewing over existing topstitching.

4 Turn the garment inside out and carefully trim out pocket fabric up to the seam allowance (Fig. 3.6).

Replace the Ribbing

"I had to have a tracheotomy and found that the necklines on my sweatshirts were too high. So I made a scoop neckline out of some of them. In the winter I like to wear turtlenecks but have not found a way to make them larger around the neck. Any ideas?"

Barb Hines
Homemaker
Dublin, OH

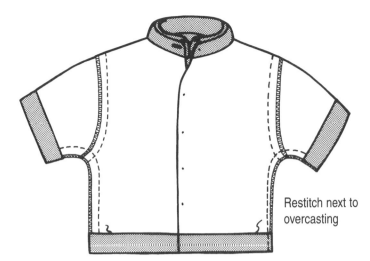

Restitch next to overcasting

Figure 3.4 You would be surprised how much can be added to the width of a blouse by letting out all the seams. Restitch seams just next to the overcast edges.

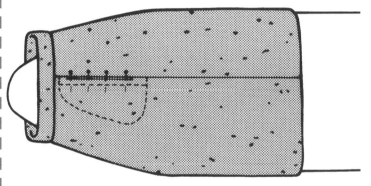

Figure 3.5 Pin pocket closed, placing pins perpendicular to the pocket opening and pinning through the lining (if applicable).

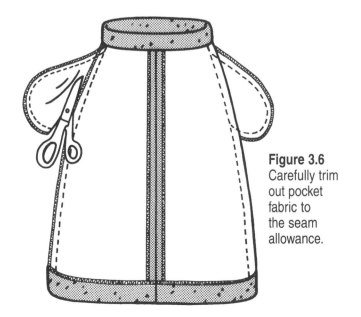

Figure 3.6 Carefully trim out pocket fabric to the seam allowance.

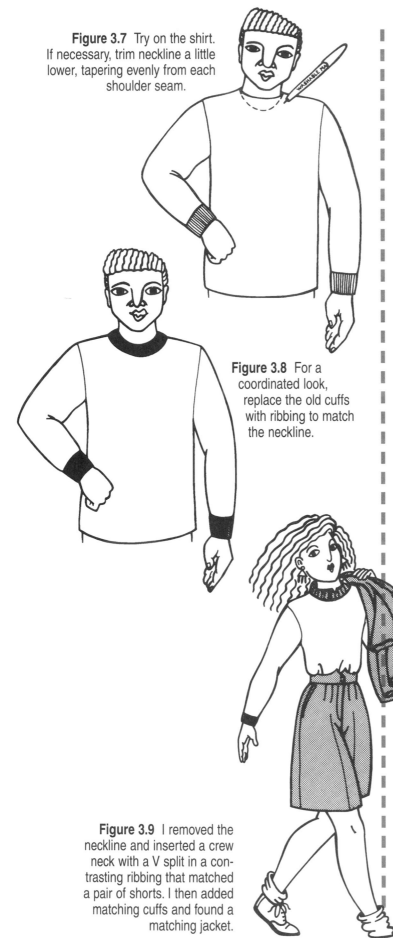

Figure 3.7 Try on the shirt. If necessary, trim neckline a little lower, tapering evenly from each shoulder seam.

Figure 3.8 For a coordinated look, replace the old cuffs with ribbing to match the neckline.

Figure 3.9 I removed the neckline and inserted a crew neck with a V split in a contrasting ribbing that matched a pair of shorts. I then added matching cuffs and found a matching jacket.

Here are a few ways to change a too-tight neckline.

...by Lowering the Neckline and Applying a Mock-Turtle Band

1 Cut off the turtleneck at the seamline, trimming away the seam allowance. Carefully try on the shirt. Is the neckline comfortable? If so, go on to the next step. If not, cut the front neckline a little lower, tapering evenly down from the shoulder seams to the center front (Fig. 3.7).

2 Using the instructions for ribbing application on pages 25-28, replace the turtleneck fabric with ribbing cut to a mock-turtle finished width of 2" (5cm) or less. If you cannot find ribbing to match the fabric, use contrasting ribbing. You may even find sock ribbing that will work (that's right, ribbing cut from a pair of socks that may have a hole in the toe). For a coordinated look to your shirt, replace the cuffs with ribbing to match the neckline (Fig. 3.8).

For even more room and comfort at the neckline, try the following Quick-Fix.

Quick-Fix Neckline Change

"I purchased a cotton knit shirt because I liked the color, style, and quality of the fabric. However, it had a mock turtleneck that I really didn't like. I removed the neckline and inserted a crew neck with a V split in a contrasting ribbing that matched a pair of shorts (Fig. 3.9). I then made and added a matching cuff to the sleeves. I now have a coordinated outfit and have added a matching jacket to the ensemble. I also made a pattern from this shirt...and have made another shirt with a color-blocked inset. This led to another pair of matching shorts, giving me a five-piece coordinating summer wardrobe."

Pam Swierczynski
Sewing instructor; Author of *Pizzazz With Color Blocks*
(Open Chain Publishing, 1991)
Redwood City, CA

...by Enlarging the Neck Opening and Adding Wider Ribbing

"I would like to know how to enlarge the neck opening on children's turtle-necks and T-shirts. Kids' heads are just plain big and they struggle putting tops on and off."

Jeanne Moser
Family friend; Mother of four
East Kingston, NH

The problem with enlarging a neckline in children's clothing is that once the opening is large enough to fit over their heads, it's sometimes too big for their small frames. For a bigger opening with good recovery, that doesn't look too big:

1 Cut off existing ribbing at the seamline. Carefully try on the shirt and check that the opening is comfortable (remember it will finish a bit larger because you will be turning under a 1/4" [6mm] for the seam allowance when you attach the new ribbing). Also measure from the cut edge to where you would like the top of the ribbing to come (Fig. 3.10). This will be the finished width of the ribbing. Because ribbing is doubled over before it is attached, remember to cut your ribbing double the finished width and add 1/2" (1.3cm) for the seam allowances.

2 Before cutting the ribbing to length and seaming it into a circle, fold it in half the long way and try it around your child's head to be sure it will fit (Fig. 3.11). Cut, seam, quarter-mark, pin, and stitch or serge the ribbing into the neckline (see pages 25-28). If you think the single ribbing looks too wide, try the following.

...by Adding a Double Ribbing

If, after cutting a larger neck opening, you think a single ribbing will look too wide, add a double ribbing.

1 Measure and cut two contrasting ribbings, one 1/2–3/4" (1.3-2cm) narrower than the other (see Fig. 2.27).

2 Seam each into a circle and fold them in half separately.

3 With the raw edges even, layer and baste them together (see pages 27-28).

Figure 3.10 To determine how wide to make the ribbing, measure from the cut edge to where you want the top of the ribbing to come. Double this measurement and add 1/2" (1.3cm) to determine ribbing cut width.

Measure for ribbing width

Mark and pin

Figure 3.11 Before cutting the ribbing to length, fold it in half the long way and try it around your child's head.

4 Sew or serge ribbing into the neckline as described on pages 25-28. Either application—the single or the double ribbing—make the neck opening larger and easier for a child to pull on. The ribbing has recovery and it comes up on the neck far enough for a neat, comfortable fit.

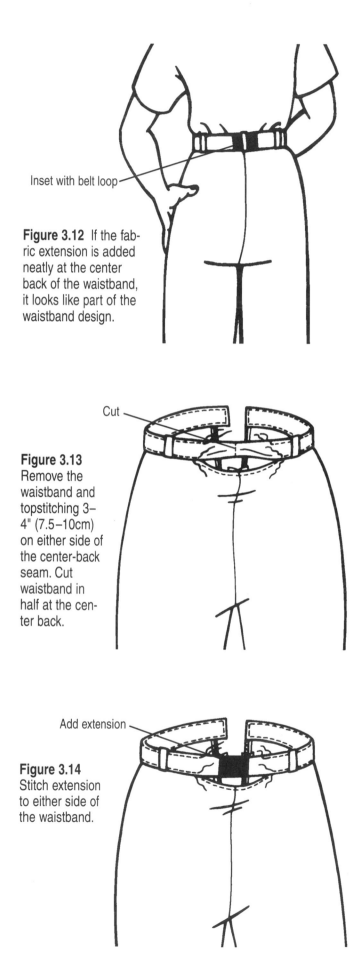

Figure 3.12 If the fabric extension is added neatly at the center back of the waistband, it looks like part of the waistband design.

Inset with belt loop

Cut

Figure 3.13 Remove the waistband and topstitching 3–4" (7.5–10cm) on either side of the center-back seam. Cut waistband in half at the center back.

Add extension

Figure 3.14 Stitch extension to either side of the waistband.

Let Out Waistbands and Pleats

...by Adding a Waistband Insert

"I have added to the waistline seams of casual pants. When waistbands are cut on the lengthwise grain, they can shrink 1/2" (1.3cm) in the first washing, making them quite uncomfortable. I've taken excess fabric from the hems, if available; fabric from the lower edge of one in-seam pocket; or fabric from a belt loop I could do without to create a waistband insert at the center back. Replacing the belt loop at the center back helps to camouflage the inset. If it is done neatly or decorated with decorative stitching, it looks like part of the waistband design (Fig. 3.12)."

Mary Griffin
Sewing specialist, Singer sewing machines
Columbus, OH

To add an insert to a waistband:

1 Remove the waistband and (where applicable) topstitching 3-4" (7.5-10cm) on either side of the center-back seam. Cut waistband in half at the center back (Fig. 3.13).

2 Try on the skirt or slacks to see how much fabric you will need for the waistband extension. Find the waistband extension fabric (as described by Mary Griffin above), and cut and interface the extension piece. Stitch it to either side of the waistband (Fig. 3.14).

3 Reattach waistband to garment, duplicating the original stitching.

4 Stitch a belt loop at center back to disguise the extension.

...by Letting Out Stomach-Hugging Bartacks and Pleats

If your stomach "blooms" below the waistline and causes some of your pants, skirts, and shorts that have stitched-down tucks and pleats to pull the pockets open, try this: Release the bartacks and the stitching from the base of the pleat to the waistband (Fig. 3.15).

...by Letting Out the Center-Back Waistband in Tailored Trousers

When you let out the center back seam in tailored trousers, you get more room at the waistline while lowering the crotch. This alteration is covered thoroughly in chapter 2 (see pages 16-17).

Let Out the Side Seam, Then Reshape the Hip Curve

1 Remove the waistband completely.

NOTE—*If you are letting out less than an inch (2.5cm), you may be able to remove the waistband only slightly past the seams to be let out; then, if necessary, an extension piece can be added to the ends of the waistband.*

Let out the seams as described earlier in this chapter (see Fig. 3.4). Remove the original stitching. Try on the skirt or slacks right side out (so that the seams are on the inside of the garment).

Sew How: Because hips and shoulders are generally higher on one side than the other, it is not a good idea to try on and fit a garment inside out. The garment will end up being fitted to the wrong side of your body.

2 Have a friend or spouse pin the side seams parallel to and following the smooth contour of your hips (Fig. 3.16). Transfer these marks to the inside of your garment, and restitch the altered side seams.

3 From the wrong side, press seams over a tailor's ham. Before reattaching the waistband, try on the garment. Do you have a smoother fit? If not, make further adjustments. You may have to clip the seam allowances in places to make the seam lie flat.

4 With your skirt or slacks on, pin the waistband onto the garment or stretch and tie a length of narrow elastic around the waistline. The bottom of the waistband or elastic will sink to your "shelf," the new waistband seamline. Mark this line with pins or chalk, then take off the garment (Fig. 3.17).

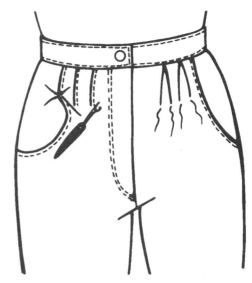

Figure 3.15 Does your stomach "bloom" below the waistband? If so, to prevent the pockets from pulling open, release the bartacks and stitching from the base of the tucks to the waistband.

Figure 3.16 Have a friend or spouse pin the side seams parallel to and following the smooth contours of your hips.

Figure 3.17 Stretch and tie a length of narrow elastic around your waistline to mark the new waistband seam placement.

Mark waist seamline

5 With right sides together, position and restitch the waistband so the seamline is along the altered waistband seamline.

NOTE—If you need more room in the waistband, see Figures 3.12, 3.13, and 3.14.

Make an Elastic Belt Extender

I have a favorite fabric belt that got too tight, so I added an elastic extender. The belt fits better, the elastic stretches for more comfort, and the elastic grips the fabric so it won't loosen as I wear it (Fig. 3.18).

Elastic extension

Front

Back

Figure 3.18 Add an elastic belt extender.

If it's too 4 loose...

When I buy clothing on sale (and if my ego lets me ignore the size labels), I often find good buys on things that are oversized, knowing that by taking my purchase in a little here or cinching it in with elastic there, I will end up with something I can wear and enjoy. You may be a shopping fiend like me, or you may be one of those enviable thin people, or maybe you're thinner in one place than another. All of these situations call for the Quick-Fixes in this chapter. I hope they can help you do some fine-tuning of some of your too-loose clothing.

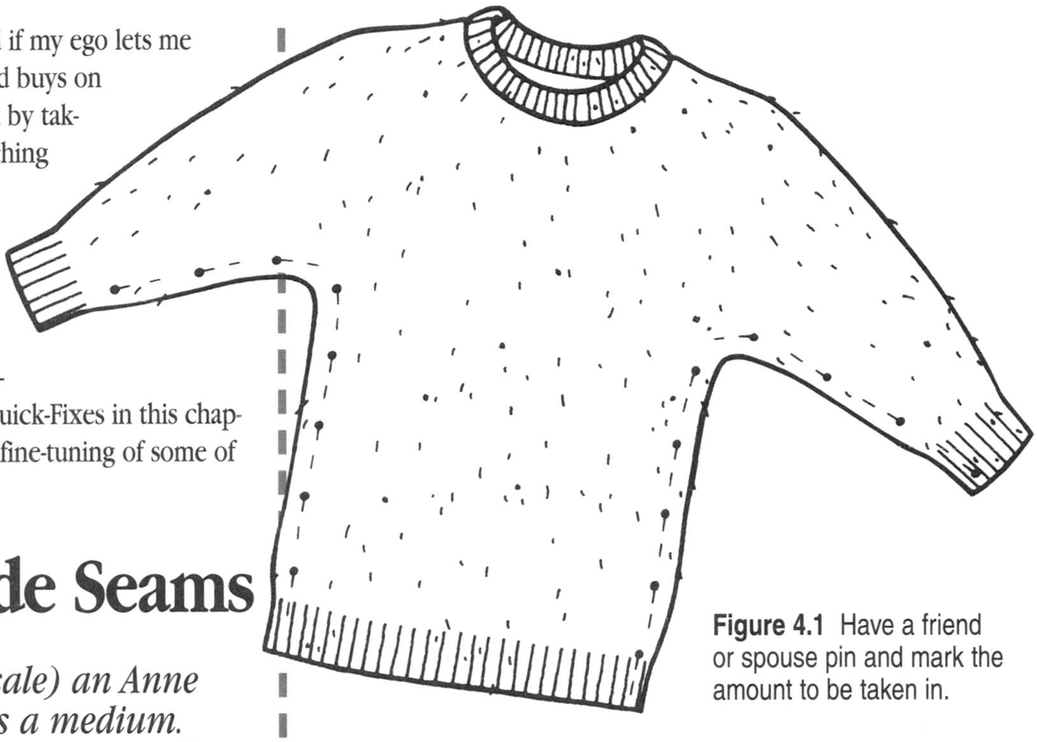

Take In the Side Seams

"I just bought (not on sale) an Anne Klein sweater that was a medium. I should have bought an extra small. I loved it so much that I serged the sleeve seam deeper to make the shoulders and sleeve length work; then I serged the underarm seam from wrist to hem and it fits just fine."

Susan (Pletsch) Foster
Retired author; Sewing and serging expert
Portland, OR

1 Try on the garment, right side out, to determine how much needs to be taken in. (Remember to try on and fit a garment right side out to be sure that prob-

Figure 4.1 Have a friend or spouse pin and mark the amount to be taken in.

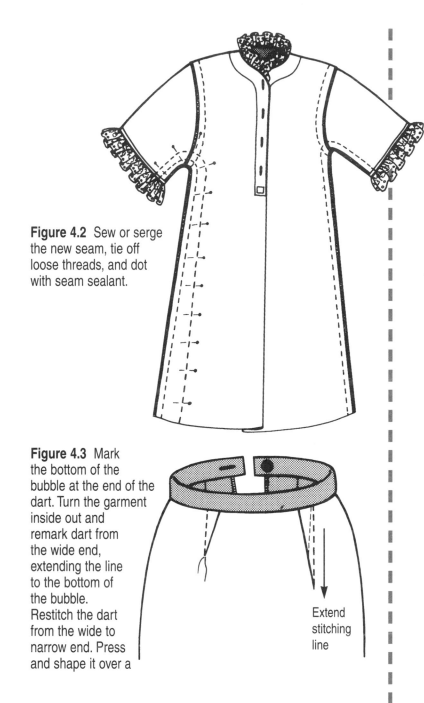

Figure 4.2 Sew or serge the new seam, tie off loose threads, and dot with seam sealant.

Figure 4.3 Mark the bottom of the bubble at the end of the dart. Turn the garment inside out and remark dart from the wide end, extending the line to the bottom of the bubble. Restitch the dart from the wide to narrow end. Press and shape it over a

Extend stitching line

Figure 4.4 Learn to tie a secure knot. (Reprinted with permission from *A Step-by-Step Guide to Your New Home Sewing Machine* by Jan Saunders [Radnor, PA: Chilton, 1992].)

lems caused by a hip or shoulder being higher on one side are marked properly.) Have a friend or spouse pin it in for you (Fig. 4.1).

2 Turn the garment inside out and transfer the marked seamline. Sew or serge the new seam (Fig. 4.2). Tie off loose threads or dot them with a liquid seam sealant.

Extend the Darts

"What's the best way to deal with pant/skirt darts that don't flatter? I've stitched them down, but there's still a 'pouch' that forms below them."

Cindy Kacynski
Editor, *Serger Update* newsletter; Free-lance editor
Peoria, IL

Extend darts to get rid of the bubble at the point.

1 Try on the garment, right side out, and have a friend or spouse mark the bottom of the bubble.

2 Turn the garment inside out and remark the dart from the wide end, extending the line to the bottom of the bubble (Fig. 4.3).

3 Restitch the dart, sewing from the wide to the narrow end. *Don't* backstitch at the point; tie a knot instead.

Sew How: Tie a knot that will not come out. Starting with a thread tail at least 7" (18cm) long, hold the threads together in one hand and form a loop (Fig. 4.4a). Bring both thread ends around and through the loop (Fig. 4.4b). Work the loop down to the base of the stitch and hold it with your thumb (Fig. 4.4c). Pull threads taut so the loop forms a knot at the base of the fabric.

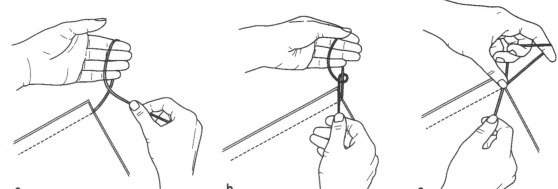

a   b   c

4 Try it on. Isn't it better? From the wrong side, press the dart toward the center over a tailor's ham to set and shape it.

Shape Up Baggy Ribbing

Use a little elastic thread and a hand needle to give a sweater a new life.

...by Reweaving It with Elastic Thread

1 Thread a large-eyed tapestry needle with a single 12" (30.5cm) length of elastic thread and knot the end.

2 Turn the sweater inside out. Starting at the seam and at the top of the ribbing, stitch through the edge of the ribs (Fig. 4.5). When you get all the way around, pull the elastic up to the right snugness *without* stretching the elastic. Tie off elastic thread ends (see Fig. 4.4).

3 Repeat for two or three rows, about 3/4" (2cm) apart.

...by Replacing It with an Elasticized Band

If the ribbing is worn out on a sweatshirt or T-shirt, you may have to replace the ribbing. My first choice is to replace it with a ribbing that is a cotton and Lycra blend. If this isn't available in your area, use ribbing and elasticize it with a little clear or "plastic" elastic.

> **Sew How:** *Plastic elastic is clear, doesn't "grow" when stitched through, creates no bulk, and is chlorine-safe so it can be used on swimwear. I also stitch it (without stretching it) into knit shoulder seams for extra stability.*

1 Reread about ribbing application in chapter 2 (see pages 25-28). After you have cut the ribbing to length, cut a piece of clear elastic so it is the exact length of the ribbing. Fold the ribbing in half the long way so the short ends are even. Fold the elastic in half the long way, too. Layer the elastic on top of the ribbing so all short ends are even.

2 Seam the ribbing, incorporating the elastic in the seam (Fig. 4.6).

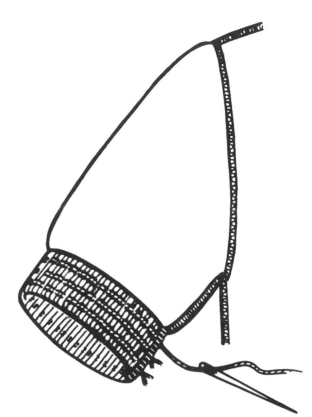

Figure 4.5 With a needle threaded with elastic thread, stitch through the wrong side of the ribs, then pull elastic to the right snugness. Tie off elastic thread ends.

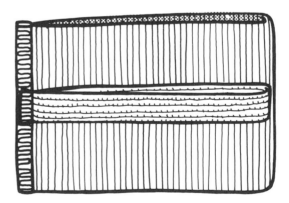

Figure 4.6 Seam ribbing incorporating the clear elastic in the seam.

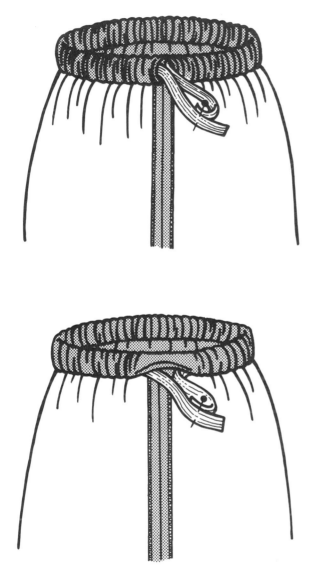

Figure 4.7 Pull elastic out of casing. Cut it, overlap the ends to make it the desired length, then pin and stitch securely.

3 Turn the band right side out so the seam is on the inside, folding the band in half over the elastic.

4 Quarter-mark, pin, and serge the band into the opening. Because the elastic is soft and the same length as the unstretched band, it has great recovery without the bulk of traditional elastic.

Shape In the Waistline

In her syndicated column, Erma Bombeck writes, "My problem with elastic is that when you finally wear it to the point where you can breathe in it and it feels comfortable, it's ready to throw away." Before you throw it away, try this.

...by Shortening the Elastic

"I bought a pull-on silk chiffon skirt that was marked down from $200 to $12—I can't buy the fabric for that. I simply tightened the elastic, and the short skirt on the right-sized person is tea length on me."

Susan (Pletsch) Foster
Retired author; Sewing and serging expert
Portland, OR

To shorten the elastic on a skirt:

1 Try on the skirt to determine how much the elastic needs to be taken in. Find where the casing stitching begins and ends or where the elastic is joined together in the casing or waistband.

2 Remove about 2½-3" (6.5-7.5cm) of stitching from either side of where the elastic is seamed together.

3 Pull a short loop of the joined elastic out through the opening in the casing, cut it, then overlap and securely pin the ends, making the elastic the desired length. You may want to try the garment on again to double-check for comfort (Fig. 4.7).

4 Stitch the elastic together. Restitch the casing or waistband as it was before.

Quick-Fix Elastic Saver — *Replace elastic that is "shot" by opening the casing about 1" (2.5cm) near a seam. Pull out the old elastic and cut new elastic a* *comfortable length plus ½" (1.3cm) for overlap. Use a bodkin, elastic guide, or Drawstring Restringer to pull the elastic through the casing. Overlap elastic ends and stitch securely. Restitch the casing.*

Even Quicker-Fix—*If you don't have an elastic-threading tool, stitch one end of the new elastic to one end of the old elastic and pull it through the casing until the new elastic is in place. To keep the new elastic from pulling completely through the casing, put a safety pin on the free end before pulling it through.*

...by Adding Elastic Inside the Waistband

"How do you make better-fitting waistbands in both adult and children's clothing? Is there a way to apply elastic to the back inside of a set-in waistband? We always just pull a belt a little tighter, but then it looks too bunchy."

Jeanne Moser
Family friend; Mother of four
Kingston, NH

To take in a waistband without altering the hips of the garment, try inserting elastic inside the back waistband. The elastic will be added from side seam to side seam, across the back.

NOTE—*If there is a zipper at center back, add two pieces of elastic from each side seam to center back.*

1 Remove the stitches holding the inside of the back waistband to the waistline, including the stitches about 1" (2.5cm) past the side seams (Fig. 4.8).

2 Cut a length of elastic that fits comfortably around the back of the waistline.

3 Stitch across the short ends to secure the elastic at the side seam ends and on the *inside* of the waistband (Fig. 4.9).

4 Restitch and secure the inside of the waistband to the waistline (Fig. 4.10).

Figure 4.8 Remove stitches holding the inside waistband about 1" (2.5 cm) past the side seams.

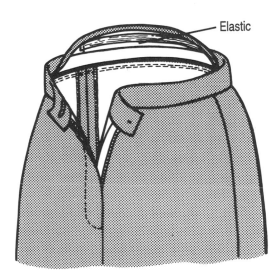

Elastic

Figure 4.9 Stitch accross the ends to secure the elastic at the side seams and on the inside back of the waistband.

Figure 4.10 Restitch and secure the inside of the waistband to the waistline.

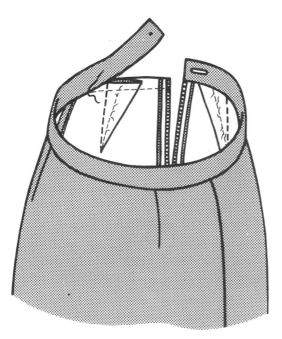

Figure 4.11 I partially remove the waistband and take the seam in. If there isn't a seam there, I make one or a larger dart to eliminate the excess fabric, says Jane Metcalf.

Quick-Fix for Shaping in a Smaller Amount of Fullness

"After losing inches around the waist, I partially remove the waistband and take in the side seams. If I can't take the garment in at the seams, I make a larger dart or take a tuck in the front to eliminate the excess fabric (Fig. 4.11)"

Jane Metcalf
Owner, Viking Sewing Center
Ann Arbor, MI

...by Adding Elastic Thread Shirring

I had a rayon challis tent dress with too much billowy fullness. To shape it in, I made a decorative belt, but when I put it around my waistline, gobs of fabric spread unevenly around my waist—neither flattering nor comfortable. To remedy this, I ran three rows of elastic-thread shirring at the waistline. The shirring kept everything where it was supposed to be, and the dress was comfortable to boot. This technique can also be used on baby and children's clothing to protect their sensitive skin.

1 Try on the dress. Stretch a strip of narrow elastic around the waistline and have a friend or spouse mark the waistline placement with pins or a fabric marker.

2 Wind a bobbin of elastic thread (see pages 8-9). Do not stretch it as it goes on the bobbin. Then thread the bobbin through normal bobbin tension. Set your machine for a 3-3.5 stitch length (9-10 stitches per inch) and use all-purpose thread as your top thread.

Sew How: *European elastic thread has the most recovery because it is rubber wrapped with cotton. Find it at your local sewing machine dealer or through your favorite mail-order source.*

3 Starting at a side seam, sew on the right side of the garment through a single thickness. Guide by the pins or chalk marks and stitch around the waistline. The fabric will shirr as you sew. Tie off the thread ends (see Fig. 4.4).

4 Repeat for as many rows as needed (Fig. 4.12).

Quick-Fix Elastic Shirring

"To shirr in a waistline that doesn't already have elastic, apply an elastic

treatment called Stitch 'n Stretch, available at your local fabric retailer or through your favorite mail-order source. It's a flat fabric tape with rows of elastic (spandex) cord threaded through it. Turn the garment inside out; then open one side seam the width of the Stitch 'n Stretch.

Cut the Stitch 'n Stretch the same length as the flat waistline circumference plus seam allowances. Pull out the spandex cords ½" (1.3cm) from each end of the woven band. Fold under the short ends of the woven band (where the spandex cords have been removed).

Pin the treatment around the waistline; then stitch along each of the blue stitching lines marked (which fall between the rows of spandex cord). **Note:** *On dark fabric use the black Stitch 'n Stretch with white stitching lines.*

Pull the elastic cords out 4-5" (10-12.5cm) at each end, and tie the cords in a knot. Pull the knotted cord ends equally from both ends to a comfortable length. Secure cords to the tape and other seam allowance, zigzagging through all layers twice. Trim away excess cord and restitch the side seam. For more information, ask your fabric retailer or see your mail-order catalog."

Nancy Zieman
President, Nancy's Notions, Ltd.;
Host of *Sewing With Nancy*, PBS television show
Beaver Dam, WI

...by Taking It In at the Center-Back Waistband Seam

This works on women's and men's tailored trousers that have a center-back seam in the waistband. This method of taking in a waistband may raise the crotch a little.

1 Try on the slacks to determine how much you need to take in. Remove the center-back belt loop.

2 Remove the stitches that hold the inside waistband in place about 3" (7.5cm) on either side of

Quick-Fix Shortening Trick
Take a leather belt to a shoemaker and have it shortened from the buckle end.

Figure 4.12 Using elastic thread on the bobbin, shirr multiple rows to shape a waistline on a lightweight tent dress.

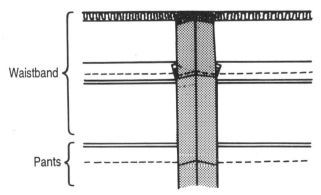

Waistband

Pants

Figure 4.13 Remove the center-back belt loop and the stitches that hold the inside of the waistband.

Figure 4.14 Flip up the waistband. Restitch the center-back seam, tapering up and into the waistline seam. Stitch straight up through the waistband.

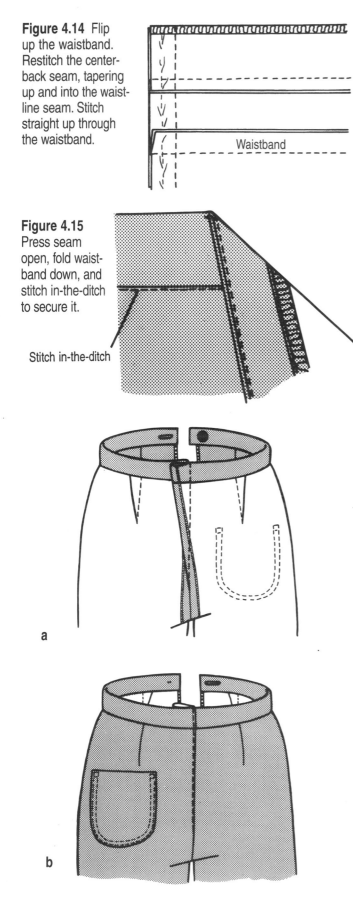

Figure 4.15 Press seam open, fold waistband down, and stitch in-the-ditch to secure it.

Stitch in-the-ditch

a

b

Figure 4.16 For slacks without a center-back seam, pinch in the needed amount and edgestitch next to the seam.

the center-back seam. Flip up the waistband; then pinch the two sides of the seam allowance together.

3 Starting about 5" (12.5cm) below the waistline seam, restitch the center-back seam, tapering up and into the waistline seam the amount needed. Then stitch straight up through the waistband (Figs. 4.13–4.15).

4 Remove the original seaming and try on the slacks. If they fit, press the seam open, fold the waistband down, and stitch in-the-ditch at the waistline seam. Restitch the belt loop in place.

Quick-Fix Variation: For slacks without a center-back seam, pinch in the needed amount at the center back and edgestitch next to the seam and through the waistband with matching thread (Fig. 4.16; see also Fig. 1.9).

Pinch In a Pleat at the Jacket Back

I was on my way to an event and made an unlined jacket to wear on the trip. Because I was in a hurry, I didn't check the fit until I had the buttons on, the buttonholes cut, and was dressed and ready to walk out the door. The jacket was *huge.* Because I did a serged Hong Kong seam finish, I didn't want to take in the fullness at the side seams, so I pinched out and stitched a pleat at the center back (Fig. 4.17). The jacket fit and everyone loved the back detail.

"I would like to be able to alter my husband's dress shirts to appear more fitted. He has a huge neck and shoulders, but his waist is more normal. The unfitted shirts are easier to find in an 18" (46cm) neck but look terrible (on him). Unfortunately, back darts look tacky and the side seams are usually double-stitched."

Carla Moore
Certified Home Economist; Consultant
Columbus, OH

Quick-Fix Variation for Too-Full Shirts—
Unfortunately, there is not an easy answer here. However, to control excess fullness permanently stitch inside the pleat at center back from yoke to hem (Fig. 4.18), or teach him this quick-fix military tuck.

Quick-Fix Military Tuck for Shirts:—*Because military shirts are standard issue, this tucking method looks well on most sizes and body shapes, and the shirts look as though they fit better than they really do.*

1 Smooth the shirt across the front to the side seams.

2 Pinch in a wide tuck on both sides, then push the tucks so the folds are to the back (Fig. 4.19).

3 Tuck the shirt in the pants, smoothing the side tucks over the hips and seat.

4 Close and zip the pants, and put on a belt.

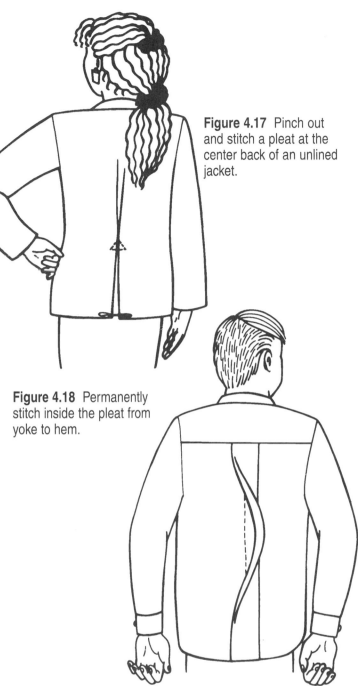

Figure 4.17 Pinch out and stitch a pleat at the center back of an unlined jacket.

Figure 4.18 Permanently stitch inside the pleat from yoke to hem.

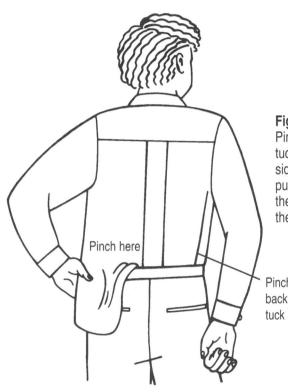

Figure 4.19 Pinch in a wide tuck on both sides, then push tucks so the folds are to the back.

Pinch here

Pinch, fold back, and tuck in

Figure 4.20 Too-full shoulders can be corrected at the center-back seam or with a beefed-up shoulder pad to fill in the excess fullness.

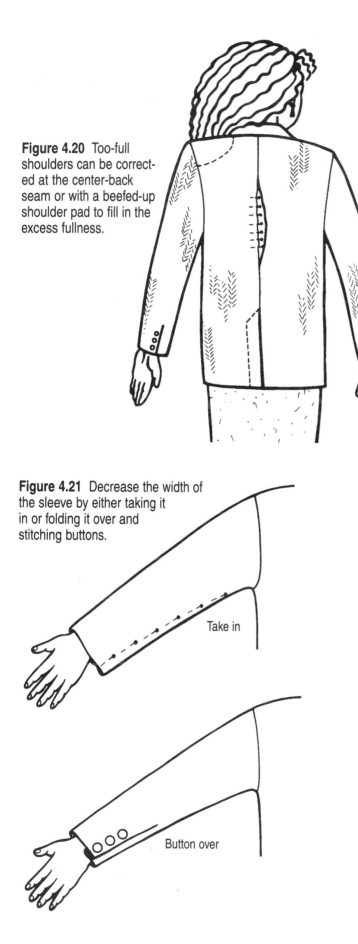

Figure 4.21 Decrease the width of the sleeve by either taking it in or folding it over and stitching buttons.

Take in

Button over

"I want to know how to get rid of fullness across the back shoulders."
Sallie Maresh
Retired civil servant (and my mother-in-law)
Ocala, FL

Quick-Fix for Too-Full Shoulders —*On ready-to-wear it is difficult to eliminate fullness across the shoulder line because the garment is already cut and constructed. For those garments without a center back seam, a beefed-up shoulder pad will sometimes fill in the excess fullness. If there is a seam at center back, simply pinch out and pin the fullness (Fig. 4.20), mark it, and then take it in from the wrong side of the garment.*

Secure a Loose Sleeve and Droopy Pocket

"Decrease the width of a sleeve to give a slimmer look by tapering or folding it over and adding some buttons (Fig. 4.21). Droopy pockets can also be tacked, buttoned, or stitched closed for a better look (Fig. 4.22)."
Jan Nunn
Sewing instructor; Professional dressmaker
Portland, OR

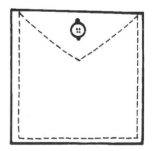

Figure 4.22 Droopy pockets can be tacked, buttoned, or stitched closed for a better look.

Serge In a Too-Big Bra Cup

"Occasionally I will see beautiful bras on sale. While they are the correct circumference, the cup is too big, so I cut it down to size by serging off the excess."

Gail Brown
Author; Sewing and serging expert
Hoquiam, WA

1 Thread the upper and lower loopers with Woolly Nylon and set for a narrow balanced 3-thread overlock (see Reference Chart A). (This softer thread in the seam is more comfortable.)

2 On the inside of each cup, pull in and pin the excess, following the original seamline (Fig. 4.23).

3 Serge the seam, leaving long-enough thread tails to tie them off (see Fig. 4.4).

Sew How: *To flatten the seam, stitch over it with the three-step zigzag stitch set on the widest width and about a 1–2 length (see Reference Chart A).*

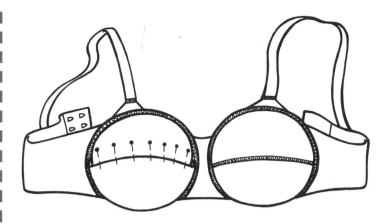

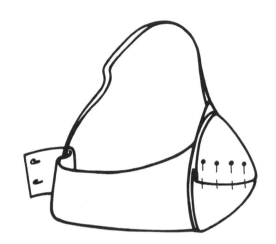

Figure 4.23 On the inside of each cup, pull and pin the excess. Serge a new seam, following the original seamline. To flatten seam, stitch over it with the 3-step zigzag stitch.

Take In Children's Clothes

An obvious approach is to take in a seam. Just remember to use a longer basting stitch that is easily removed when the child grows to the next size.

Quick-Fix Tip

"I take in side seams on my children's clothing, lining and all. In a few months it will have to be let out anyway, and as long as it looks okay from the right side without being bunchy, this shortcut really works."

Gail Brown
Author; Sewing and serging expert
Hoquiam, WA

Add Durability, Warmth, and Figure-Flattering Comfort

Add Durability: Bring In the Reinforcements

...by Restitching Seams to Stabilize Them

"One of my pet peeves is cheap thread on ready-to-wear that disintegrates after a few washings. This is a particular problem on serged children's clothing, but I also had it happen on a pair of my (moderately expensive) cotton/Lycra stirrup pants. Any tips?"

Anne Marie Soto
Fashion and sewing consultant; Free-lance sewing journalist
Teaneck, NJ

"Inexpensive loosely knitted sweaters and tops often need reinforcement at the cuffs and lower edges. Quickly serging over the high-stress areas before wearing the garment saves time later (Fig. 5.1)."

Tammy Young
Author; Sewing and serging expert
San Francisco, CA

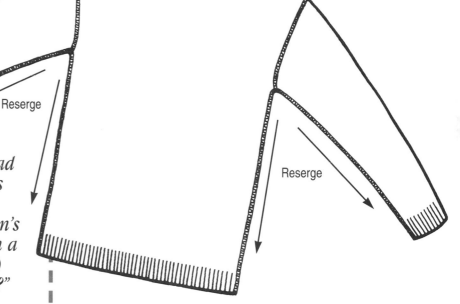

Reserge

Reserge

Figure 5.1 Serging over high-stress areas before wearing the garment will save time later. Use a balanced 3-thread overlock, with Wooly Nylon in the upper looper and all-purpose serger thread in lower looper (see Reference Chart A).

"I have mainly done repair work, especially in my daughter Melissa's knit stirrup pants and leggings, by reserging over broken seams."

Pati Palmer
President, Palmer/Pletsch Publishing
Portland, OR

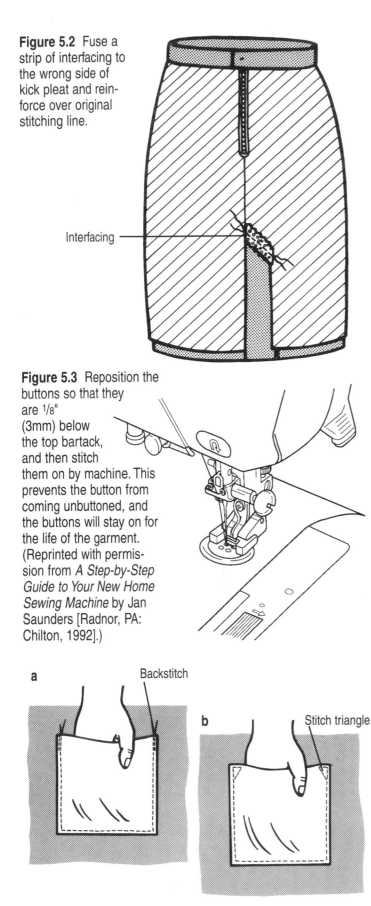

Figure 5.2 Fuse a strip of interfacing to the wrong side of kick pleat and reinforce over original stitching line.

Interfacing

Figure 5.3 Reposition the buttons so that they are ⅛" (3mm) below the top bartack, and then stitch them on by machine. This prevents the button from coming unbuttoned, and the buttons will stay on for the life of the garment. (Reprinted with permission from *A Step-by-Step Guide to Your New Home Sewing Machine* by Jan Saunders [Radnor, PA: Chilton, 1992].)

a

Backstitch

b

Stitch triangle

Figure 5.4 Backstitch over original stitching. Topstitch a triangle. Then bartack over the stitching with a short satin stitch.

To stabilize seams on knits, use Woolly Nylon in your bobbin and restitch stress areas with a tiny zigzag stitch (see Reference Chart A). On wovens, thread the top and bobbin with an all-purpose cotton-wrapped polyester and reinforce stress areas.

In addition to reinforcing stress areas, be careful not to "cook" the garment in a too-hot dryer. Check the care label for more information.

Quick-Fix for a Kick Pleat—For a kick pleat that has already ripped or to reinforce one before it does, fuse a piece of interfacing under the stress area. Then, stitch over the original topstitching from the right side. Remember to use matching thread and the same stitch length as the original stitching (Fig. 5.2).

...by Resewing Buttons

"I always remove and resew buttons on ready-to-wear garments, especially my husband's dress shirts. This only takes a few minutes when done by machine. Commercially sewn buttons are positioned in the center of the buttonhole. Instead, move the buttons up slightly so the thread shank sewn through the button is about ⅛"(3mm) below the top bartack (Fig.5.3). This causes the button to slide to the top of the buttonhole, which prevents the button from coming unbuttoned. A dab of seam sealant on the threads ensures that the button will stay on for the life of the garment."

Suzy Poor
Sewing instructor; Sewing and serging expert
Artesia, CA

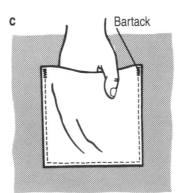

c

Bartack

...by Reinforcing Pocket Tops and Slits

Reinforce a pocket top or a slit by fusing a piece of interfacing on the wrong side of the garment, then doing *one* of the following:

- Backstitching over original stitching (Fig 5.4a)

- Topstitching a triangle (Fig. 5.4b)

- Bartacking with a short, 3-width satin stitch (Fig. 5.4c; see also Reference Chart A)

To reinforce a slit or pocket top that has already ripped, reinforce the back of the fabric as described earlier; then stitch over it with decorative hand or machine stitch, or cut and stitch a decorative tab of synthetic suede or leather to cover the rip (Fig. 5.5).

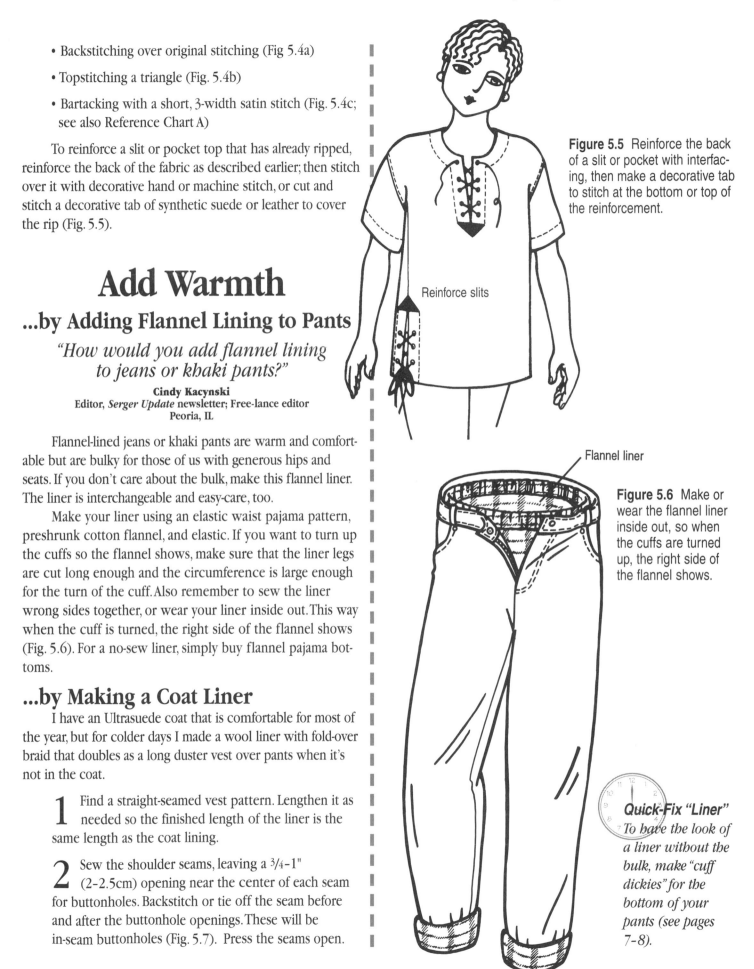

Reinforce slits

Figure 5.5 Reinforce the back of a slit or pocket with interfacing, then make a decorative tab to stitch at the bottom or top of the reinforcement.

Add Warmth

...by Adding Flannel Lining to Pants

"How would you add flannel lining to jeans or khaki pants?"

Cindy Kacynski
Editor, *Serger Update* newsletter; Free-lance editor
Peoria, IL

Flannel-lined jeans or khaki pants are warm and comfortable but are bulky for those of us with generous hips and seats. If you don't care about the bulk, make this flannel liner. The liner is interchangeable and easy-care, too.

Make your liner using an elastic waist pajama pattern, preshrunk cotton flannel, and elastic. If you want to turn up the cuffs so the flannel shows, make sure that the liner legs are cut long enough and the circumference is large enough for the turn of the cuff. Also remember to sew the liner wrong sides together, or wear your liner inside out. This way when the cuff is turned, the right side of the flannel shows (Fig. 5.6). For a no-sew liner, simply buy flannel pajama bottoms.

Flannel liner

Figure 5.6 Make or wear the flannel liner inside out, so when the cuffs are turned up, the right side of the flannel shows.

...by Making a Coat Liner

I have an Ultrasuede coat that is comfortable for most of the year, but for colder days I made a wool liner with fold-over braid that doubles as a long duster vest over pants when it's not in the coat.

1 Find a straight-seamed vest pattern. Lengthen it as needed so the finished length of the liner is the same length as the coat lining.

2 Sew the shoulder seams, leaving a ³/₄–1" (2–2.5cm) opening near the center of each seam for buttonholes. Backstitch or tie off the seam before and after the buttonhole openings. These will be in-seam buttonholes (Fig. 5.7). Press the seams open.

Quick-Fix "Liner"
To have the look of a liner without the bulk, make "cuff dickies" for the bottom of your pants (see pages 7–8).

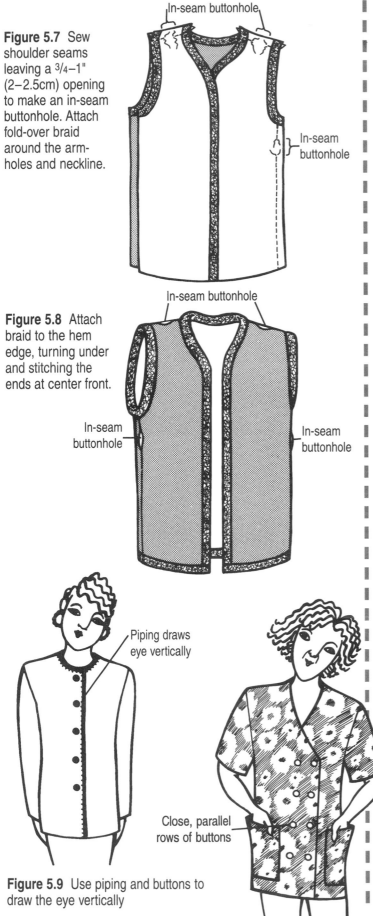

Figure 5.7 Sew shoulder seams leaving a 3/4–1" (2–2.5cm) opening to make an in-seam buttonhole. Attach fold-over braid around the arm-holes and neckline.

In-seam buttonhole

In-seam buttonhole

Figure 5.8 Attach braid to the hem edge, turning under and stitching the ends at center front.

In-seam buttonhole

In-seam buttonhole

In-seam buttonhole

Piping draws eye vertically

Close, parallel rows of buttons

Figure 5.9 Use piping and buttons to draw the eye vertically

3 With the side seams open, attach the fold-over braid around the armholes and neckline.

4 Sew the side seams leaving another 3/4-1" (2-2.5cm) opening at the top for in-seam button-holes. Backstitch or tie off the seams before and after the buttonhole openings, then press the seams open.

5 Attach fold-over braid to the bottom of the liner, turning under the ends at center front (Fig. 5.8).

6 Sew large flat buttons to the inside of the coat at the shoulder and side seams. Turn the liner so the seams are right side out. Button in the liner through the in-seam buttonholes. For another look with the same liner, turn it right side out and wear it on the outside of the coat.

Add Figure-Flattering Lines

...by Dressing Thinner without Losing Weight

Whether you are on a diet or are happy with your figure as it is, there are ways to dress thin. The following ideas are my personal favorites. To learn more, read *Flatter Your Figure*, by Jan Larkey (Prentice-Hall, 1991), available through your local book store, or write the author:

Jan Larkey
Flatter Your Figure—Information
P. O. Box 8258
Pittsburgh, PA 15218

Another excellent reference is *Clothes Sense*, by Barbara Weiland and Leslie Wood (Palmer/Pletsch Associates, 1985), available through your local fabric retailer, or write to:

Palmer/Pletsch Associates
P. O. Box 12046
Portland, OR 97212

The following do's and don'ts may help you weed out your closet or help you plan your future clothing purchases.

The Do's and Don'ts of Dressing Thinner

DO'S

Do... use piping or buttons to draw the eye vertically (Fig. 5.9). If you use two parallel rows, make them close together (see "Make a Double-Breasted Jacket Single Breasted" in chapter 3).

Do... appear taller by combining the same colors and values (Figs. 5.10-5.12).

Do... buy or make a garment with enough fitting ease (see Reference Chart D). Wrinkles on a too-tight outfit create horizontal lines (Fig. 5.13) "Straighten" unwanted curves by wearing loose rather than tight-fitting clothing that cups around those curves.

Do... choose styles to fit your hips and tummy, even if you need to take in the waistband a little (see suggestions in chapter 4) for a good fit. Loose waistbands are much less noticeable than clothing that accentuates your figure challenges.

Do... create visual diversions toward your assets (Fig. 5.14). A great scarf or accessory draws attention to your face. Remember, the size of your accessories should increase or decrease with the size of your body, shoulder pads, and/or clothing (the bigger the look, the bigger the jewelry).

Do... "adjust your bra straps to lift your low or full bust to mid-chest," writes Jan Larkey, author of *Flatter Your Figure* (Prentice-Hall, 1991). "Many women think they are short-waisted when they are just low-bosomed!"

*Do...*wear prints near your figure assets because they are usually more interesting than solids. An all-over print can also camouflage figure faults, but the scale of a print from repeat to repeat is important. A 1/2-2" (1.3-5cm) repeat in a medium all-over print looks good on most figures. A large-scale print will work on medium- to large-boned figures.

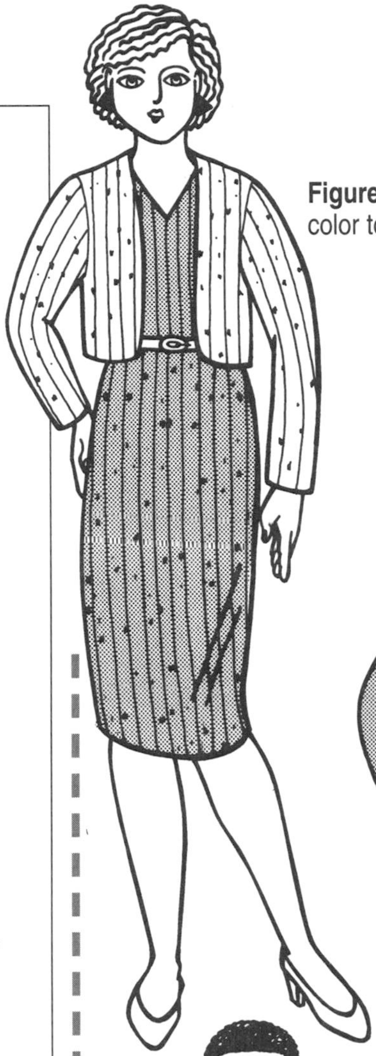

Figure 5.10 Wear inside garments of one color to look taller and slimmer.

Figure 5.11 Wear outside garments of one color to look taller and slimmer.

Figure 5.12 Wear one color head to toe (such as the jacket and pants here) to look taller.

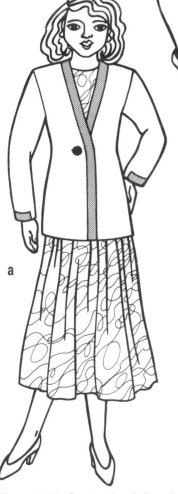

Figure 5.13
Wrinkles on a too-tight outfit create horizontal lines.

Figure 5.14 Create visual diversions away from your liabilities and toward your assets. Here two different looks play down the hips while drawing attention to the face.

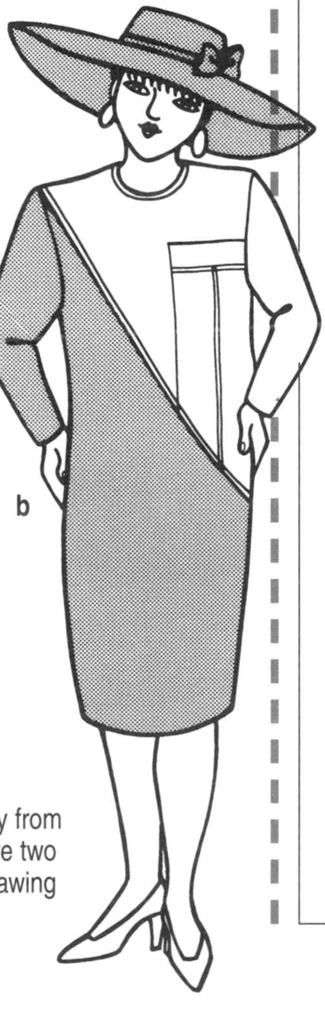

Do... eliminate cuffs on walking shorts and trousers to eliminate another horizontal.

Do... remove back patch pockets from slacks or jeans to divert the eye's attention somewhere else. Remember, everyone else sees you coming *and* going.

Do... wear shoulder pads. Lose five pounds in the hips by making your shoulders look wider.

DON'TS

Don't... cut your figure in half (i.e., half top, half skirt). To get a more pleasing and proportioned look, think in thirds. Nature (rams' horns and snail shells) and architecture (Egyptian pyramids and the Parthenon) are proportioned roughly into a 2-to-3 rather than a 1-to-2 relationship. Think of the shape of a door or a piece of paper. They are taller than they are across and it's more interesting. This "Golden Mean" or two-thirds rule teaches us to dress so that one-third is on top, and two-thirds is skirt or slacks, or vice-versa (Fig. 5.15).

Don't... look rounder. If you have a round face and a round body, choose angular detailing, such as welt pockets on a slant, pointed lapels, and squared-off jacket hems.

Don't... buy or make clothing out of nubby, puffy, thick, or textured fabrics that add unneeded pounds. Choose flat weaves in fabrics that drape close to the body. For example, two layers of drapey wool jersey or crepe is generally more flattering than a tweed suit.

Don't... wear clunky shoes or those with ankle straps. The first adds weight, while the other visually cuts the length of the leg and widens the ankle.

Don't... wear clothing that has horizontal lines where you are the broadest.

Don't... wear a wide or contrasting belt if your waistline is thicker than 33" (84cm). If you want to wear a belt, choose one that is thin and the same color as the garment, and wear it under a jacket so only the buckle shows. The decorative buckle catches the eye and stops it from looking around the waist circumference.

...by Adjusting Length and Proportion

"Poorly stitched hems or incorrect lengths can ruin the look of a garment. Try adjusting the length of a skirt or dress to improve the proportion. Nothing makes a jacket look as dumpy as sleeves that are too long."

Marla Kazell
Professional dressmaker; Custom tailor
Tigard, OR

"I will especially address the full-figured woman because to me, improving ready-to-wear means making sure the details such as closures, hem lengths on sleeves and skirts...and the style lines (outline or silhouette of the garment) are in proportion.

• Never wear a sleeve that is too long, because it looks sloppy. Cuff and collar buttons should be moved to make them snug without being tight.

• Make sure the hem is even front and back. Some can be evened at the bottom. For others, it will be necessary to take excess length from the waist [see '...by Taking Up a Flared Skirt from the Waistline' in chapter 1].

• The fullness at the pant hems and sleeve ends must be controlled by using darts or open-ended pleats (Fig. 5.16)."

Gale Grigg Hazen
Instructor; Author;
Sewing machine, serger, and knitting machine expert
Saratoga, CA

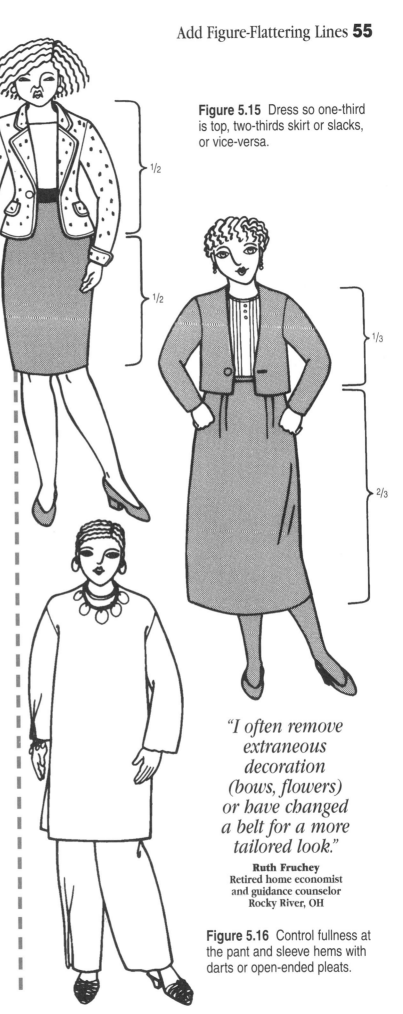

Figure 5.15 Dress so one-third is top, two-thirds skirt or slacks, or vice-versa.

1/2

1/2

1/3

2/3

"I often remove extraneous decoration (bows, flowers) or have changed a belt for a more tailored look."

Ruth Fruchey
Retired home economist
and guidance counselor
Rocky River, OH

Figure 5.16 Control fullness at the pant and sleeve hems with darts or open-ended pleats.

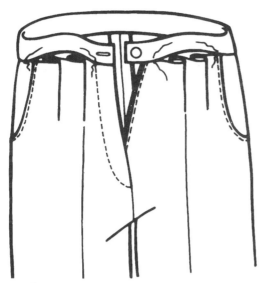

Figure 5.17 Turn pleats so the folds are toward the center front and so they open toward the side seams.

...by Making Tummy-Trimming Pleats

"On some skirts and slacks, the pleats at the waistline are pressed so they open toward the center front. This isn't flattering when you carry weight in your stomach. I change the pleats so they are pressed to the other side."

Lisa Kushwara
Sewing instructor; Avid machine and hand quilter
Austin, TX

"According to the consumer response, the number-one problem that frustrates women is the protruding abdomen. Darts or pleats that go toward the center front, especially in slacks, will accent the curve in the abdomen. To solve: Rip out the waistband seam, turn the pleats toward the side seams, and resew."

Jan Larkey
Author, *Flatter Your Figure* (Prentice-Hall, 1991)
Pittsburgh, PA

To follow Lisa's and Jan's tips:

1 Loosen a few stitches holding the waistband on and past either side of the pleats.

2 Turn the pleats so the folds are toward the center front and they open toward the side seams. Tuck pleats back into the waistband and restitch (Fig. 5.17).

...by Adding Shoulder Pads (a Plus or Your Pet Peeve?)

"Shoulder pads are necessary to fill the space between your body and the garment shoulder line. You may need to change the thickness, depending on the slope of your shoulders. You can also change the placement of the shoulder pads, depending upon the width of your shoulders. Change the shoulder pads to fit you."

Marla Kazell
Professional dressmaker; Custom tailor
Tigard, OR

Are shoulder pads one of your pet peeves? Then learn:

• Why not to eliminate them

• What to do when they are destroyed by the dry cleaners

• How to reduce garment fullness at the shoulders and necklines to use with smaller pads

• How to keep from looking like a football player

Even though the trend of late is away from the over-padded look, most women are reluctant to give up shoulder pads because we look better with them than without them. If you're still not convinced, read on.

Sleeves made for shoulder pads are cut with longer sleeve caps, and jackets and bodices with a straighter shoulder line. This extra space can be altered or reduced slightly, but for the most part they should be left alone to maintain the integrity of the shoulder line. Other reasons we need shoulder pads are that:

• A person's narrowing, sloping, or hollow shoulders can be made to look more normal with the addition of a shoulder pad

• A large bust can appear slightly smaller with a bigger-looking shoulder line

• Shoulder pads preserve the shape of a garment when it's on a hanger

If you're still not convinced you need your shoulder pads, this point bears repeating: You visually lose five pounds in the hips by making the shoulders appear wider.

...by Making Shoulder Pads Removable

If your shoulder pads are removable, you don't have to send them to the dry cleaners to be mangled, you can avoid football shoulder pad build-up (shoulder pads on top of shoulder pads), and you can replace them with pads that fit your figure and make you look better. Here are two easy ways to do it.

"I always remove the shoulder pads from ready-to-wear and use one of the three pairs I keep in my closet that fit my frame and my style perfectly. All I have is the hook side of a Velcro strip sewn on each shoulder pad, which grabs on to any garment (Fig. 5.18)."

Cindy Kacynski
Editor, *Serger Update* newsletter; Free-lance editor
Peoria, IL

"I dislike shoulder pads that are not compatible with the care of the garment, so I make mine detachable with snaps. Remove the shoulder pads, noting the difference between right and left sides. If there is a difference, I use black snaps on the left side and chrome on the right. This way I match colors and have the correct pad in place on the garment. My favorite technique for lining up snap parts is first to sew the pointed side to the side of the pad that does not touch the body. Rub white chalk over the point of the snap. Push the snap against the garment to mark the position for the other snap. They line up perfectly."

Naomi J. Blodgett
Certified Home Economist; Consultant
Columbus, OH

...by Replacing Shoulder Pads

"I would love to know how and if sleeves with shoulder pads can be changed to wear no shoulder pads or smaller ones."

Veda Rose
Certified Home Economist
Columbus, OH

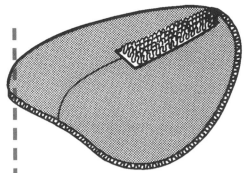

Figure 5.18 "Sew the hook side of a Velcro strip on each shoulder pad.

Sew How

An excellent booklet and patterns are available called "Shape Your Shoulders With Shoulder Pads." For information, write to the author: **Belva Barrick, M.S., C.H.E,.** *5643 West Townley Avenue, Glendale, AZ 85302*

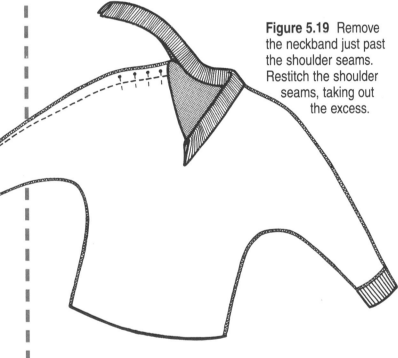

Figure 5.19 Remove the neckband just past the shoulder seams. Restitch the shoulder seams, taking out the excess.

Because set-in sleeve caps are elongated to accommodate shoulder pads, and armcyes (armholes) are cut to fit the sleeve, the alteration to reduce the size of the shoulder pads is a job for a skilled dressmaker (see chapter 9). However, I was able to easily reduce the size of a shoulder pad on a dolman sleeve. Here's how.

1. Remove the shoulder pad. Try on the garment, right side out, and pin out the necessary fullness.

2. Remove the neckband just past the shoulder seams. Restitch or reserge the shoulder seams, taking out the excess fabric (Fig. 5.19).

3. Replace the neckband as before. Install a smaller pad.

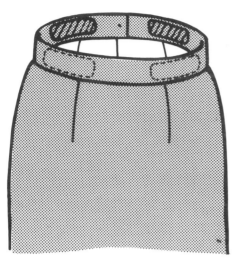

Figure 5.20 Cut and fuse or stitch 2–3" (5–7.5cm) strips of synthetic suede to the inside of your waistbands to keep shirts tucked in. If making a waistband from scratch, line the inside with it.

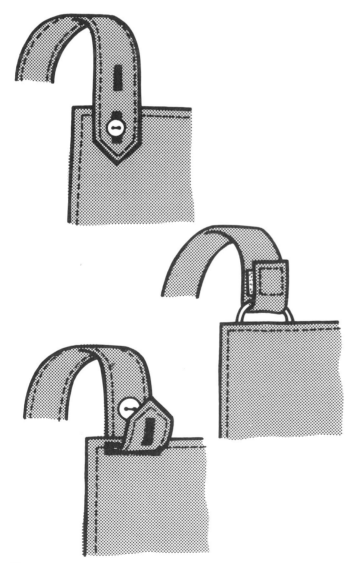

Figure 5.21 If you remove a buckle, replace it with a large button or Velcro on the strap and pull it through a buttonhole or loop.

Add Comfort

...by Using Quick-Fix Comfort Tricks

- If your nylon tricot slip rides up, wear it inside out. The ribs in the tricot grab the ribs in your pantyhose and climb. By turning the slip inside out, the smooth side of the tricot and prominent rib in your pantyhose are perpendicular.

- If the elastic on your underwear and nightgown bothers you, wear them inside out. The smooth fabric, rather than the rough texture of the elastic, will be against the skin.

- If care or designer labels scratch your neck, remove them and resew them into a side seam.

...by Making an Un"tuck"able Waistband

"I sew or fuse four strips of Ultrasuede or waistband tabs [available through your local retailer or mail-order source] inside the waistband of skirts and trousers. The texture of the synthetic suede keeps shirts and blouses tucked in all day. The strips should be ½" (1.3cm) narrower than the waistband, and about 2–3" (5–7.5cm) long. Cut one for each side and one for the front and back. These strips can be fused in place, hand stitched or edgestitched by machine. If making a garment from scratch, the entire waistband can be lined with it (Fig. 5.20)."

Suzy Poor
Sewing instructor; Sewing and serging expert
Artesia, CA

...by Adding Comfortable Closures

"Oshkosh B'gosh uses hard buckles on their overalls. The fabric they use is always so durable that it's worth buying the overalls, but the buckles break, are hard for a child who is potty training to unfasten, and when an infant wears them, their little chins and

cheeks get pinched. If you remove the buckle, replace it with a large button or Velcro on the strap and pull it through a buttonhole or loop (Fig. 5.21)."

Jeanne Moser
Family friend; Mother of four
East Kingston, NH

...by Adding a Quick-Serged Lining

"I often add a lining to an unlined skirt or slacks."

Jan Nunn
Sewing instructor; Professional dressmaker
Portland, OR

For a pleated or full skirt, you may want to seek the services of a professional dressmaker (see page 116-117). However, if you wish to line a skirt with a back kick pleat, try this.

1 Cut the front lining on the fold, and back lining as shown in Figure 5.22. The lining should be cut 1" (2.5cm) shorter than the hemmed skirt length. Rather than cutting a vent, cut a gentle curve ending just above the pleat.

2 Sew or serge the side seams together and press the seam allowance together or to one side.

3 Open the lining flat and quickly finish the curved and bottom edges with a balanced 3-thread overlock or narrow hem (Fig. 5.23; see also Reference Chart A).

4 Stitch the center-back seam together at the 5/8" (1.5cm) seamline, starting 1" (2.5cm) above the curve. If there is a zipper at the center back, stitch the center-back lining seam to the bottom of the zipper opening, then backstitch and/or tie off thread ends. From there, baste the rest of the seam allowance together. Press the seam open, then topstitch around the basted seam allowance. Remove basting stitches to create a slit for the zipper.

5 Remove the stitches holding the inside waistband in place. Pin the lining into the waistline, pinning at center front, center back, and side seams. Lining will be fuller than the waistline opening.

6 Set your machine for a moderately long stitch (about 3-3.5) and use the embroidery foot.

7 Starting at the zipper opening, place the top of the skirt and lining under the foot, lining side down. Begin sewing slowly, holding the skirt layer firmly in your right hand at the first pin and preventing it from

feeding normally through the machine. At the same time, let the lining feed normally. The feed dogs feed the lining into the waistline, automatically easing in the excess fullness. Continue this process from pin to pin. Once the lining is attached, stitch the inside waistband back in place.

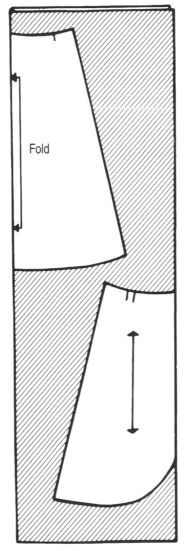

Figure 5.22 Cut front and back lining so they're 1" (2.5cm) shorter than the hemmed skirt length.

Serge-Easy Tip
For a lot more information on serging, read The ABCs of Serging, *by Tammy Young and Lori Bottom (Chilton, 1992),* Serged Garments in Minutes, *by Tammy Young and Naomi Baker (Chilton, 1992), and* Serge a Simple Project, *by Tammy Young and Naomi Baker (Chilton, 1994).*

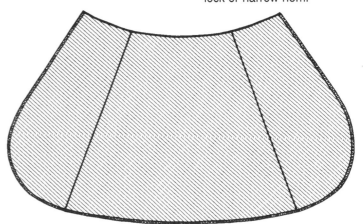

Figure 5.23 Open lining flat and finish the curved and bottom edges with a balanced 3-thread overlock or narrow hem.

Quick-Fix  Repairs

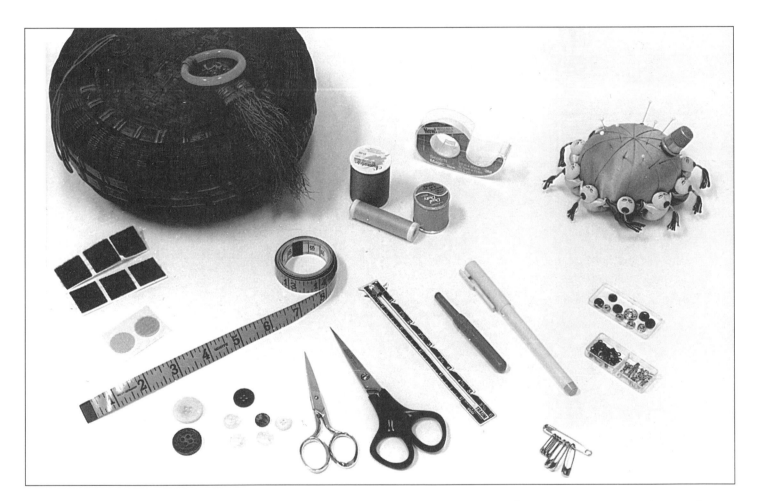

Figure 6.1 Quick-Fix Survival Kit: the basic sewing supplies needed for Quick-Fix repairs.

In researching this chapter, I discovered two books devoted to mending basics, such as repairing holes, tears, and splits. Due to my space limitations (and because this book focuses on *Quick*-Fixes), I recommend these books to learn more in-depth techniques. Both books are available through your local fabric or sewing-machine retailer, or by mail-order. Call or write for information on the retailer near you.

Fear of Sewing
Power Sewing
95 Fifth Avenue
San Francisco, CA 94118
1-800-845-7474

Clothing Care and Repair
Singer Reference Library
Cy DeCoss Incorporated
5900 Green Oak Drive
Minnetonka, MN 55343
1-800-828-2895

Quick-Fix Survival Kit

Every household or dorm room needs a few sewing supplies. Here is a list of essentials available at any fabric store or sewing mail-order source (Fig. 6.1) and recommended by Barbara Gash, sewing columnist at the *Detroit Free Press*. Since many of my friends outside the industry don't sew, I put these items in a basket as a gift. I always include quality products (instead of the five-spools-for-a-dollar-type thread). Any recipient of this gift has been thrilled to have everything they need in one place for Quick-Fix repairs.

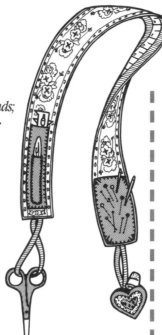

Quick-Fix Gift

I have made sewing chatelaines for friends; this puts almost everything they need for hand sewing at their fingertips (Fig. 6.2). A pincushion on one end holds needles and pins; a pouch hung below holds a thimble; the pocket on the other side holds a seam ripper and a 6" (15cm) hem gauge; a pair of embroidery scissors hangs below the pocket. On the side of the chatelaine that touches the neck, I also stitch a tape measure.

Figure 6.2 A sewing chatelaine makes a great gift.

The Quick-Fix Survival Kit

Assorted-sized hand needles

Needle threader (for needle threading and pulling in snags)

Thimble to protect the middle finger on the sewing hand

All-purpose (cotton-wrapped polyester) thread in assorted basic colors (the Rainbow Thread Braid described later in this chapter saves you the time, trouble, and space limitations of finding small spools in the basic colors)

Transparent monofilament thread

Straight pins (preferably glass-headed so they won't melt if pressed over)

Pincushion

1/2" (1.3cm) transparent tape (for zipper repair and temporarily taping a hem, ribbon, or appliqué)

Small embroidery scissors for clipping threads

Seam ripper or surgical seam ripper for "un-sewing" sewn and serged stitches (see page 127)

6" (15cm) metal hem gauge

Tape measure

Safety pins

Snaps, hooks, and eyes

Extra shirt buttons

Velcro hook-and-loop fasteners

Lint remover to lift off unwanted threads

Helpful Repair Aids and What They Do

Although these items are not essential, they make Quick-Fix repairs a snap (Fig. 6.3). These items, often referred to as sewing notions, are generally found grouped together on the wall around the perimeter of fabric stores.

Res-Q Tape and Res-Q Tabs

This paper-backed double-faced tape holds fabric to fabric. Use it to eliminate "gaposis" between blouse buttons and to temporarily hold hems that have ripped out (a must for any desk drawer at work). It can also keep bra straps up and surplice blouses closed.

> *"Easily remove paper backing from the Res-Q tape by turning down one corner 1/4"(6mm), pressing tape to tape. That tape corner now sticks to itself for easy peeling."*
>
> **Clotilde**
> President, Clotilde, Inc.
> Ft. Lauderdale, FL

Button Safety Pins

Pin on special or decorative shank buttons for easy changing and cleaning. The hump goes over the button shank.

Emergency Shirt Buttons

Great for traveling and will work when you don't have time or an extra shirt button or needle and thread handy. Push the point on the underside of the emergency button through the fabric. Place the snap over the point, push, then break off the point. Button it through your buttonhole. To remove the button, cut off the plastic shank with a sharp pair of embroidery scissors.

Rainbow Thread Braid

This 29-color braid is made of 350 threads cut 28" (71cm) long. Work the point of a hand needle under one strand and pull it out of the woven braid. Great for traveling or your Quick-Fix Survival Kit.

Elastic Thread

Use this to pull in stretched-out sweater cuffs or bagged-out sock tops, or to shirr in a too-big waistline or sleeve (see pages 9, 39, and 43).

Liquid Seam Sealant

Use Fray Check, Stop Fraying, or No-Fray to prevent raveling on the edge of laces or trim. Use it to reinforce cut edges of a buttonhole, or to prevent serged threads from unraveling.

Liquid Fabric Mender

This clear mending adhesive mends fabrics without sewing. Apply a thin coat of the adhesive and place the patch over a hole immediately; then press the patch and the fabric together with your fingers. The mend is dry after a half hour but gains maximum strength overnight. Later, I'll tell you how it worked on a vinyl coat I repaired (see pages 65-66).

It Stays!

This water-soluble roll-on body adhesive stops pantyhose from drooping, your bra strap from slipping, and helps to keep bathing suit leg openings down (when you aren't swimming, of course).

Glue Stick

Use this to temporarily glue-baste an appliqué, zipper, or button in place.

Figure 6.3 Helpful repair aids include Res-Q Tape and Res-Q Tabs, button safety pins, Emergency Shirt Buttons, Rainbow Thread Braid, elastic thread, liquid seam sealant, Liquid Fabric Mender, glue stick, paper-backed fusible web, liquid fusible web, Knit Fixer, bodkin, elastic guide, Drawstring Restringer, Zipper Safety Hook, Zipper Pull Repair Kit, Zipper Rescue Kit.

Teflon Pressing Sheet

This small, translucent, nonstick pressing sheet is used to prevent fusible adhesive from sticking to the iron and/or the ironing surface. Use it with fusible web, paper-backed fusible web, liquid fusible web, or as a press cloth on fabrics that need lower iron temperatures such as ripstop and nylon taffeta.

Paper-Backed Fusible Web

This notion is available by the yard or cut into 1/4-3/4" (6mm-2cm) widths. Just iron it on paper side up, peel off the paper, then fuse up a hem, and attach trim or ribbons. Fusible web makes any fabric fusible, so it's great for patching and appliqué.

Liquid Fusible Web

Apply this to the wrong side of the fabric; set it permanently by ironing on the wool setting. To protect the ironing surface, use a Teflon pressing sheet. Use it to permanently attach ribbons, appliqués, trims, and patches. This adhesive is completely removable if it is washed out before ironing, but is resistant to washing and dry cleaning after heat-setting.

Knit Fixer

Fix snags and pull loose threads to the wrong side of the fabric with this miniature latch hook (see pages 66-67).

Bodkin and/or Elastic Guide

Thread elastic or ribbon onto the bodkin or guide, then slip it through a casing. Elastic guides prevent twisting and snagging.

Drawstring Restringer

Restring a sweatshirt hood or waistline casing with the restringer. Slip the blunt end through the casing from eyelet to eyelet. Thread string through the loop in the restringer and slowly pull until the end of the string appears. Tie large knots or use cord locks at both ends of the drawstring so that it won't pull out again.

Zipper Pull Repair Kit

Fix zippers that have lost their pull. Insert the steel wire through zipper slide and push a new 1⅝" (4cm)-long pull onto a locking wire. Repair a camera case, briefcase, handbag, or tote bag with this extra-large sturdy pull.

Zipper Rescue Kit

This kit includes 32 sliders in four sizes most commonly used in outdoor gear. It also includes six bottom stops, six top stops, a spool of thread, a curved needle, a chunk of beeswax (that is run over the thread so it will not tangle), and a repair manual (see the source list in the back of the book for mail-order information).

Zipper Safety Hook

Control old run-away zippers. Fasten the C-hook around the button shank. Hook the bottom of the fastener into the lower opening of the zipper pull so the zipper stays up.

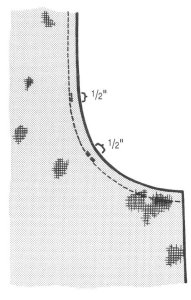

Figure 6.4 Restitch the seam by hand or machine starting 1/2" (1.3cm) from the split and backstitching at the beginning and end of the repair stitches.

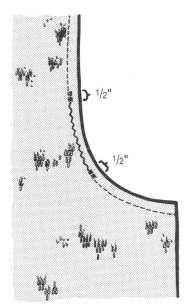

Figure 6.5 Mend a split seam in a woven fabric using a short straight stitch; mend a knit using a small zigzag stitch.

Sew Easy Tip

If your sewing machine has stretch or knit stitches, use one of them to repair a seam (see Reference Chart A).

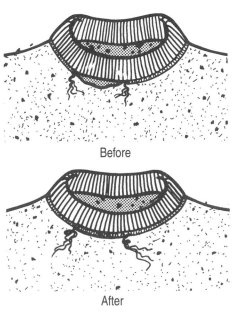

Figure 6.6 Mend a split in a sweater seam with a serged 3-thread or 3/4-thread overlock or a stretch stitch from your conventional machine. Dot threads with seam sealant to prevent original serged stitching from unraveling where the repair begins and ends.

Before

After

The Hole Story

Often a seam at a stress point, such as an underarm seam, side seam, or waistline, will pull out and tear. To fix it, stitch over the old seamline. Here's how.

Mend a Split Seam

If the seam allowance is still intact, remove the broken and ripped stitches. Restitch the seam by hand or machine, starting 1/2" (1.3cm) from the split and backstitching at the beginning and end of the repair stitches (Fig. 6.4), adhering to the following guidelines as needed.

- For a woven fabric, use a straight stitch; for a knit use a small zigzag (Fig. 6.5).

- To mend a split seam in a sweater, use a 3-thread or 3/4-thread overlock (Fig. 6.6, see Reference Chart A).

- To reinforce a stress area such as an underarm or crotch seam, use an elastic straight stitch (sometimes called a straight stretch stitch) where the needle takes two stitches forward and one back (Fig. 6.7).

Mend Leather, Suede, and Vinyl

"What can and cannot be repaired when it comes to special fabrics such as leather, suede, or vinyl?"

Carol McGuire
Publisher, *American Fastener Journal*
Columbus, OH

Often with leather, suede, faux suede, or vinyl, stress points rip or tear where the seam has been perforated by the stitch. To repair one of these fabrics:

1 Following the manufacturer's directions, glue the tear or rip, butting the edges together with one of the liquid adhesives mentioned in the "Helpful Repair Aids" section. To help set the glue in the tear, place a strip of masking tape on the right side of the garment and perpendicular to the tear. Let the glue dry completely before the next step (Fig. 6.8).

2 Leather, suede, and some faux suedes can withstand the heat of a *cool* iron (always test first on an inconspicuous inside seam). On these fabrics, reinforce the tear by ironing a piece of fusible tricot (look for trade names such as Easy-Knit, Fusi-Knit, Knit Fuze, or French Fuse at your local fabric retailer or through a mail-order source listed in the back of the book) on the back of the tear so that the patch goes beyond the tear about 1/2" (1.3cm) (Fig. 6.9).

Mend Ripstop Nylon or Nylon Taffeta

For ripstop or nylon taffeta, make a fusible patch with a low-temperature iron, paper-backed fusible web, and a Teflon pressing sheet.

"If the area to be patched can accommodate it, I prefer to patch ripstop or nylon taffeta with an appliqué because it looks better and stays longer than a fused patch. However, if the appliqué is not in an acceptable location, fuse a patch like this:

1. Trim away loose threads and/or fiberfill from around the hole. Fuse a piece of paper-backed fusible web onto the wrong side of the patch fabric following the manufacturer's instructions and using a Teflon pressing sheet over the fabric. This prevents the nylon from melting (Fig. 6.10a).

2. Leaving the release paper on, cut a patch slightly larger than the hole. (Circle shapes fuse better and are less conspicuous on solid fabrics. The corners of a square or rectangular patch have a tendency to curl after some wear.)

3. Remove the release paper and fuse the patch to the garment, again using the Teflon pressing sheet over the work (Fig. 6.10b)."

Arlene Haislap
President, The Green Pepper, Inc.
Eugene, OR

Quick-Fix Alternative for Vinyl—*For vinyl, however, fusing is not an option, so try this: Using one of the liquid adhesives listed in the "Helpful Repair Aids" section, follow the manufacturer's directions and glue the tear together as described for leather (see Figs. 6.8, 6.9). After the glue is dry, remove the tape and glue a patch of sturdy woven fabric behind the rip as well.*

NOTE— *I just repaired the back vent of my vinyl raincoat this way. For extra support, I cut a patch of faux leather and glued it over the original stitching by dotting*

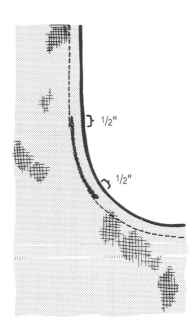

Figure 6.7 Reinforce a stress area such as an underarm or crotch seam, using a machine elastic stretch stitch that takes two stitches forward and one back.

1/2"

1/2"

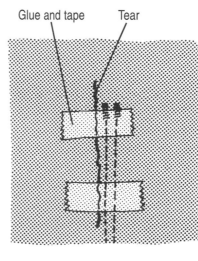

Glue and tape   Tear

Figure 6.8 Glue the tear or rip together with a liquid adhesive. On the right side of the garment, place a strip of masking tape perpendicular to the tear. Let the glue dry completely before removing the tape.

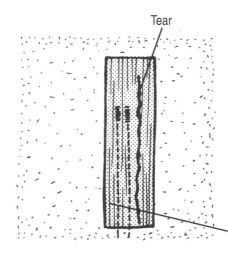

Tear

Figure 6.9 To reinforce the tear on leather, suede, or faux suede, fuse a piece of fusible tricot on the back of the tear using a cool iron.

Fusible tricot

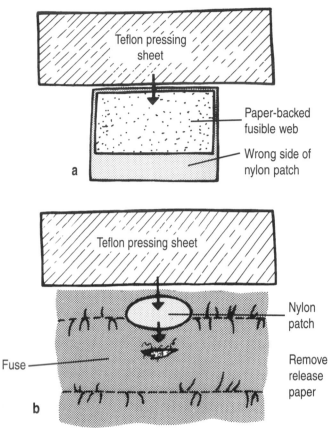

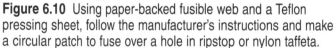

Figure 6.10 Using paper-backed fusible web and a Teflon pressing sheet, follow the manufacturer's instructions and make a circular patch to fuse over a hole in ripstop or nylon taffeta.

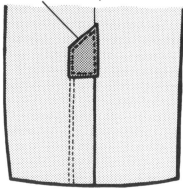

Figure 6.11 To mend a tear in vinyl, glue it together. Glue another piece of reinforcing fabric to the wrong side of the tear. Cut a faux leather patch large enough to cover the torn area and dot glue on the perimeter of the new patch. Finger-press it into place. Let the glue dry completely. Stitch through the patch and the vinyl, reinforcing the fabric with a long straight stitch to prevent further ripping.

the adhesive around the edge of the patch. After the glue was dry, I topstitched the patch in place using a long straight stitch and sewing through the patch, vinyl, and lining so it won't rip again (Fig. 6.11).

Mend a Snag

Rather than cutting off a pulled thread or snag, which would create a hole and run in the fabric, pull the snag through to the wrong side of the garment with a Knit Fixer or needle threader. From the wrong side, poke the latch hook or wire up through to the right side of the fabric so the latch or wire is open. Pick up the snag, then pull the tool back through. The latch or wire automatically closes while pulling the snag to the back of the fabric (Fig. 6.12).

Goof-Proof Zippers

Lightweight zippers are usually inserted as a centered or lapped application. Centered means that the zipper is centered in the seam so there is an equal amount of overlap on either side to hide the zipper teeth. A lapped application has a wide overlap that covers the zipper teeth on one side and an underlap stitched next to the teeth on the other side of the zipper. Within those two categories, you will also see heavier zippers. Separating zippers on jacket fronts, for example, are centered zippers; fly-front zippers found in jeans or trousers are lapped zippers.

In this section, you'll learn how to replace all of these zippers, as well as how to tackle other zipper bugaboos.

Put Zippers Back on Track

If a zipper pull comes off-track and the teeth are in good repair, rather than replace the zipper, put the pull back on track.

1 Remove the metal stop at the bottom of the zipper, working a metal nut pick or staple pull under the prongs.

2 Zip the pull back on track from the bottom.

3 Replace the zipper stop or stitch a few hand or machine stitches at the bottom of the zipper.

Sew-Easy Tip: When buying a replacement zipper, buy one that is at least 1" (2.5cm) longer than the opening. It is easier to replace because the pull is out of the way of the presser foot while you are stitching. Once it is stitched in, the zipper is shortened at the top to fit the opening

Replace a Centered Zipper

1 Remove the broken zipper by clipping stitches with embroidery scissors or a seam ripper. Rip back the waistband about 1" (2.5cm) on both sides of the zipper. Machine baste the seam together from the bottom of the zipper opening to the top, using a long stitch. With the new zipper closed from the wrong side of the garment, place the zipper teeth over the seam with the stop at the bottom of the basting stitches. Tape-baste across the back of the zipper (Fig. 6.13).

2 On the right side of the garment, place a strip of 1/2" (1.3cm)-wide transparent tape or zipper guide tape such as Straight-Tape (available through you fabric retailer or mail-order source) the length of the zipper, centering the seamline under the tape. This will be your stitching guide (Fig. 6.14).

3 Attach your zipper foot and adjust it to sew one side of the zipper, first stitching across the bottom of the zipper and then sewing up alongside the transparent or zipper-guide tape. Repeat for the other side of the zipper sewing up the other side. (This two-step process ensures that plaids and stripes will match after the basting stitches are removed.)

4 Remove the guide tape and basting stitches; *then move the zipper pull to the bottom of the zipper.* Trim the zipper at the top edge by cutting the zipper tape so that it is 1/2" (1.3cm) above the seamline. Be careful: Don't, for example, try on the garment before you secure the top of the zipper or the pull will come off. Tuck the zipper into the waistband or facing and restitch it as it was before, using your standard presser foot (Fig. 6.15).

Replace a Lapped Zipper

1 Remove the old zipper, ripping stitches at the waistband about an inch (2.5cm) on either side of the zipper. Pin and/or hand baste the new zipper to underlap so that the teeth are close to the fold and the stop is at the bottom of the opening. Using your zipper foot, stitch the basted side of the zipper, starting from the bottom and sewing up (Fig. 6.16).

2 With the zipper closed, baste the overlap so that it just covers the machine stitches on the underlap. On the topside of the garment, place a strip of 1/2" (1.3cm)-wide transparent or zipper-guide tape the length of the zipper so that one edge is even with the

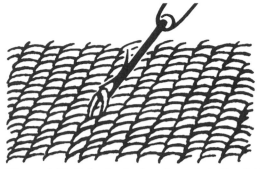

Figure 6.12 Poke the tool up through to the right side of the fabric so the latch or wire is open. Pick up snag, then pull the tool back through.

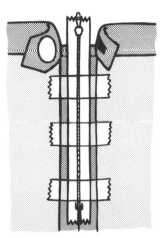

Figure 6.13 Machine baste the seam together. On the inside of the garment, place zipper stop at the bottom of the basting stitches so the teeth are centered over the seamline. Tape-baste zipper into position so the pull is up on the zipper tape, out of the way.

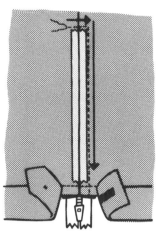

Figure 6.14 On the right side of the garment, place a strip of 1/2" (1.3cm) guide tape the length of the zipper, centering the seamline under the tape. The straight edges of the tape will be your stitching guide.

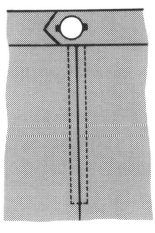

Figure 6.15 From the right side and starting at the bottom of the zipper, stitch next to the guide tape, sewing up to the waistline seam. Next, sew across the bottom of the zipper and up the other side of the guide tape as before. Shorten the zipper from the top. Position and restitch the waistband.

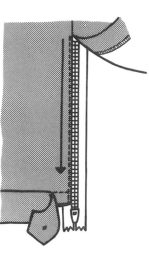

Figure 6.16 Remove old zipper; pin and/or hand baste the zipper to the underlap so the teeth are close to the fold and the stop is at the bottom of the opening. Stitch the first side next to the teeth, sewing from the bottom up.

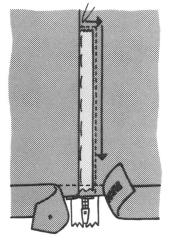

Figure 6.17 Hand baste the overlap. Place a strip of 1/2" (1.3cm) transparent tape even with the seamline. Stitch the other side of the zipper, sewing next to the transparent tape.

Stitch in-the-ditch

Figure 6.18 Remove transparent tape and basting stitches. Open zipper so the pull is at the bottom stop. Cut off excess zipper tape 1/2" (1.3cm) above the original seamline. Tuck in zipper and stitch in-the-ditch, using a

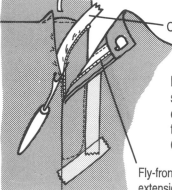

Old zipper

Figure 6.19 Mark the topstitching line on the fly-front extention with transparent tape or Fly Front Zipper Guide.

Fly-front facing extension

seamline. This will be your stitching guide. Using your zipper foot, sew across the bottom of the zipper and up, guiding the needle next to the guide tape (Fig. 6.17).

3 Remove the guide tape and basting stitches. *Then move the zipper pull to the bottom of the zipper.* Cut off the top of the zipper so that the zipper tape is about 1/2" (1.3cm) above the seamline. Tuck the zipper tape into the waistband or facing and restitch it as it was before (Fig. 6.18), using a standard zigzag presser foot and guiding the needle in the crack of the seamline (also known as stitching in-the-ditch). If you have a guide on your blindhem foot, guide it down the ditch as you sew. The guide opens the seam; then, after stitching, the seam allowance closes over the stitches so they are almost invisible. Use this same stitch in-the-ditch technique to catch facings, too.

> **Sew How:** *Before restitching the waistband or facing above a lapped or centered zipper, backstitch over the top of the zipper tape across the coil several times so the pull won't come off-track.*

Replace a Fly-Front Zipper

Do you have a pair of jeans or pants in your repair pile that have been there awhile because the zipper needs to be replaced? Fix them in an hour or less. You'll feel as though you have added another pair of pants to your wardrobe in less time than it takes to shop for a new pair. All you need is a replacement zipper, transparent tape or a Fly Front Zipper Guide (available through your local fabric retailer or a mail-order source), and a jeans needle (size 90/14; see Reference Charts B and C). It will probably take you longer to read the directions than to complete the task, so think of this as part of your learning curve. The next zipper replacement should go much faster.

> **Sew How:** *Often it's easier to replace a zipper longer than the opening so that you don't have to stitch around the zipper pull. However, I have found when replacing a metal jeans zipper that I am more successful using a zipper the exact length needed for the opening.*

1 Mark the original topstitching line on the fly-front extension by drawing over the stitches with chalk (for dark-colored jeans) or water-erasable marker (for light-colored jeans), or lay a strip of transparent tape or a Fly Front Zipper Guide next to the stitching (Fig. 6.19).

2 Unzip the zipper and remove the old zipper, carefully ripping the stitches by snipping them with sharp embroidery scissors or a seam ripper. Make notes on how the zipper was installed (I usually draw a

sketch for myself for reference). Note that the fly-front extension side is usually stitched in two steps. Rip back the waistband just far enough to remove the old zipper.

3 Open out the fly-front facing extension. With right sides together, either pin or hand baste the zipper so that the left edge of the zipper tape as you look at it is even with the left edge of the facing extension. Stitch along the left edge of the zipper tape, sewing from the bottom up (Fig. 6.20).

4 Unzip the zipper and turn the fly-front facing extension under to its original position. Pin the other side of the zipper in place so the zipper tape is sandwiched between the underlap and extension and the fold is next to the zipper teeth (Fig. 6.21). Before stitching, zip up the zipper to be sure that everything is positioned correctly and the zipper and fly front are smooth. If everything looks okay, hand baste, then machine stitch the other side of the zipper close to the teeth.

5 Move the pull to the bottom of the zipper, and if necessary, shorten the zipper at the top, leaving 1/2" (1.3cm) of zipper tape and teeth above the original waistband stitching line (Fig. 6.22). On the side with the underlap, tuck the top of the zipper under the waistband and restitch.

6 Topstitch the fly front, guiding the needle next to the transparent tape or Fly Front Zipper Guide and using thread and a stitch length similar to what was originally used. Restitch the waistband as it was before (Fig. 6.23).

Add an Oversized Separating Zipper

"In the past, I have removed skimpy separating zippers in children's clothing and sewn in oversized ones in their place. That improvement turned out to be a stroke of genius...if I do say so myself. This way the kids have an easier time zipping their own jackets."

Libby Anderson
Teacher; Mother of two
Amherst, OH

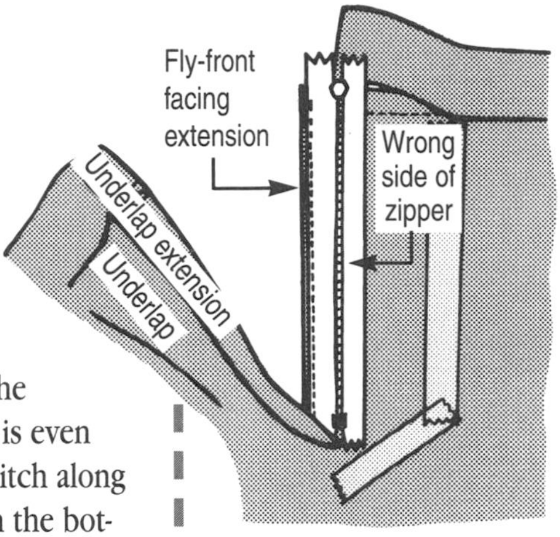

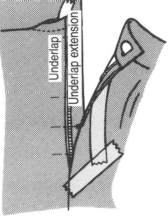

Fly-front facing extension

Underlap extension

Underlap

Wrong side of zipper

Figure 6.20 Open out fly-front facing extension. With right sides together, either pin or hand baste the zipper so the left edge of the zipper tape as you look at it is even with the left edge of the facing extension. Sew along the left edge of the zipper tape, sewing from the bottom up.

Underlap

Underlap extension

Figure 6.21 Open the zipper. Pin the other side of the zipper so the zipper tape is sandwiched between the underlap and underlap extension, and the fold is next to the zipper teeth. Zip zipper and check that the zipper and fly front are smooth. If they are, unzip again, then machine stitch the other side of the zipper close to the teeth.

Figure 6.22 Cut off excess zipper tape (if necessary). On the side with the underlap, tuck the top of the zipper under the waistband and restitch.

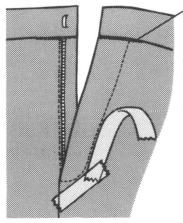

Stitch in-the-ditch

Figure 6.23 Topstitch the fly front, guiding the needle next to the transparent tape or Fly Front Zipper Guide and using thread and stitch length similar to what was originally used; restitch the waistband, catching the top of the zipper tape in the stitching. Reattach the waistband by stitching in-the-ditch.

Figure 6.24 Separate the replacement zipper. Pin, baste, and finger-press one side of the zipper to the lining side of the jacket so the pull faces to the outside. Stitch the first side of the zipper, sewing through a single layer of lining while guiding the presser foot down the middle of the zipper tape.

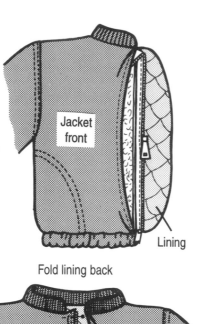

Fold lining back

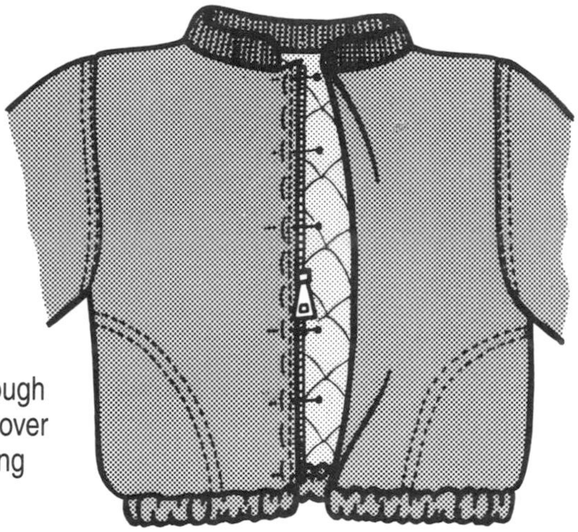

Figure 6.25
Align jacket lining with jacket front, pin, and baste; then topstitch through all layers, sewing over the original stitching line.

To insert an oversized separating zipper:

1 Buy a replacement zipper the length of the opening.

2 Remove the old zipper with sharp embroidery scissors or a seam ripper by carefully snipping the stitches. Separate the replacement zipper. Open the lining flat where the zipper is to be replaced; then pin, baste, and finger-press the first side of the zipper to the *lining* so the pull faces to the outside. Using a zipper foot, stitch the first side of the zipper, sewing through a single layer of lining while guiding the presser foot down the middle of the zipper tape (Fig. 6.24).

3 Pin and baste the jacket front over first side of the zipper, pinning through all layers. Using your zipper foot and a 3–3.5 (8–10 stitches per inch) stitch length, topstitch over the original zipper topstitching line (Fig. 6.25).

4 Zip on the second side of the zipper. Align the jacket lining and pin, baste, finger-press, and stitch as before. Pin, baste, and topstitch the second side of the jacket front as before (Fig. 6.26).

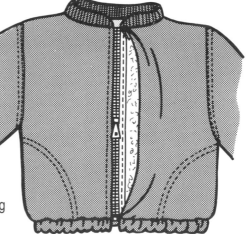

Figure 6.26 Zip on second side of zipper. Align jacket lining; pin, baste, and stitch jacket front and lining together, sandwiching the zipper in between as before.

Sew How: *If you can't find an oversized zipper the exact length you need, buy one longer than you need. Then, instead of cutting off the zipper at the top as described earlier for other applications, either fold over the tape on a coil zipper (Fig. 6.27), or remove teeth and put on a new stop for a molded-tooth zipper (Fig. 6.28). For more advice and specific details on replacing, repairing, or installing zippers for use in backpacks, tote bags, duffle bags, sleeping bags, and outdoor wear, consult The Green Pepper, Inc., 3918 W. First Avenue, Eugene, OR 97402; (503) 345-6665, or for orders only: 1-800-767-5684, fax (503) 345-6671. They offer an inexpensive information leaflet on coil zippers, molded-tooth zippers with reversible pulls, single pulls, nonseparating, one-way separating, and two-way separating zippers. This company also has a wide range of sport-type zippers available in many colors.*

Home Improvement

At night, I am usually cold because my husband throws off all the covers. To keep the peace, I have solved this problem by making a blanket that is a double thickness on my side and a single thickness on his side. For our queen-size bed, I bought a king-size blanket, put it on the bed, and fit it so there was enough drop on both sides, but doubled where I need it. In Europe they solve this problem by putting two duvets on each double bed.

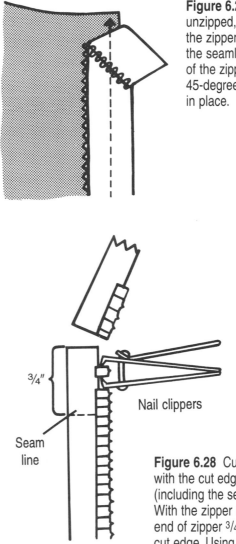

Figure 6.27 With the zipper unzipped, cut off the top of the zipper 3/4" (2cm) above the seamline. Fold each side of the zipper over itself at a 45-degree angle and stitch in place.

3/4"

Nail clippers

Seam line

Figure 6.28 Cut off zipper even with the cut edge of the fabric (including the seam allowance). With the zipper unzipped, mark end of zipper 3/4" (2cm) below the cut edge. Using finger nail clippers, pull teeth off the ends of the zipper above the marks. Pin zipper in place, folding the extra tape at a 45-degree angle and including two teeth as shown. Stitch.

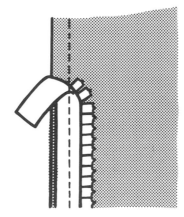

Part II

Quick-Fix Embellishments and Time-Saving Strategies to Upgrade Your Wardrobe

Have you wanted to breathe new life into a comfortable old favorite? Then you'll love "Embellishments in an Evening or Less." In chapter 7, find the inspiration for no-sew embellishments (no experience needed), quick embellishments (if you sew a little), and how to let your sewing machine or serger do all the work (if you sew a little more).

"Care and Feeding of Your Wardrobe" (chapter 8) includes information on care labeling, how to "get the red out" when you've accidentally washed a red sock in the white load, and Quick-Fix spot removal tips. Also, see how to recycle or restyle clothing once it's past improving.

Have you owned a pair of pants that looked great the first few times you wore them, but lost their charm after several washings? Learn how to evaluate clothing quality, along with a little about fiber content and fabric structure, in chapter 9. Before you know it, you'll be able to make "Savvy Shopping" decisions as they relate to your budget and lifestyle, helping you look better with less. You'll even discover tricks for shopping with and for your kids. I think you'll enjoy the section, so let's start!

Embellishments in an Evening or Less

Pompom

Movable eyes

Ribbon bow

Sleeves to match pants

Figure 7.1 Add glitter, bells, bows, pom-poms, and movable eyes to existing appliqués; add pockets and sleeves to match skirts or pants.

Have you walked through an airport or shopping mall and thought to yourself, There goes someone who just bought a new sewing machine. You know what I'm talking about—every flat surface is covered by machine embroidery, ruffles, and ribbons.

It seems everything these days is embellished. But there is a fine line between appropriate and too much. In this chapter I'll attempt to give you a few appropriate ideas that have worked for me and others. Maybe one of these ideas is something you always wanted to try, but you didn't have the first idea about where to put it or how to do it. Or perhaps you are teaching others to have fun embellishing and need some ideas. These ideas come in handy when you need something fast for a special occasion and don't have the time or budget to go shopping.

I hope something in this chapter will spark your imagination, then move you to tastefully embellish something you already own in an evening or less.

Sources of Inspiration

"I try to express my style through the use of jewelry and accessories but enjoy learning other ways to add to ready-to-wear by unique, but appropriate sewing ideas."

Barbara Kaufmann
Homemaker
Richmond, VA

In a department store, I can usually spot a creative person two departments over. She is turning everything inside out, talking about it with a friend, or making sketches. I, too, find my best sources of inspiration are "snoop shopping" and perusing mail-order catalogs. While department stores and boutiques carry the latest styles and fashions, the mail-order catalogs carry clothing that sets itself apart from all the others, giving us great sources for "borrowing" ideas. I also pull pictures and line drawings out of the newspaper and children's coloring books. I save stationery and artful calendars, and if I see a great design on a piece of china or linen I've found in a catalog, that also goes in my ever-expanding idea file. Other great sources are o.p.i.'s (other people's ideas). Here are some favorites.

No-Sew Embellishments

Glue-on Bells, Bows, and Glitter

"I have taken ready-to-wear, especially children's clothing, and added glitter, bells, bows, pom-poms, and movable eyes. I have also added pockets on sleeves of tops with fabric to match skirts or pants (Fig. 7.1)."

Maxine Constantine
Bausch & Lomb
Madison, WI

1 Prewash the garment. Use a permanent washable glue to attach the bells, bows, pom-poms, or movable eyes. Do not use white craft glue; it will wash out. Look for one of these.

Solvent-based permanent glue
(washable and usually, but not always, dry cleanable)

Beacon Chemical Company's Fabri Tak

Bond's 527

EZ Fabric Glue

Magic American Chemical's Fabric Mender Magic

Plexi 400 Stretch Adhesive

Washington Millinery's Bridal Glue

Waterproof glues
(can be washed but generally not dry cleaned)

Aleene's OK-to-Wash-It

Dritz Liquid Stitch

Jurgen's Jewel & Fabric Glue

Plaid's Glu-N-Wash

Collin's Unique Stitch

2 Test glue on the underside of a seam allowance to check for colorfastness and texture. If it is safe, apply glue to the wrong side of fabric or decoration using your finger, a brush, or the bottle. Nancy Ward, author of *Stamping Made Easy* (Chilton, 1994), spreads glue with an old credit card. (For more information on glues, adhesives, and fusibles, read *The Crafter's Guide to Glues* by Tammy Young [Chilton, in press].)

3 Position the decoration and wait until the glue is completely dry, usually 24 hours, but read the recommended times on the product.

Sew How: *For more ideas on making designer clothes for the little people in your life, read* Petite Pizzazz *by Barb Griffin (Chilton, 1990).*

Stencil, Paint, Transfer, or Fuse

"I have stenciled things (shirts, etc.), and I have painted with the kids, using puffy paints and sponge painting techniques. I have also colored leaves to print on shirts using the crayon transfers (Fig. 7.2)."

Jane Thomas
Inept seamstress (sews only under pressure [her words]);
Elementary school teacher (and my college roommate)
Troy, MI

Here's how to transfer leaves onto fabric.

1 Select leaves that have good texture and veining, and that aren't too dry.

2 Using Dritz Transfer Crayons, Sulky Iron-on Transfer Pens, Jones Tones, or Tulip Fabric Paint (all available through your local fabric or craft store or by mail-order), color or paint the back of each leaf, using different colors for each. If you use fabric paint, slip a piece of cardboard under the area to be painted or use a cardboard T-shirt frame (available at craft stores) to prevent the paint from bleeding through.

3 Individually press the leaves (color side down) onto a preshrunk light-colored or white cotton shirt, arranging leaves into a pleasing design as you go.

4 For additional texture and dimension, machine stitch or dribble a bead of fabric paint over the most dominant lines. If you machine stitch, stabilize the underside with tear-away stabilizer.

No-Sew Tip: Read more about fabric painting techniques in Nancy Ward's Fabric Painting Made Easy *(Chilton, 1993).*

Stick It On, Peel It Off

Have you ever used a sticky note? You know, those little yellow slips of paper that stick temporarily to just about anything? Using the same kind of glue, you can transform laces, crests, appliqués, trims, ribbons, even shoulder pads into removable accents for temporary enhancement or embellishment. The secret is pressure-sensitive adhesive, and there are a number of brands on the market.

Aleene's Tack-It Over & Over

Clotilde's Sticky Stuff

Dritz Insta Tack

Faultless' Bead Easy Re-Apply Adhesive

Plaid's Stickit Again & Again

As with any glue, test on a seam allowance or like fabric scrap for colorfastness.

1 Using a disposable brush or credit card, apply glue to the wrong side of the appliqué, crest, or trim.

2 Let the glue dry as recommended by the manufacturer (usually 24 hours). It will dry clear and tacky.

3 Position the item and apply hand pressure. At the end of the evening, peel off the decoration, store it on waxed paper, then use it again. The glue stays tacky for many wearings.

NOTE— *Some of these glues are temporary until they have been on the garment for over 24 hours; then they become permanent. Read the label carefully.*

Quick-Fix Embellishments, If You Sew a Little

Before starting a new project, *change the sewing machine needle.* Refer to Reference Charts B and C to match the needle with your fabric and technique.

Figure 7.2 Color the backs of leaves with transfer crayons, iron-on transfer pens, or fabric paint; press on the fabric, then outline with fabric paint or stitching.

Figure 7.3
Decorate an existing jacket with press-on gold swirls, anchor, and red, white, and gold stars scattered randomly across the right lapel and shoulder.

*"I bought a boring silk noil jacket and skirt recently because they fit decently, the price was right, and I could wear them immediately (rather than constructing them from scratch).
I decorated the jacket with wonderful fusible gold swirls on both sleeves, a red and gold anchor on the breast pocket, and red, white, and gold stars scattered randomly across the right lapel, spilling over onto the right shoulder. Now the outfit is NOT boring and looks as though I spent days at my computer sewing machine embroidering (Fig. 7.3).
I love when that happens!"*

Janet Penwell
Wearable artist; Designer; Sewing instructor
Indianapolis, IN

Add, Baste, Cover, Create

"Improved ready-to-wear projects I have completed (Fig. 7.4):

• *Added metallic bows to a plain black sweater for an instant holiday look*

• *Basted a sequin appliqué to a sweater for a party, then took it off again for normal wearing*

• *Covered a ready-to-wear tie with buttons*

• *Added braid to a ready-to-wear jacket*

• *Created a detachable lace collar for a dress*

• *Added a label collage to a thrift store men's vest"*

Linda Turner Griepentrog
Editor, *Sew News* magazine
Peoria, IL

Follow Linda's example, attaching these items by hand or machine. For a temporary, removable accent, use liquid pressure-sensitive adhesive on the back of each embellishment (see "Stick It On, Peel It Off" earlier in this chapter).

Sew How: For the latest in fashion sewing, read Sew News *magazine, a monthly publication available through your local fabric or sewing machine store or write or call:*

Sew News
P.J.S. Publications, Inc.
News Plaza
P. O. Box 1790
Peoria, IL 61656
(309) 682-6626

Add Buttons

"I am going to sew buttons around the neckline of a ready-to-wear jewel-neck T. Should I interface?"

Robbie Fanning
Author; Series editor, Chilton Books;
Publisher, *The Creative Machine* newsletter
Menlo Park, CA

Interface only under heavy buttons stitched to a single layer of fabric. To do this, cut a bias strip of ½" (1.3cm)-wide fusible tricot and fuse it under where the but-

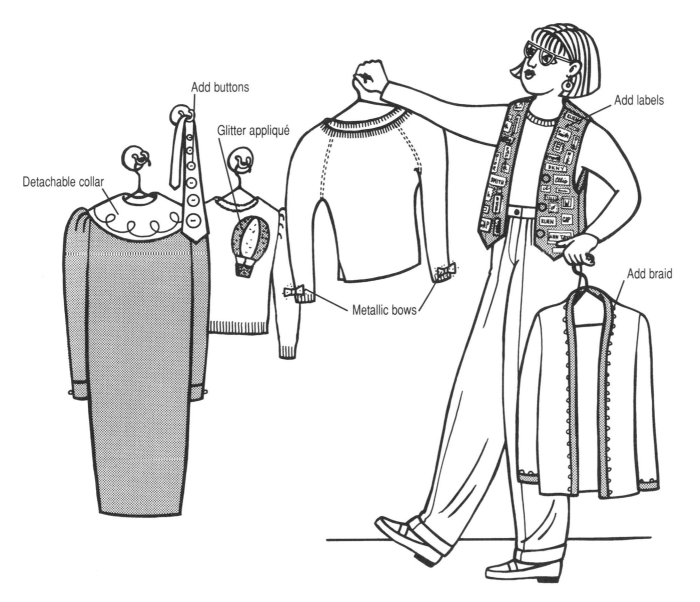

Add buttons

Glitter appliqué

Detachable collar

Add labels

Metallic bows

Add braid

tons will be stitched, following the manufacturer's instructions. Then sew the buttons on by hand or machine (Fig. 7.5; see also pages 126–127).

Fuse and Serge a Yoke

To give a casual shirt a lift, Gail Brown adds a contrasting yoke using hand-woven Guatemalan fabric. Simply cut, finish, fuse, and stitch.

1 Lay out the shirt and trace the shape of the front and/or back yokes by placing tissue paper over the yoke and tracing over the seamlines using a water-soluble marker. Do not add seam allowances.

Sew How: I save large blank sections of tissue paper I remove from commercial patterns to use for tracing off smaller pattern pieces. When I don't have any on hand, I use Do-Sew pattern tracing material or pattern tracing cloth.

Figure 7.4 Add a metallic bow to or baste a sequin appliqué on a sweater; cover a tie with buttons; add braid to a jacket; create a detachable lace collar for a dress; and add a label collage to a thrift store vest.

2 Cut out a contrasting yoke. On the wrong side and around the perimeter of the accent fabric, fuse on strips of 1/4" (6mm)-wide paper-backed fusible web, following the manufacturer's instructions.

3 Remove the release paper. Sewing from the right side, finish around all edges. The fusible web acts like staystitching, so the fabric won't stretch (Fig. 7.6).

Sew-Easy Tip: If you don't have a serger, finish the edges with a narrow zigzag (3 length [9 stitches per inch], 3 width), guiding the fabric halfway under the foot so the needle stitches into the fabric on the left, and falls off the raw edge on the right.

Figure 7.5 Fuse fusible tricot to the wrong side of a single fabric layer to interface under the buttons, as on this decorated jewel T-shirt.

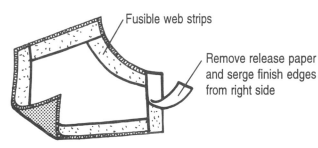

Fusible web strips

Remove release paper and serge finish edges from right side

Figure 7.6 Fuse paper-backed fusible web around yoke accent and finish the edges. Fuse the yoke accent over existing yoke and topstitch it in place.

"My daughter and I take work shirts and plain-Jane clothes and 'spiffy them up.' We use decorative threads and stitches, and we almost always change the buttons. When my daughter is the designer, she's more apt to wear her creation and we both have fun in the process."

Nancy Bednar
Sewing specialist, Bernina of America
La Grange Park, IL

Serge-Easy Tip: *Serge-finish around all edges with a balanced 3-thread or 3/4-thread overlock. If your serger has a differential feed, set it on the plus setting (between 1 and 2) to control the stretch.*

4 Place the wrong side of the yoke to the right side of the shirt, lining up the finished edges of the accent yoke with the original yoke seamlines. Tuck loose serged threads between the yoke and shirt front and pin into place. Fuse and let it cool; then topstitch the yoke with a straight stitch or double needles.

Sew How: *This idea first appeared in the April 1993 issue of* Serger Update. *For more information on the latest sewing and serging techniques, subscribe to the* Update *newsletters.* Sewing Update *comes out every other month, and* Serger Update *is a monthly. For more information, write or call:*

Update Newsletters
P.J.S. Publications, Inc.
2 News Plaza, P. O. Box 1790
Peoria, IL 61656
(309) 682-6626

Add Interchangeable Lacing, Cuff Dickies, and Covered Buttons

Do you have a jacket in your closet you just can't part with but are not wearing? Try this restyling idea.

In chapter 1, we made cuff dickies (see pages 7-8) to creatively shorten a too-long jacket sleeve. I have taken this idea further and have a set of cuff dickies, laces, and covered buttons I use to give a plain black jacket two different looks.

1 Make the cuff dickies as described on pages 7-8. If you make them out of Ultrasuede as I did, don't add hem allowances or serge-finish. The following lacing idea was adapted from one I learned from Viking Sewing Machine Company educator, Patti Jo Larson.

2 You will be creating eyelets or buttonholes that are 5/8" (1.5cm) apart and 5/8" (1.5cm) from the edge of the top collar and lapels. Using a disappearing dressmaker's chalk or marker, mark lines 5/8" (1.5cm) apart and perpendicular to the edge of the top collar and lapels. Next, mark lines 5/8" (1.5cm) from and *parallel* to these finished edges. On the front lapel, stop marks above where the fabric turns at the button and buttonhole.

3 Where the lines intersect, make eyelets or small buttonholes with thread to match the fabric.

4 Before cutting the laces, thread a strand of thread or dental floss over and through the eyelets to determine the length needed. Cut lacing strips of Ultrasuede ¼–⅜" (6mm–1cm) wide and across the grain. Thread lacing around and through the eyelets, cutting lacing to length *plus* ½" (1.3cm) for the turn back after you know how long to make them. Attach pressure-sensitive adhesive to both ends of the lace or use small pieces of hook-and-loop fastener on the lace and on the underside of the upper collar and lapels.

5 Now make covered button(s) to match the lacing. Find button-covering sets and instructions in the notion section of your local fabric store.

6 Attach and turn back the cuff dickies; thread the lacing through the eyelets, fastening the ends under the collar and lapels with hook and loop fastener or with pressure-sensitive adhesive. Attach the covered button with a button safety pin (see page 62) and voilà! A new jacket. Wear the jacket with or without the trim for two different looks, or make other sets for different slacks, skirts, and dresses. So many looks...so little time (Fig. 7.8).

Letting Your Sewing Machine or Serger...

Appliqué It

"I love to take a basic item, a crew neck sweater, plaid skirt, and the like, and add bits of fabric appliqués to enhance it and give it a designer look on a shoestring budget. You can get exactly the colors and quality you want, and all at a reasonable price."

Barb Griffin
Free-lance designer; Author
Ft. Collins, CO

An appliqué is a piece or pieces of fabric applied to the surface of another base fabric to create a design.

1 To appliqué the easy way, start with a piece of fabric larger than the appliqué for the appliqué fabric. Next, fuse a piece of paper-backed fusible web to the wrong side of the whole appliqué fabric, following

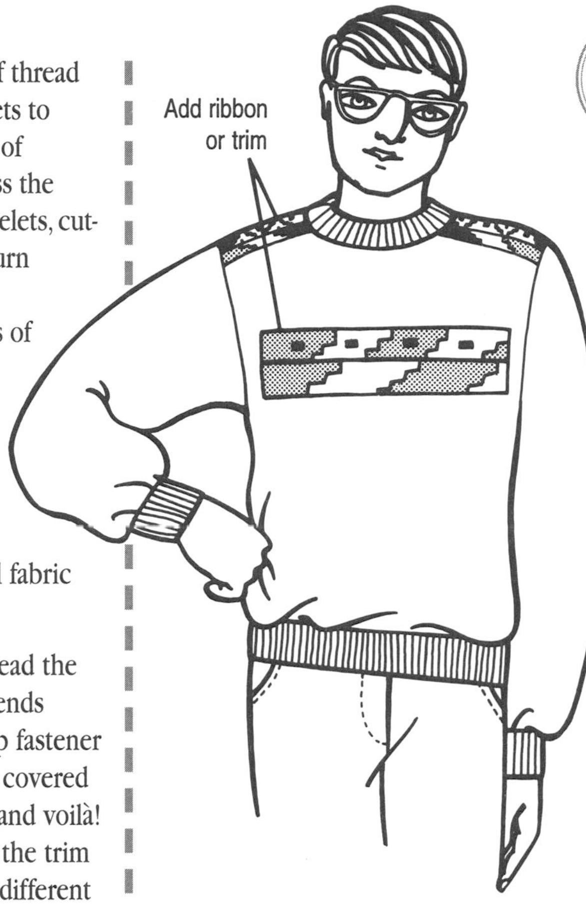

Add ribbon or trim

Quick-Fix Embellishment
Using the fusing technique explained in "Fuse and Serge a Yoke," add a wide trim or fabric border to the front of a sweatshirt and make matching epaulets (Fig. 7.7).

Figure 7.7 Back a border or trim with strips of paper-backed fusible web, fuse in place, then topstitch.

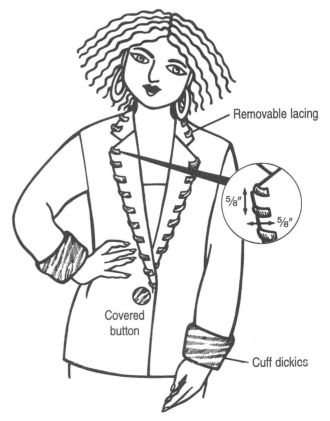

Removable lacing

5/8" 5/8"

Covered button

Cuff dickies

Figure 7.8 Make and attach cuff dickies, lace the eyelets, and pin on the button for an instant new look to an old jacket.

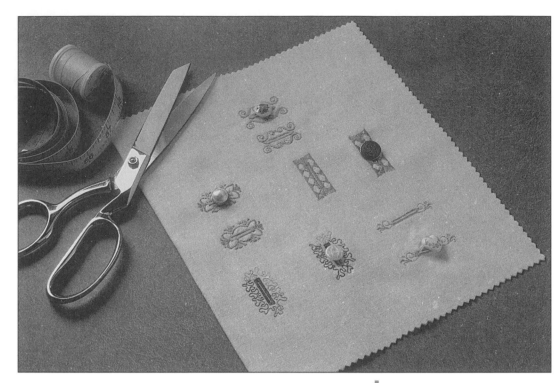

Figure 7.9 Jane Burbach of Elna, Inc., adds open machine embroidery stitches around buttonholes.

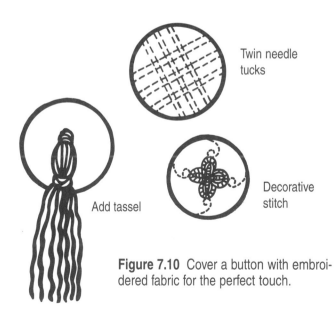

Twin needle tucks

Add tassel

Decorative stitch

Figure 7.10 Cover a button with embroidered fabric for the perfect touch.

the manufacturer's instructions. Then cut out the appliqué shapes. This way, you can fuse the shapes to the base fabric and they won't shift while sewing.

2 If you are appliquéing more than one shape, place the shape that is farthest away onto the base fabric first. For example, if there are two clouds in the sky, fuse the cloud that is farthest away first, and then fuse the closer cloud so that the scene will be in perspective.

3 After positioning and fusing the appliqué fabrics, stitch around them either by yarn tracing (see page 21) or by satin stitching around each shape using a short 2.5- to 3-width zigzag and an embroidery foot.

Button It

When are buttonholes not just buttonholes? When Jane Burbach, Elna (sewing machine company) sales and product training manager, makes them. Simply whipstitch the buttonhole closed to stabilize it and decorate around it with a fairly open decorative stitch or stitches. The stitches should not pucker or pull because the area around the buttonholes is stabilized with interfacing. Remove whipstitches; then button (Fig. 7.9). To do this on something you have made from scratch, do not cut the buttonhole open until after you've finished embellishing.

Sometimes I can't find an appropriate button for a project, so I embroider fabric and use it to cover buttons, adding just the touch I need (Fig. 7.10).

Convert It

Convert and transform a pullover sweater or sweatshirt—cut it, embellish it, and make it better (Fig. 7.11). In this project, you'll turn an ordinary sweatshirt or sweater into an attractive, more stylish cardigan with a bit of woven braid or trim and some plaid or print fabric. You'll also love the ideas in Mary Mulari's book, *Sweatshirts with Style* (Chilton, 1993). The following instructions are for a woman's cardigan. For a man's cardigan, put the ribbing band on the right side and the ribbing facing on the left.

1 Preshrink your washable sweatshirt or sweater and the woven trim and plaid or print fabric you'll use to decorate your cardigan.

2 Draw a line down the center front of the shirt or sweater from the neckline to the hem or waistline ribbing. Cut the shirt or sweater open on the line, cutting through the front layer only. You have just converted your shirt into a cardigan.

3 Cut off the bottom ribbing, cutting through the seam allowance. If the ribbing is knitted to the bottom of the sweater, machine baste just above the ribbing before cutting it off.

4 Finish the hem edge (see Reference Chart A), and then turn it up and topstitch it with thread that matches the fabric. To stitch a sweater hem with recovery, see page 138.

5 Place, pin, and stitch the woven braid or trim so that it is even with the finished hem edge. Stitch matching trim above the sleeve ribbing.

6 Cut two 3" (7.5cm)-wide strips of a plaid or print fabric the length of the center front plus about 2" (5cm) to shape the neckline curve. Lay the strips on the cardigan front and draw the neckline curve on the top edge of each strip so that it falls just under the ribbing; then cut the curve. Cut the bottom edges of the strips even with the hemline fold.

7 Fuse narrow strips of paper-backed fusible web around the perimeter of both fabric strips. To fuse the strips around the neckline curves, pinch in and shape the fusible web, leaving the paper on the web as you go. When the paper is removed, the web will be smooth.

Sew-Easy Tip: For clean, pinked or scalloped edges, leave the release paper on and use the scalloping blade on your rotary cutter or pinking shears to pink around three sides (two short ends and the longest side) of the strip; then remove the release paper (Fig. 7.12).

Serge-Easy Tip: Remove the release paper and serge-finish around three sides (two short ends and the longest side) of the strip with a short, balanced 3-thread overlock, using decorative thread in the upper looper.

8 Fuse one plaid strip down each side of the cardigan center front opening. Topstitch close to the

Pink or serge-finish

Figure 7.11
Make a conversion sweatshirt. Cut down the front, remove the bottom ribbing, hem, and add fabric strip appliqués and trim.

Face with ribbing

Woven trim

Side seam tucked and buttoned

Pink or serge-finish

Figure 7.12 Serge-finish or pink around three edges, then face and add ribbing to the center front. If the bottom is too baggy, fold and button over a tuck at the side seams.

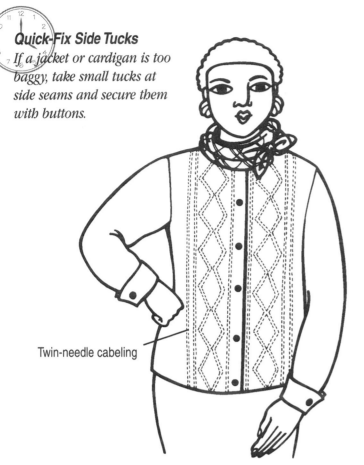

Quick-Fix Side Tucks
If a jacket or cardigan is too baggy, take small tucks at side seams and secure them with buttons.

Twin-needle cabeling

Figure 7.13 Transfer your design to jacket front, then stitch over the lines with wide twin needles and matching thread, creating a cable on a plain boiled-wool jacket.

"The most creative thoughts on improving ready-to-wear are all the beautiful embellished one-of-a-kind garments I have stitched on my Viking sewing machine. With its Pictograms, Omnigrams, and professional monogramming and embroidery capabilities, I can take a plain blouse or dress and turn it into a designer garment. With time so short due to my job, I will sometimes skip the construction steps and actually purchase the basic garment to embellish. Thus, I have all the fun of personalizing my clothing and gifts and expressing my own creativity in spite of a tight schedule."

Sue Hausmann
Vice-president, education and merchandising,
Viking White Sewing Machines;
Host of *The Art of Sewing*, PBS television show
Cleveland, OH

finished edge around the two short ends and the longest side of each strip.

9 Using the bottom ribbing you cut off in step 3, cut two ribbing strips 2 1/2" (6.4cm) wide and the length of the center front plus 1/2" (1.3cm) for seam allowances.

10 Fold one ribbing strip in half the long way and finish the short ends; turn the ribbing right side out. Serge or stitch this ribbing strip to the edge of the left side of the cardigan; you will be sewing through both the cardigan fabric and the plaid strip to attach the ribbing (see Figs. 2.23–2.26).

11 The second ribbing will be used to face the right side of the cardigan opening. Fold and press a 1/4" (6mm) hem on the two short ends of the ribbing band. Fuse a strip of paper-backed fusible web to the wrong side of *one* long side of the ribbing; leave the release paper on.

12 Place the un-fused edge of the ribbing along the right center front of the cardigan, with right sides facing. Stitch or serge the strip to the cardigan front using a 1/4" (6mm) seam allowance and catching the narrow hems at both ends of the ribbing in the seam.

13 Press the ribbing to the inside of the cardigan. Remove the release paper, and fuse the other side of the ribbing to the wrong side of the cardigan to secure it.

14 To finish the cardigan, decide on the number of buttons and buttonholes needed and mark them (you may want to look at a cardigan of similar length to determine button placement). Sew buttons on the ribbing band and sew corresponding buttonholes on the plaid strip on the right edge of the cardigan.

Sew How: *Make your buttonholes vertical rather than horizontal so they don't "fishmouth" out of shape.*

Decorate It

I discovered one of the simplest decorating ideas in *Threads Magazine* (an upscale sewing, knitting, and fiber arts magazine for the purist), available through your local fabric retailer or write to:

Threads Magazine
The Taunton Press, Inc.
63 S. Main Street, P. O. Box 5506
Newtown, CT 06470-5506

Threads sponsored a Readers' Showcase in Issue 37 (Oct./Nov., 1991), where readers submitted ideas they have used in their creative sewing. My favorite entry was Joy Landeira's "Aran" boiled-wool jacket. Joy created a cable design on boiled-wool yardage using a wide double needle (see Reference Charts B and C). Rather than buying the boiled-wool fabric (at $50 per yard), the matching fold-over braid, which can be found for around $7 per yard, and decorative buttons, I adapted this idea to a reasonably priced ready-made boiled-wool jacket costing well under $100.

> **Sew How:** *If your sewing machine has a side-loading bobbin, the double needle sits in the machine sideways and will not work.*

Machine Readiness Checklist

stitch: straight
foot: transparent embroidery or embroidery
stitch length: 3-3.5 (7 - 9 stitches per inch)
stitch width: 0
upper tension: tighten slightly; for a more pronounced tuck, tighten more
accessories: 4-6mm-wide size 90 stretch double needle (see Reference Charts B and C), matching thread to the fabric. When threading double needles, threads should reel off each spool in opposite directions to prevent tangling (see your Operating Manual).

1 Decide on your design by working it out on tracing paper first. Do something simple such as a few straight lines with a large, possibly intersecting zigzag pattern as shown in Figure 7.13.

2 Mark your design on the front and back of the jacket with a disappearing fabric marker or chalk (see page 123).

3 Because there is one thread on the bobbin that shares itself with the two top threads, a slight tuck is pulled up in the fabric, creating the cable look we want.

4 Starting on the right side and at the top, begin sewing. As you get to a place where you need to change direction and if it is a slight angle, leave the needles in the fabric and pivot slightly. If the angle is more defined, raise the needle so it is barely out of the fabric, lift the foot slightly, pivot so the needles graze the fabric, lower the presser foot, and continue.

5 When you get to the end, pull the threads to the back and tie them off. Continue in this way until you have completed the design (Fig. 7.13).

> **Sew How:** *To "un-sew" double-needle stitching easily, pull the bobbin thread.*

Embroider It

These instructions are a variation of the double-needle method used for the boiled-wool jacket (see "Decorate It" on the facing page).

1 Prepare your materials and machine following the Machine Readiness Checklist at left *except:*

• Use a 2.5-3mm size 80/12 Universal double needle (see Reference Charts B and C)

• Choose thread that contrasts with the fabric

• Set your stitch length to 2.5-3 (10-12 stitches per inch)

2 On the right side of the garment, use a disappearing fabric marker or chalk to draw the crosshatches shown in Figure 7.14 on the yoke, cuffs, or pockets of a garment.

3 Stitch over the lines made in step 2, and then pull the threads to the back of the garment and tie them off.

4 At each intersection of stitching, place a stud, sequin, or button. For the center of each diamond shape, choose a single motif and stitch. Pull threads to the back and tie them off; then put a drop of seam sealant on the knot.

NOTE——*If you have sensitive skin, test dry seam sealant against your skin to see if it will irritate you.*

Quick-Fix Embellishment Tip: *For plaids and large gingham checks, skip the double needle work and embroider single motifs on every white square, for example. Remember to use stabilizer under each stitch.*

Embroider It in Combination

Once you have mastered adding decorative stitches to plain fabric, use your decorative stitches in combination with one another to create interest anywhere on a garment (Fig. 7.15). This idea was adapted from a recent issue of *The Elna Magazine* (No. 34-190, p.3). A number of the sewing machine companies publish a magazine specific to their brands. Check to see if your local dealer carries them or can get them for you, or write to the specific sewing machine company listed in the sources in the back of the book. What I like so much about these publications is that the ideas are tastefully decorative without being overdone.

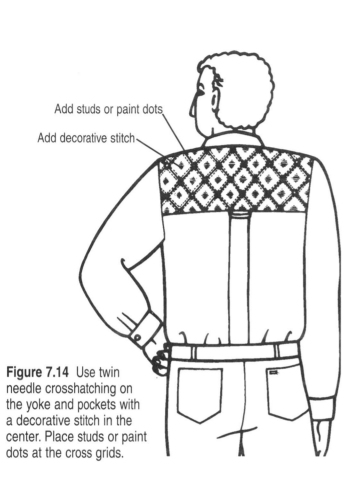

Add studs or paint dots

Add decorative stitch

Figure 7.14 Use twin needle crosshatching on the yoke and pockets with a decorative stitch in the center. Place studs or paint dots at the cross grids.

"Decorative machine stitches in rayon, metallic, or the new Renaissance thread are my favorites. Chambray shirts are a natural for decorating. Use double-needle crosshatching across the back yoke and on the pockets with a decorative stitch in the center; studs placed on the cross grids give a great effect. Also cross-stitching around the collar and pocket flaps adds just that little extra (Fig. 7.14)."

Linnette Whicker
Educational consultant, Pfaff Sewing Machines
Paramus, NJ

1 Select your stitches (no more than 10).

2 Select your colors, keeping the total number to four or five. Jackie Dodson, designer and author of *Twenty Easy Machine-Made Rugs* (Chilton, 1990), *How to Make Soft Jewelry* (Chilton, 1991), *Quick Quilted Home Decor* (Chilton, 1993), and co-author with Jane Warnick of *Gifts Galore* (Chilton, 1992), finds colored pictures of anything (a sunset, flower garden, painting) and duplicates those colors with threads, fabric, and paint. "You'll find color combinations you have never thought of," she says.

3 Repeat your design. Using a copy machine, enlarge the grid in Figure 7.16 so it fits the area you wish to embellish. Keep it simple and stitch it again and again.

Quick-Fix Embellishment — To achieve combination embroidery instantly, use woven braid, available through your local fabric or craft store, and stitch strips of it on either side of the button placket.

Reverse Embroider It

Stitch around the collar, front tab, and cuffs, using a decorative thread or cord in your bobbin and sewing upside down (that is, from the wrong side).

Machine Readiness Checklist

stitch: feather or other open motif
foot: embroidery
stitch length: appropriate for the stitch
stitch width: 4-9 (test it first on like fabric and thicknesses)
accessories: size #5 pearl cotton, 6-strand embroidery floss, crochet cotton, baby yarn threaded on your bobbin (be sure the fiber content of what you use in your bobbin is compatible with the way the garment will be cared for after embroidering). You may have to loosen the bobbin tension slightly or bypass it altogether (see your Operating Manual).

1 Wind your bobbin with decorative cord by putting it on the bobbin winder and gently guiding it on by hand as the bobbin winder turns. If your machine winds the bobbin in the machine, wind the decorative thread on the bobbin by hand.

2 Test the stitch and settings on like fabric and similar thicknesses. Fine-tune the stitch until you get the look you want (Fig. 7.17).

3 Starting at an inconspicuous place and with the right side of the fabric down, stitch around the desired areas. After you have completed a row of stitching, check your thread supply in your bobbin. You may have to reload. Pull threads to the back with a large-eyed tapestry needle or needle threader and tie them off.

Sew How: If you love these results and want to read more about decorative effects created by your sewing machine, look for Know Your Sewing Machine, *by Jackie Dodson (Chilton, 1988).*

Hemstitch It

"My favorite way to improve ready-to-wear is to add hemstitching. Several times I have found garments (mostly blouses) of acceptable construction, quality, and price that were appropriate for hemstitching. I have used the Parisian hemstitch (point de Paris, pin stitch) as a topstitch on collars or cuffs, over the stitching line of folded tucks, on hems, and around neck and armbands. I have also used it to appliqué lace or embroidered motifs onto purchased garments (most recently on tab-front blouses). Once I saw a designer linen blouse with hemstitching for $150 and a similar blouse on sale for $35. Naturally, I bought the second one and hemstitched it myself (Fig. 7.19)."

Carol Lafin Ahles
Co-author, *Know Your Elna*; Columnist, *Creative Needle* magazine;
Teacher; Fine machine artist
Houston, TX

Hemstitching was originally done as a way to secure hems and finish edges on fine European linens—thus the word "hemstitching."

A large machine needle is used to create a hole; then a very fine darning thread and very dense stitch is used to sew in and out several times to keep the hole open. Hemstitching, often referred to as French hand-sewing by machine, is most successful on woven fabrics such as 100% cotton and 100% linen. Due to my space limitations, I will show you where you might want to add some hemstitching, then refer you to two excellent magazines that specialize in this fine machine

Figure 7.15 Use your decorative stitches in combination with one another to create interest anywhere on a garment.

Figure 7.16 Enlarge the grid at left to fit in the area for embellishing; repeat the same design again and again.

Reverse embroidery

Figure 7.17 Add reverse embroidered feather stitching around the collar, cuffs, and pocket flaps.

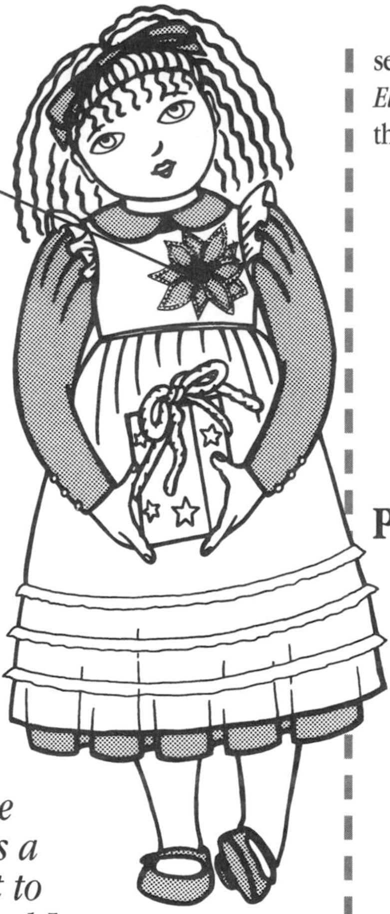

Figure 7.18 Hemstitch a poinsettia to appliqué on an organdy apron worn over a velvet dress.

Hemstitched appliqué

"One of my favorite memories of improving ready-to-wear involved a purchased red velvet Christmas dress for my daughter, Hilary. I made a white organdy apron to go over the dress. I hemstitched a large piece that I used as a poinsettia appliqué on the apron skirt. Then I machine stitched loops of white pearl cotton to the poinsettia center. It was a stunning improvement to the purchased dress. Need I say, she looked like an angel (Fig. 7.18)."

Flo Perk
Vice-president sales, Brewer Sewing Supplies
Chicago, IL

sewing. If you have an Elna, read chapter 11 in *Know Your Elna*, by Jackie Dodson with Carol Ahles (Chilton, 1989). Now the magazines:

Creative Needle
1 Apollo Road
Lookout Mountain, GA 30750
1-800-443-3127 or (706) 820-2600

Sew Beautiful
518 Madison Street
Huntsville, AL 35801-4286
(205) 533-9586

Personalize It

"I do free-machine embroidery, appliqué, and art-to-wear clothing. The word 'personalize' describes more what I do. My New Home makes nice embroidery that I stitch on cuffs or button flaps to personalize plain blouses. On a ready-made T-shirt or sweatshirt, I embellish with machine embroidery using my New Home scanner. To do this I use a copy machine and copy a print fabric. Then I enlarge or reduce the design, scan it in, and stitch the design. Tops and slacks look ready-made. My grandchildren like copying cats, dogs, and trains that I stitch onto T-shirts, too."

Mary Mueller
Sewing Enthusiast
Berkeley, FL

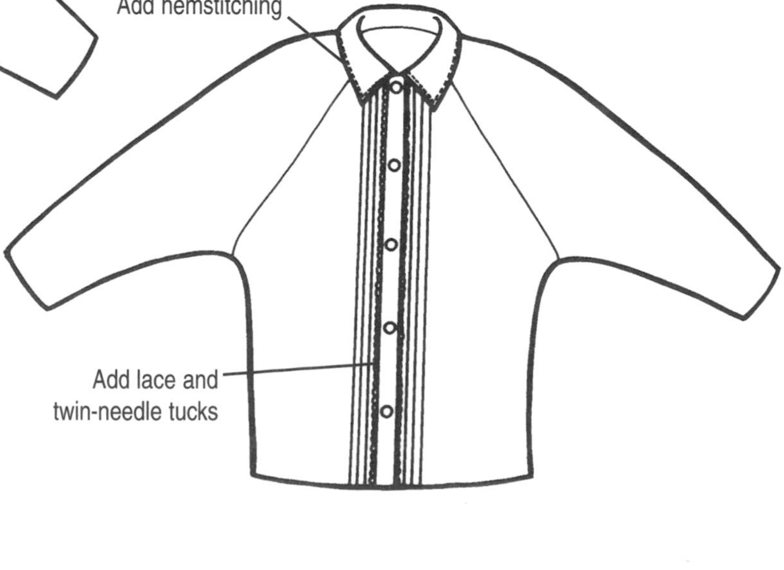

Figure 7.19 Hemstitch and add lace to the front tab of a linen blouse.

Add hemstitching

Add lace and twin-needle tucks

Today's incredible computerized sewing machines make it possible for you to do what Mary describes, and much more. But if you are new to sewing or are reentering the craft and have an older model, don't let an older or less-sophisticated machine stop you from putting your creative touch both on ready-to-wear and on items you make from scratch. Here's one personalizing idea for a shirt, blouse, dress, or piece of children's clothing that is lined with a contrasting plaid or print.

Thread top and bobbin with a contrasting color to the solid fabric. Sewing from the lined side, outline the design of the plaid or print. The shapes are then stitched through to the solid side, adding texture and color (Fig. 7.20).

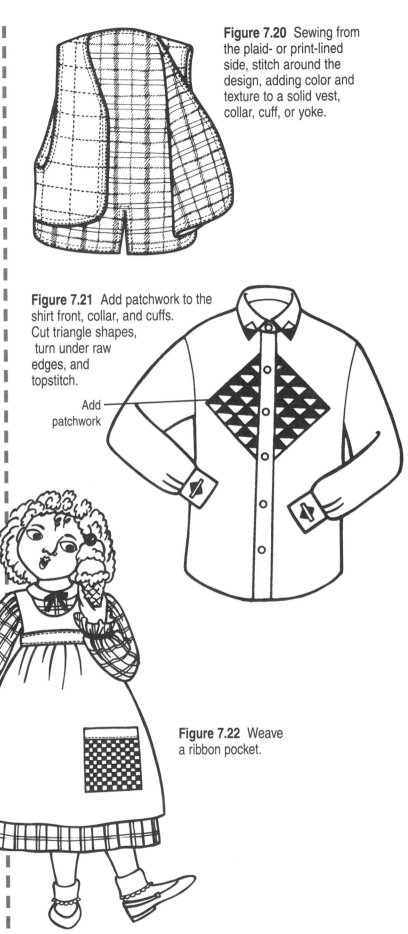

Figure 7.20 Sewing from the plaid- or print-lined side, stitch around the design, adding color and texture to a solid vest, collar, cuff, or yoke.

Piece It

"Improving ready-to-wear can be achieved through construction changes, appliqué, patchwork designs, or embellishment of laces, buttons, bangles, and/or beads."

Donna Wilder
Coordinator of the Fairfield Fashion Show, Fairfield Processing Corp.
Danbury, CT

Add a patchwork motif to the front of a shirt or jacket. If you don't know how to create the motif, purchase a preprinted patchwork fabric, or recycle parts of an old quilt you are no longer using (Fig. 7.21). Again, due to space limitations, I will refer you to another book to read more about it. Read *Mary Mulari's Garments with Style* (Chilton, 1995).

Figure 7.21 Add patchwork to the shirt front, collar, and cuffs. Cut triangle shapes, turn under raw edges, and topstitch.

Add patchwork

Weave It

"I have woven ribbons to make a pocket, which is a favorite embellishing technique (Fig. 7.22)."

Robbie Fanning
Author; Series editor, Chilton Books;
Publisher, *The Creative Machine* newsletter
Menlo Park, CA

To make a 4" (10cm) square oven-ribbon pocket, you will need 4 1/2 yards (4.2m) of 1/4" (6mm) ribbon of the same color for a plain weave. If you want to use contrasting colors, divide the total length of ribbon by the number of colors.

Figure 7.22 Weave a ribbon pocket.

1 Cut a square of fusible interfacing or paper-backed fusible web the size of the finished square, adding a 1" (2.5cm) seam allowance all the way around (for this example, a 6" [15cm] square). Draw the *finished* square on the interfacing or fusible web.

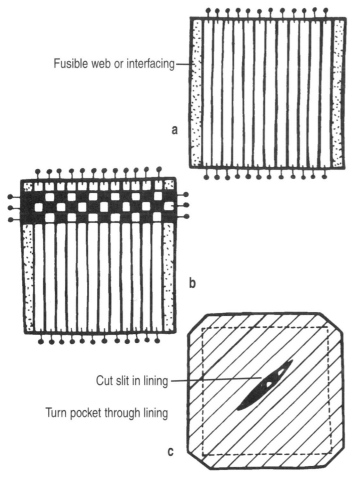

Fusible web or interfacing

a

b

Cut slit in lining

Turn pocket through lining

c

Figure 7.23 Weave ribbon anchoring with pins on either end. Fuse to interfacing or fusible web. With right sides together, sew lining to ribbon pocket. Trim seams, cut a slit through the lining, and turn pocket through the slit and attach.

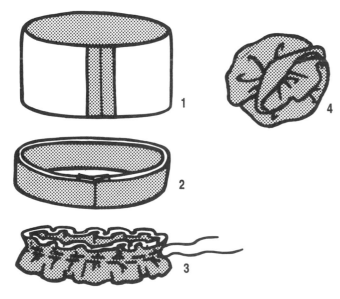

Figure 7.24 Sew each strip into a circle, fold over lengthwise and gather raw edges, pull up the gathers, tie, and twist into flower shapes.

2 Place the fusible side up and pin it to a piece of corrugated cardboard or an empty cardboard bolt (used to hold fabric and available at your local fabric store) so that the pins are in the seam allowance (outside of your drawn lines). (The June Tailor Quilter's Cut 'n Press has a padded surface that also works well for this technique.)

3 Begin weaving, anchoring the ribbon with a pin on either end, angling the pins away from the square, and weaving up to the lines you drew in step 1 (Fig. 7.23a and b).

4 Using a moderately hot dry iron, fuse ribbons to the interfacing from the top. Once the square has cooled, remove it from the board, turn it over, and iron it again, following the manufacturer's fusing instructions. Now your woven ribbon is ready to be turned into a pocket.

5 Cut a lining the same size as the entire pocket square. If you have used fusible web, remove the release paper. With lining and woven ribbon right sides together, stitch around all four sides at the 5/8" (1.5cm) seam allowance. Trim seam allowance to 1/2" (1.3cm), trimming corners as shown in Figure 7.23c.

6 Slit the back of the lining, turn the pocket through the slit, and press. Fuse or hand catch-stitch the slit closed. Stitch the pocket in place as desired.

Sew How: *Look for more ideas in Ceci Johnson's* Quick and Easy Ways with Ribbon *(Chilton, 1993).*

Topping It All Off
"I have decorated hats to go with specific outfits."

Jean Van Koughnett
Artist of wearable art
La Grange, IL

1 Take a man's plain black fedora—secondhand or new from a hat shop. Choose a ribbon for banding (1 1/2" [4cm] is a good width). Steam it into a nice curve and sew it in place (don't glue—you may want to change it later).

2 Construct flowers of a fairly crisp fabric (I use lamés in gold and silver with jersey backing). Flowers are cut in strips of fabric. For a flower Jean uses two 6" (15cm) strips. Sew each strip in a circle,

fold over lengthwise, wrong sides together (like ribbing), and gather the raw edges (you may have to overcast or serge-finish them first). Pull up and fasten gathers, tie, and twist into flower shapes (Fig. 7.24).

3 Tack to hold the flower shape and cover the gathers. The flower centers may be beaded or covered in some other way. Attach the flowers to the hat band in a cluster or all around. This method produces a flat flower unless the fabric is very stiff. Experiment with different sizes and shapes for more interest (Fig. 7.25).

Figure 7.25 Attach the flowers to a hat band in a cluster or all around.

Care and Feeding of Your Wardrobe

Care Labeling and What It Means

You routinely check the ingredients in the food you buy; why not do the same for clothing? Read and follow the instructions on the care labels stitched into your clothing.

The care labeling rule was established by the Federal Trade Commission in 1971, and although the care labels may not be totally accurate and there may be more than one way to clean, dry, and press a garment, manufacturers are only obligated to give you one method. Care labeling also establishes who is responsible if garments are damaged in the care process.

To help you to better understand what the care labels really mean, refer to the Consumer Care Guide for Apparel, on pages 94-95. Better yet, photocopy and post it in your laundry area.

Life's a Bleach and Then You Dye, or Colors Wanted and Unwanted

Get the Red Out

Have you ever accidentally washed a red sock with a white load? If so, be aware of two products available through your local fabric store or favorite mail-order source that will help you get those clothes white again.

Tucks

Figure 8.1 Put a contrasting pocket collage over an ink stain.

Quick-Fix Pocket Collage
My husband's pen leaked all over his dress shirt. I couldn't get to the stain fast enough and couldn't remove it, so I put a contrasting pocket collage over the stain and shortened the sleeves for myself (Fig. 8.1).

"The recommended care procedures (on the care labels) will keep your apparel looking nice longer, as well as help extend the item's wear life."

Bette Jo Dedic
Cooperative extension specialist, textiles and clothing,
University of Kentucky
Lexington, KY

Table 8.1

Consumer Care Guide For Apparel

This guide is made available to help you understand and follow the brief care instructions found on permanent labels on garments. Be sure to read all care instructions completely! (Reprinted with permission from the American Apparel Manufacturers Association.)

"I use Top Job on a scrub brush and elbow grease. It takes out the spot on washable clothes every time."

Ray Saunders
Retired civil engineer (and my dad)
Columbus, OH

	WHEN LABEL READS:	IT MEANS:
MACHINE WASHABLE	Machine wash	Wash by any customary method including commercial laundering (If no bleach statement is made, then all types of bleach may be used)
	Do not commercially launder	Use laundering methods designed for residential use or use in a self-service establishment
	Warm wash / Warm rinse	Use warm water or warm washing machine setting 90° F to 110° F (hand comfortable)
	Cold wash / Cold rinse	Use cold water from tap or cold washing machine setting (temperature up to 85° F)
	Bleach when needed	All bleaches may be used when necessary
	No bleach	No bleaches may be used
	Only non-chlorine bleach when needed	Chlorine bleach may not be used
MACHINE WASHABLE	Wash separately	Wash alone or with like colors
	Delicate or gentle cycle	Use appropriate machine setting (slow agitation and reduced time)
	Durable press cycle / Permanent press	Use appropriate machine setting (cool down or cold rinse before short spin cycle)
	No spin	Remove wash load before final machine spin cycle
NON-MACHINE WASHING	Hand wash	Launder only by hand at hand comfortable water temperature (If no bleach statement made, all bleaches may be used)
	Hand wash with like colors	Launder only by hand with colors of similar hue and intensity
HOME DRYING	Tumble dry	Dry in tumble dryer at specified setting — high, medium, low or no heat

• *Dylon Run Away*—This product will whiten and remove dye stains from whites washed by mistake with colored items. The manufacturer recommends wearing rubber gloves, dissolving the product in the hottest tap water, and letting the garment soak for two hours. Then remove the garment and wash as normal.

• *Rit Color Remover*—This product is recommended not only for getting the "red" out but also for removing or reducing old colors before redyeing something, and for removing faded, spotted, or streaked color. It also helps remove brown iron rust stains on white fabric washed in hard mineral water. Use this color remover in the washer or use it by hand.

Wash the Gray Away

Products such as Dylon Double Duty and Rit Fabric Whitener & Brightener are designed to get the "gray" out of nylon, cotton, rayon, acetate, linen, silk, and wool. These products whiten whites and remove stains (e.g., wine, gravy, sauce, blood, perspiration, grass, egg, chocolate, fruit juice, fat, makeup, tea, and coffee) when used by hand or in the washing machine. Neither contains chlorine bleach, so they are safe on

	WHEN LABEL READS:	IT MEANS:
HOME DRYING	Tumble dry Remove promptly	Same as tumble dry, but in absence of cool-down cycle remove at once when tumbling stops
	Drip dry	Hang wet and allow to dry with hand shaping only
	Line dry	Hang damp and allow to dry
	No wring No twist	Hang dry, drip dry or dry flat only. Handle to prevent wrinkles and distortion
	Dry flat	Lay garment on flat surface
	Block to dry	Maintain original size and shape while drying
IRONING OR PRESSING	Cool iron	Set iron at lowest setting
	Warm iron	Set iron at medium setting
	Hot iron	Set iron at hot setting
IRONING OR PRESSING	Do not iron	Do not iron or press with heat
	Steam iron	Iron or press with steam
	Iron damp	Dampen garment before ironing
MISCELLA-NEOUS	Dry clean	May be dry cleaned by normal method or in coin operated dry cleaning machine
	Professionally dry clean	Included with this term will be other instructions to be followed by your professional dry cleaner

Quick-Fix Tip

When washing anything with a spot or taking it in for dry cleaning, it's important to know what the spot was and how long it has been there. For example, if there is a coffee stain on your linen tablecloth, the stain is treated differently if it had milk or cream and sugar in it than if the coffee was black.

colors. Both caution you to follow the fabric care labeling instructions.

See "A Spot Is on—A Stain Is In" later in this chapter for more information about stain removal.

Is Your Dye Running?

If you are looking for a foolproof method of setting color in dyed fabric, the news is not good. According to the International Fabricare Institute, color loss and running problems are epidemic. Finding colorfast dyes that work on a variety of fabrics is difficult because what works well on 100% cotton, doesn't dye the same on a blend. You may have read

that adding $1/2$ cup salt to a gallon of water and soaking the garment (about the size of a large sweatshirt) for 30 minutes will help to set the dye. This has been disproved for most fabrics, but it may work for you.

Fade for Fashion

If you have the opposite problem and want to safely fade a fabric for a worn or antique look, fade up to six yards of fabric with Jupiter's fabric fading kit. Write to:

Fabric Fading Kit by Jupiter
6801 N. 21st Avenue, Suite O
Phoenix, AZ 85015

Now that you have a little knowledge about caring for washable fabrics, here's a word about dry cleaning.

Isn't Dry Cleaning, Dry Cleaning?

In 1840, a clumsy French tailor named Jolie Bolin spilled his kerosene lamp onto his not-so-clean tablecloth. When the liquid dried, the cleaning world took a quantum leap forward, and dry cleaning was born.

The dry cleaning fluid commonly used today is called perchlorethylene, or "perc" for short, and is great for getting out a wide range of stains. But it is not the only dry cleaning method. All types of dry cleaning solvents (perc, petroleum, fluorocarbon) can be used on a garment when the label says "Dry Clean." If the garment needs special handling, the label will say "Professionally Dry Clean," followed by specific instructions.

Table 8.2
Deciphering Dry Cleaning Labels

If the Label Says	It Means
Dry Clean	Use any of the available cleaning solvents (perc, petroleum, fluorocarbon) to commercially dry clean the item
Professionally Dry Clean, Fluorocarbon, or Petroleum	Use fluorocarbon or petroleum to commercially dry clean the item (do not use perchlorethylene)
Professionally Dry Clean, Reduced Moisture	Reduce the moisture added to solvent so that the solvent's relative humidity decreases
Professionally Dry Clean, Cabinet Dry Warm, No Steam	Cabinet dry at a temperature up to 120 degrees F; do not tumble dry; do not use steam when pressing, when finishing, in steam cabinets, or in steam wands

Regarding Warnings: If any part of the dry cleaning process will harm the item, the label must say "Do Not," "No," "Only," or other clear language must be used.

A Spot Is On —A Stain Is In

If you don't attack the spot right away, it soon becomes a stain that takes a lot more work to remove, even on those wonderful Stainmaster, Stainguard, Teflon, and Scotchgarded fabrics. So remember these three rules:

1. *Get rid of the worst of it first.* Most spots have some bulk that glob or puddle on the surface. Scrape it up, loosen it, or mop it up any way you can before applying any cleaner or solvent.

2. *Use a clean, absorbent white cloth like terry cloth or (my favorite) a clean cloth diaper.* Many of us tend to grab an old dirty rag to get up a spot or stain, and then we can't see if we got up most of it or made it worse because the dirt or dye from the rag has rubbed onto the surface that had the spot.

3. *Use the right cleaner for the job.* Success in stain removal depends on using the right cleaner or solvent to dissolve and emulsify the base. For example, say your kids tracked in tar on the carpet. After ten tries of getting it up, making a bigger mess each time, you finally blot on a bit of paint thinner; the stain almost jumps off the carpet. You matched the cleaner with the base. Then you try the same paint thinner method to remove spaghetti sauce that has splattered on your husband's dress shirt, but it doesn't work. The reason is that the food stain is an organic protein that is removed beautifully with liquid dishwashing soap, formulated to break down food deposits in the sink.

In researching this topic I quickly realized that there are as many systems for stain removal as there are stains, so I will give you some Quick-Fix stain removal tips to handle a few of the common ones. But there's another excellent guide and a new stain removal kit I have used with good results.

Professor Barndt's Stain Removal Guide, by Herb Barndt (Doubleday, 1992, $2.99 U.S., $3.50 Canada) is a book I picked up at the grocery store checkout line. Its small, convenient size makes it a handy reference to keep near your laundry area. The author is a leading authority on the science of stain removal. An associate professor at the Philadelphia College of Textiles, he is the director of the Grundy Center for Textiles Product Evaluation, where he and his staff run the Stain Hotline (215-951-2757, M-F, 9:00 A.M.-4:00 P.M. EST), fielding questions in stain removal from around the country. This handy pocket guide discusses seven stain removal formulas on the fold-out cover, using common household and cleaning products. Inside, just look up the stain, then refer to the method on the front cover to remove it. Easy!

The Color It Gone Stain Remover Kit has five color-coded bottles of nontoxic liquid formulated for different bases. In the kit you get an alphabetized stain removal chart that tells you which color bottle to use for over 150 stains. Look for this kit at your local fabric retailer or through a mail-order source.

Quick-Fix Stain Removal Tips

Remember that no one spot removal technique will work 100% of the time on all fabrics, but these methods may make stain removal a little easier.

Blood (Fresh)

If you have pricked your finger and have just a drop on the fabric, spit on it or chew a ball of white thread and dab the thread on the blood spot. Your saliva has the same pH and removes the stain without a trace (and in most cases without leaving a ring). This trick has been used by dressmakers throughout history.

For bigger blood stains, blot or scrape up all that you can using a dull butter knife. For washables, flush out the stain with cold water. Then make a paste of dry Biz or Axion and water, or use a liquid detergent (Era Plus or Wisk) and apply it to the stain. Wait 30 minutes and launder as directed on the care label. If the stain persists, fill an eye dropper with an ammonia and water solution (diluted 1:1), and then spot the spot. Do not use ammonia, Era Plus, or Wisk on wool or silk.

For nonwashables, treat with cold water, then spot with the white vinegar and water solution (diluted 1:1). Always test on a seam first.

Blood (Dried)

Soak washables in a cool saltwater bath. Rinse. If the stain persists, use a solution of several tablespoons of ammonia to a pint of water. If you still see a spot, use Biz or Axion and water to make a paste over the spot. For nonwashables, moisten the stain with cool salt water; then rinse with cool plain water. Then spot with the white vinegar and water solution (diluted 1:1). *Do not use ammonia or Biz, Axion, Era Plus, or Wisk on wool or silk.*

Coffee

For washables, spread the stained fabric over a large bowl and pour a lot of boiling water directly through the stain from a distance of about one foot. If a milk product was used in the coffee, spot with K2r or dry cleaning solvent. If the spot remains, fill an eye dropper with a white vinegar and water solution (diluted 1:1). For nonwashables, knead a liquid low-alkali soap (Woolite, Ivory, or Lux) directly into the stain. Let it stand for five minutes. Add a little water and work it in so it foams, and let it stand for another five minutes. Flush it out with cool water. If the stain persists, treat with an eye dropper of white vinegar and water (diluted 1:1). For milk products, treat again with K2r or dry cleaning solvent.

Greasy Foods

Scrape off all the gunk you can using a dull butter knife. Using dry cleaning solvent or K2r, sponge over the spot. If that doesn't work, on washables, spot using a detergent paste of Biz or Axion and water. (This may work on nonwashables, but test it first.) Bleach any remaining stain with an eye dropper of white vinegar or lemon juice and water (diluted 1:1). Again, pretest on nonwashables.

Ink (Ballpoint Pen)

Sponge with diluted dishwashing detergent (20 parts water:1 part soap) first. If the stain persists, saturate with cheap hairspray; then blot it dry. If it's still there, brush the spot with alcohol, acetate, or nonoily nail polish remover, using a brush that is safe for the fabric. If a yellow stain remains, try rust remover. I have also had success removing ink with a stain stick called Wink.

Tar and Grease

Scrape off all that you can with a dull butter knife first. Remove the rest of the stain with paint thinner, dry cleaning solvent, or K2r. Let it dry, then blot with diluted dishwashing detergent (20 parts water:1 part soap) for spotting. If the spot persists, apply dishwashing detergent in a higher concentration on the spot, let it stand for five minutes, and then wash (washables) or flush (nonwashables) with cool water.

Bleach Spots

I was pouring liquid bleach into the washing machine and some splashed on my brand new navy blue shorts and bleached out spots. I was sick about this and thought of redyeing the shorts, which probably would have worked fine, but I didn't have the dye or the time. Instead, I found a navy permanent marker and colored over the spots. It hasn't washed out and if you didn't know the spots were there, you'd never see them.

Figure 8.2 Replace scratchy neck ribbing in a sleep shirt with a knit tube cut from an old T-shirt sleeve. This way you don't have to seam the new ribbing into a circle.

Berry and Food Stains

"For nasty berry and food stains, I dissolve a Polident tablet in a little bit of water to make a paste. Then I gently brush it on the stain with an old toothbrush. I let it sit for awhile (sometimes overnight). The stain usually comes out."

Ruby Harrison
Retired, Civil Service (and my husband's aunt)
Ocala, FL

To Recycle, Restyle, or Donate...That Is the Question

If some of your clothing has unremovable stains, is the wrong color or style, or you want to give it one last chance before donating it to the charity of your choice, try one of these ideas.

Recycle

MAKE A PLAN

"Whether you're interested in recycling or conserving your clothing budget, pick a garment from the back of the closet, something that hasn't seen the light of day for many months or even years. Make it a personal challenge to update or improve the garment so you'll want to wear it now. Often by studying current ready-to-wear or clothing catalogs, you'll spot a trim idea or detail that you can add with even the most basic sewing skills. Once the improved garment appears in public again, someone is sure to say, 'Is that something new you're wearing? It looks great!' Accept the compliment—you deserve it."

Mary Mulari
Designer; Author of creative sewing books
Aurora, MN

FOR COMFORT, RECYCLE T-SHIRT SLEEVES

"I needed to replace the scratchy neck ribbing on my husband's cotton/wool sleep shirt. He got impatient waiting for me to do it (too bad he doesn't know someone who sews), so he ripped off the ribbing and replaced it with a tube of cotton knit he had cut from an old T-shirt sleeve (Fig. 8.2).

*This way he didn't have to seam the
new ribbing into a circle
(see pages 26–28)."*

Robbie Fanning
Author; Series editor, Chilton Books;
Publisher, *The Creative Machine* newsletter
Menlo Park, CA

CUT OFF A DRESS TO MAKE A TUNIC

*"I shortened no-waistline dresses
into a tunic-length top."*

Tammy Young
Author; Sewing and serging expert
San Francisco, CA

Make this easy change by cutting off the dress so it is the
desired length plus hem allowance. To make a vent in the
tunic, un-sew the side seam the desired vent length; then
backstitch where the seam ends above the vent. Pin and gently press up the hem. When you get to the side-seam vents,
fold and press the seam allowance over the hem allowance;
then stitch the hem as described on page 133 (Fig. 8.3).

CUT EXTRA COLLAR STAYS

I saw collar stays on the dresser the other day that said
"Holiday Inn" and I asked my husband what they were. When
he loses or breaks a collar stay, he takes the "Do Not Disturb"
sign off the hotel door and cuts a new one (Fig. 8.4).

RECYCLE PANTYHOSE

Although this was in my first book, *Speed Sewing,* it
bears repeating. I recycle pantyhose two ways: (1) When I get
a run above the knee, I cut them off and make knee-highs. Cut
hose off, leaving enough nylon to encase elastic at the top of
each knee-high. Stitch elastic in, using a stretch stitch. (2) If I
have one good leg and one bad leg of two pair of pantyhose, I
cut them apart at the seam and reserge the two good legs
together.

Restyle

SET UP A SYSTEM

*"With too many things to do, too little
time, a budget, and an unsatisfied
appetite for magnificent clothes, I get
very excited about adding a clever
touch to a ready-made garment.
Here's what I do.
Periodically, I clean out my closet,
remove the clothes I don't wear, and
contribute them to a 'reject box.' When
I first contribute a garment to the reject*

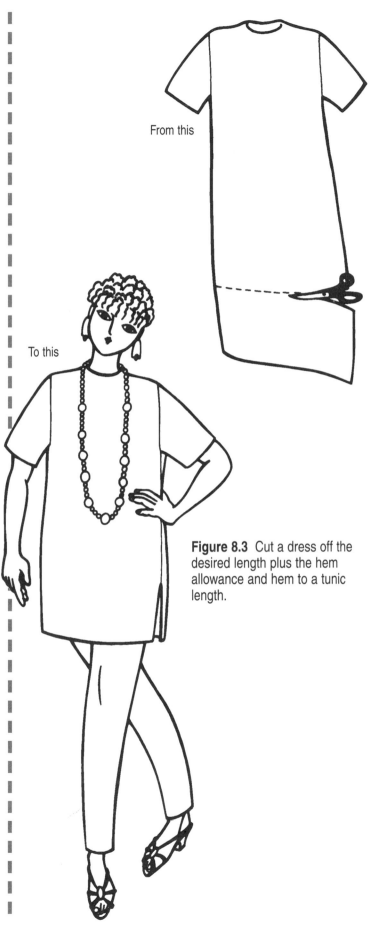

From this

To this

Figure 8.3 Cut a dress off the
desired length plus the hem
allowance and hem to a tunic
length.

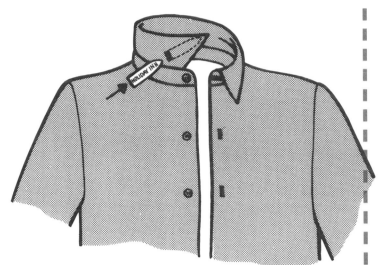

Figure 8.4 Cut extra collar stays.

Figure 8.5 Restyle a wedding dress.

box, I usually have some kind of aversion to it. I let the garment sit there for about six months until I can be objective about it; then I pull it out again and let my imagination go wild. When I think I have nothing to wear, I head for the reject box in the basement, retrieve an outdated garment, and with simple but innovative modifications, I create a unique addition to my wardrobe. If you don't have a reject box, secondhand stores are full of hidden treasures just waiting for creative TLC.

The ready-made opportunities are endless. Consider any touches you can add to a garment you're making from scratch; they can usually be added to a ready-made garment. Wade through pattern books, catalogs, and retail stores for details, embellishments, or even structural updates that can be applied. If worst comes to worst and you can't think of anything to do with a garment, use the fabric for an accessory or to trim another garment, or give it away to your favorite charity."

Lori Bottom
Author; Sewing and serging expert
San Anselmo, CA

Sew How: *For lots of creative ideas on how to restyle your wardrobe and personalize sewing patterns for creative design, read* Make It Your Own *by Lori Bottom and Ronda Chaney (Chilton, 1994).*

RESTYLE A WEDDING DRESS

"I once let out a mother's wedding dress

(1965) for a daughter's wedding (1985). Tight capped sleeves became full shoulder-padded leg-of-mutton sleeves.
I removed the old train and made a new bustle, then covered the old champaign stains with trim. I no longer do this type of work because it is too labor-intensive; however, within a family or for a friend, it becomes a labor of love (Fig. 8.5)."

Victoria Waller
Creative director, Hollywood Trims
Los Angeles, CA

NOTE FROM JAN—*If you would like to restyle a wedding dress, but don't feel qualified to, see "Working with a Dressmaker" in chapter 9.*

REUSE OLD OR FAUX FUR PIECES

"Jan, I know you have done considerable work with fur and fake fur. Maybe you have done some work restyling furs. Can you share some ideas for doing something with those old pieces of silver fox, mink, Persian lamb that were used to decorate collars and cuffs from years back?"

Vicki Mantel
Friend; Sewer; Mother of five
Dyer, IN

These days, using animal fur is not politically correct, so although I will explain how to use some of the old fur pieces, you can use faux fur in lieu of animal fur in all of these areas. The best faux fur I've found is distributed by Donna Salyers, syndicated columnist and founder of Fabulous Furs. For more information on fur by the yard, fur coat patterns, and ready-to-wear, write or call toll-free for a free catalog:

Fabulous Furs
700 Madison Avenue
Covington, KY 41011-2412
1-800-848-4650

Even though your fur pieces may be old, updating them is easy by putting them on a more fashionable garment of today. Sometimes they don't even need to be restyled. First, check that the pelt is in good condition by pulling back the lining. The leather should be smooth and supple without tears or cracks. Pull on the hairs: Do they stay attached? If so, the fur

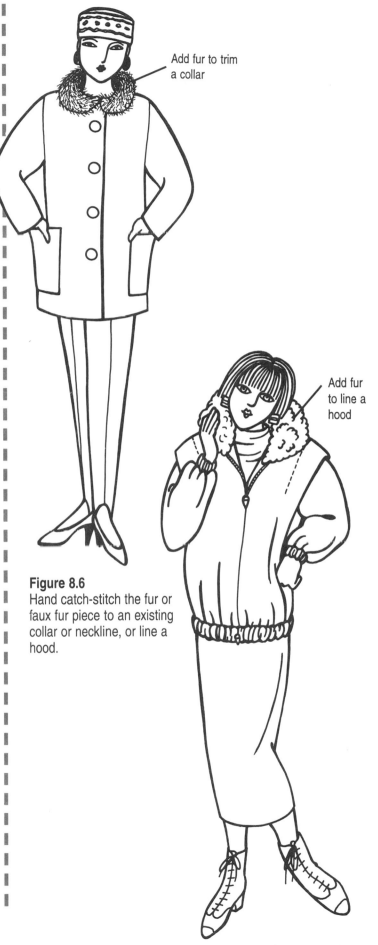

Add fur to trim a collar

Add fur to line a hood

Figure 8.6
Hand catch-stitch the fur or faux fur piece to an existing collar or neckline, or line a hood.

Figure 8.7 Cut up sweater pieces from an old worse-for-the-wear sweater and incorporate them into a new garment.

is worthy of your attention. For odder-shaped pieces, fashion a fur yoke, or line the inside of a hood (Fig. 8.6). If the fur piece is not lined, line it with good-quality satin. Then hand catch-stitch the fur piece to an existing collar or neckline. Fur and faux fur is dramatic, warm, and easily removed for cleaning.

REUSE OLD SWEATER PIECES

"I have taken old sweaters, cut them up, and incorporated these sweater pieces into a new garment (Fig. 8.7)."

Mary Jolly MacLeod
Owner, Midwest Sew and Vac II
Independence, MO

REVAMP YOUR STIRRUP PANTS

"How can I make stirrup pants fit more comfortably for longer legs?"

Kim Dolson
Elementary teacher; Mother of two
Dublin, OH

Quick-Fix 'Em Longer Add longer elastic stirrups.
1. Remove or cut off the existing stirrups, and rehem the bottom of each leg by topstitching a 1/4" (6mm) hem (see page 133).
2. Pin a longer-than-needed strip of 1" (2.5cm)-wide elastic to create a new

stirrup. Adjust for a comfortable length, and attach the elastic stirrup by stitching over the topstitching (Fig. 8.8).

Quick Fix 'Em Shorter *Cut off the stirrup pants, adding elastic lace to make a pair of leggings or bicycle shorts (Fig. 8.9).*

1. Cut off pants to the desired length plus seam allowances.

2. Measure elastic lace and cut it to a comfortable length, adding seam allowances. Overlap the lace ends and zigzag over the overlap with a 3 width, 2 length zigzag.

3. Overlap elastic lace, placing the wrong side of the lace to the right side of each leg and about 5/8" (1.5cm) from the raw edge. Zigzag as before.

MAKE THE MISSING PIECE

"I purchased a blazer on sale for $35. The lapel was trimmed beautifully with gold metallic thread and pearls. There was even a blouse to match for only $10 with the same trim on the neckline. I believe the reason no one purchased them was because there

Figure 8.8 Pin a longer-than-needed strip of 1" (2.5 cm)-wide elastic to create a new stirrup, adjust for a comfortable length; stitch, then cut off the excess.

Add elastic for comfortable length

Figure 8.9 Overlap elastic lace, placing the wrong side of the lace to the right side of each leg, and about 5/8" (1.5cm) from the raw edge, then zigzag.

Quick-Fix Transformation

"Cut off stirrup pants and use them as wind socks!"

Ted Maresh
Dealer operations manager
(and my husband)
Louisville, KY

Too short

Just right

Figure 8.10 When you find part of an outfit on sale, make the missing piece to coordinate.

wasn't a bottom piece to complete the outfit, so I bought them both. They were winter white lightweight wool. I took the jacket to the fabric store and bought fabric of a similar texture that was close in color and made a pair of walking shorts. I got the fabric and lining on sale so I spent approximately $15. For about $60, I have a complete outfit that I would have spent hundreds for, and no one knows that the shorts were not part of it (Fig. 8.10)."

Diana Bade
Executive secretary, Kwik-Sew Pattern Company
Minneapolis, MN

"I deal with a lot of unique body shapes that ready-to-wear garments were not made to fit. I have been able to resurrect many garments. One of my rules for making the garment look professional is to let the fabric be in charge. Don't try to change the grain, and press each seam as you redo it."

Lorraine "Pete" Redifer
For Pete's Sake—tailoring and alterations
Portland, OR

ADD BELT CARRIERS

*"Occasionally I will add thread belt
carriers to a dress so the belt
doesn't slip or shift."*

Beth Mauro
Education director, American Home Sewing and Craft Association
New York, NY

Machine Readiness Checklist

stitch: zigzag
foot: embroidery
stitch length: 0.5-1
stitch width: 3-5
accessories: filler cord such as dental floss, embroidery floss, multiple strands of thread to match, elastic thread, or pearl cotton

1 Place the filler cord under the presser foot and zigzag over it to cover the cord (Fig. 8.11).

2 Thread the covered filler cord through a large-eyed tapestry needle. On the garment underside pull the cord through the seam allowance below the seamline and knot it. Insert the needle in the seam allowance above the seamline. Leave enough room for the belt to pass easily through the loop of the cord. Knot the cord on the underside (Fig. 8.12).

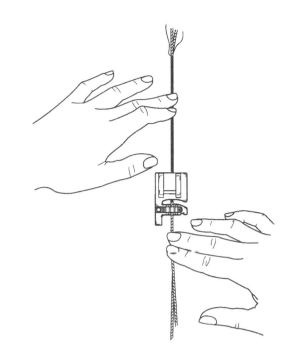

Figure 8.11 To add a belt carrier, zigzag over filler cord. (Reprinted with permission from *A Step-by-Step Guide to Your New Home Sewing Machine* by Jan Saunders [Radnor, PA: Chilton, 1992].)

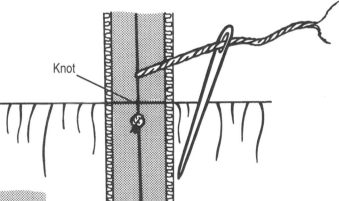

Knot

Figure 8.12 Thread covered cord through a large-eyed tapestry needle, pull it through the seam allowance, and knot both ends, leaving enough room for the belt to slide smoothly.

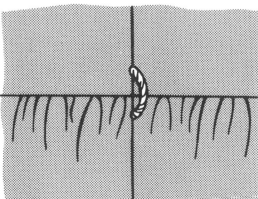

Savvy Shopping

What Does Quality Really Mean?

"How do I evaluate quality of ready-to-wear clothes? What should I look for?"

Karen Bennett
Director of consumer affairs,
Big Bear Stores Co.
Columbus, OH

I take for granted that everyone knows how to evaluate clothing quality because Mom trained me so well. My training ground was a little off-price dress boutique in Cleveland, Ohio, where I learned about gorgeous fabrics and saw French seams and Hong Kong seam finishes. I learned that clothing that was both underlined and lined wrinkled less, and when we could get

Figure 9.1 Fiber determines the look, feel, wear, and care of a garment.

MADE OF:
50% Cotton
20% Polyester
10% Acetate
8% Acrylic
6% Rayon
4% Silk
2% Spandex

bound buttonholes on a garment that fit and for a good price to boot, it was a real bargain. The boutique is not there anymore, but the experience of finding beautifully made clothing for a fraction of the original price spoiled me.

Since my early shopping education, other sources have confirmed what my mother knew when shopping for ready-to-wear. Ronda Chaney, co-author with Lori Bottom of *Make It Your Own* (Chilton, 1994) and co-chair of the home economics department, Cañada College in Redwood City, California, and Nancy J. Rabolt, Ph.D., associate professor of consumer and family studies at San Francisco State University, conducted a study called "Perceptions of Apparel Quality." Their results were published in the *F.I.T. Review* (Fall, 1990), a publication of the Fashion Institute of Technology in New York. "Retail buyers must have the training and experience to purchase quality goods that their target market demands. Careful inspection of goods, especially of workmanship and fabrication, is vital to meet today's consumer quality expectations."

Even though, as consumers, we demand quality at a good price, it's important to bone up on what makes a piece of clothing a good buy. After considering a garment's fiber content, fabric structure, and fashion cycle, use my Power Shopping Checklist on page 112 to check the quality of the garment construction to make sure your potential purchase qualifies for your wardrobe. After a few informed shopping trips, you will know quality when you see it.

Consider the Fiber

"What I need for my lifestyle is clothing that is made out of fabric that does not wrinkle easily, needs little or no ironing, can be worn in many ways, and is inexpensive. It should also pack easily without a lot of bulk."

Carol Evans
Commercial real estate agent
Columbus, OH

A fiber is the material that is spun into yarn and then woven or knitted into fabric. The fiber used in a garment determines how comfortable it will be to wear, how it will hold the color, and how easy it is to care for.

Cotton, linen, silk, and wool are natural fibers. They breathe, drape well, and take dyes well, but they shrink and/or fade when washed, wrinkle, and often stretch out of shape.

Acrylic, acetate, and rayon are man-made fibers. Nylon, polyester, and spandex are synthetic fibers.

Man-made or synthetic fibers may or may not take dye

well, often don't breathe, but are washable and often don't wrinkle as much as natural fibers. Because there are advantages and disadvantages to each, many of today's easy-care fabrics are natural and man-made fibers blended with synthetics. Become familiar with the fibers listed in the following thumbnail sketch. They are the ones you're most likely to find listed on apparel labels. For more information on natural, man-made, and synthetic fibers (and a whole lot more) read *Claire Shaeffer's Fabric Sewing Guide, Updated Edition* (Chilton, 1995).

NATURAL FIBERS

Cotton is the most common and economical of the natural fibers. It is machine washable and has a strong, stable fiber that can be rugged enough to be made into denim, or fine and supple enough for dress shirts. Blend cotton with polyester and you have a fiber that breathes and is easy-care.

Linen is another natural fiber best known for wrinkling. This lightweight and often loosely woven fabric can be blended with synthetics, which usually wrinkle less. Linens and linen blends are used in clothing for spring and summer.

Silk is a natural fiber best known for its dye affinity and fine denier (diameter of the fiber). It is mostly used in spring and summer clothing. However, silk successfully blends with other fibers, both man-made and natural, to add beauty and a fine hand (drapability and smoothness) to the fabric.

Wool is the warmest of the natural fibers. Because wool must be combed to stretch the fiber straight before it is spun into a yarn, it must be dry cleaned or hand washed in cold water. Have you ever washed a wool sweater in hot water and wondered why it shrank so much? When wool is washed, the fiber crimps down, shrinking back to the way it grew on the animal.

Worsted wool is a type of wool that is lightweight and made of fine, tightly woven threads that give it a smooth look with a soft drape. It's good for year-round wear because wool breathes. Worsteds also hold a good crease in a trouser or skirt and don't wrinkle easily. *Woolens* are made of loosely woven yarns used to create a Harris tweed or wool flannel. Primarily for winter wear, the loosely woven yarns do stretch, causing baggy knees and seat.

MAN-MADE FIBERS

Acrylic is a man-made cellulosic fiber (made from fibrous plant materials) that is soft, warm, resistant to oil and chemical stains, but sometimes stretches and pills (those little balls that appear in high-wear areas). You will find this in a lot of sportswear fabrics, such as sweatshirting.

Acetate is another cellulosic fiber often used in suit linings. It won't shrink, is moth resistant, has wonderful drapability, and is inexpensive, but often breaks down and tears or shreds after moderate wear.

Rayon is a cellulosic fiber manufactured from plant materials such as wood pulp. It breathes, drapes beautifully, dyes well, but wrinkles. It also requires dry cleaning or hand washing in cold water. In the 1920s it was used to imitate silk, but at a much lower price. Today it is used alone or blended with other fibers to look like silk, linen, and wool.

SYNTHETIC FIBERS

Nylon was the first fiber to be produced by chemical synthesis. It is exceptionally strong, elastic (when wet), abrasion resistant, lustrous, and easy to wash, with low moisture absorbency. Nylon is common in swimwear, and many man-made and natural fibers are often blended with nylon because of its strength and versatility.

Figure 9.2 Sales can be good indicators of the fashion cycle.

Quick-Fix Wool Wisdom
To make a wool washable, preshrink it in warm water and dry it in a dryer before making it into a garment. The fabric shrinks and is a little thicker than before, but is washable.

Polyester is a synthetic fiber that doesn't wrinkle, stretch, or shrink. It is easy to dye, resistant to most chemicals, and easily washed. Polyester often doesn't breathe very well, so it is best when blended with other fibers or specially treated so it will breathe better.

Spandex is a synthetic fiber that is lightweight, soft and smooth, and stronger and more durable than rubber. Spandex is used alone or is blended with other fibers in athletic apparel, bathing suits, and support and surgical hose.

Consider the Weave

Plain weaves have interlacing horizontal and vertical threads similar to those in a woven pot holder or a pie crust and are quite durable.

Well-made buttonholes

Buttons sewn on securely

Plaids match

MADE OF 70% WOOL 30% SILK DRY CLEAN ONLY

Short, even edgestitching

Generous hem and seam allowances

Hem stitched invisibly

Figure 9.3 Always check for good garment construction.

"I don't buy that much ready-to-wear to begin with. If I don't like it the way it is, I don't buy it."

Ann Price Gosch
Free-lance sewing columnist
Seattle, WA

Quick-Fix Buttonhole Tip
To prevent threads from wrapping around the button and pulling it off, dribble a line of seam sealant (Fray Check, No-Fray, or Stop Fraying) between the rows of buttonhole stitching.

Satin weave is a variation on the plain weave in which vertical threads overlap several horizontal threads and provide a lustrous surface. Because of the longer horizontal threads, the fabric is beautiful but not as durable as the plain weave.

Crepe has a pebbly surface, is lightweight, and generally is used in women's clothing. It is drapable but snags easily.

Twill weaves are easy to recognize because they have dominant diagonal ridges. This durable weave is commonly seen on denim. Common twill weaves are also gabardine (known for its durability) and serge, which has a shiny appearance that gets shinier over time. Don't take a salesperson's word that a twill weave is more durable than a plain weave. Variables include how finely the yarns are spun, the uniformity of the yarn sizes, and how tightly the fabric is woven.

A Word about Knits

Knits are constructed with a series of lengthwise loops called ribs and crosswise stitches called courses (see page 123). Because of this fabric structure, knits have different properties than wovens.

- Knits have more give than wovens

- Knits conform to the shape of the body better than wovens

- Knits generally have lengthwise stability and stretch across the grain (around the body)

- Knits are not as wind resistant as wovens, so you'll find a woven nylon taffeta windbreaker more comfortable on cold and windy days than a knitted sweatshirt

- Knits are more wrinkle resistant than woven fabrics

- Knits shrink more frequently and in larger amounts than wovens

- Knits don't ravel but may curl or run

"Looking professional at all times is a must, so I prefer knits to eliminate wrinkles and for comfort all day. To improve on the look, I may change jewelry, shoes, or other accessories. I also prefer solid fabrics rather than prints that may look busy and go out of style."

Bev Montgomery
Real estate agent
Bay Village, OH

Consider the Fashion Cycle

Gail Brown says, "When you see it as a close-out at discount stores, it's on its way out." Fashion trends have cycles. Trendy fads are introduced, rise, peak, then fall (what comes to mind as this goes to press are stirrup pants, as illustrated in Fig. 9.2).

Don't waste your money but still be in fashion. Buy a few of the trendy items and use them almost as a fashion accessory. Then stick to the classics so you'll have a closetful of fashionable clothing.

Consider the Garment Construction

Now that you know a little about the fiber content, fabric structure, and the fashion cycle, check out the garment construction. Before buying anything, you may also want to "snoop shop" to evaluate both construction and style. If you sew, you may decide to make something you see, doing it better and for less. If you don't sew, you may decide to have a dressmaker make it for you (see page 116).

Characteristics of a Good Suit

Ask yourself these questions to discover if a suit is worthy of your consideration:

- Is it made of quality fabric?

- Is the coat/jacket fully lined?

- Does it have four buttons at the sleeves with hand-made or keyhole buttonholes?

- Does it have a two-piece sleeve?

- Does it have a natural, not overpadded shoulder?

- Does it have a dull horn button opening at the waist in direct line with welt pockets (men)?

- Is it a good fit? If so, it should:

  —lie smooth across the back of the collar

  —not gap at the lapel

  —have pants that are comfortable and that don't bind when sitting and walking

  —have extra pant length that breaks (a slight fold at the crease in front) below the knee

  —fit smoothly at the waistline

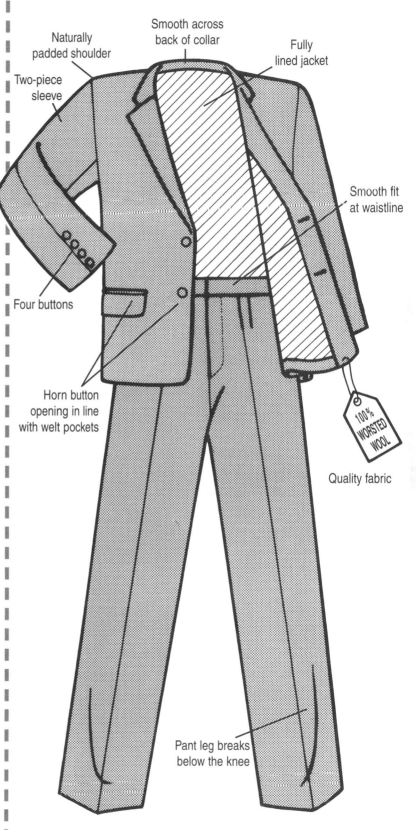

Figure 9.4 Here's what to look for when buying a suit.

Figure 9.5
Take your Power Shopping Checklist along with you when you make your next clothing purchase.

Power Shopping Checklist

_____Do the plaids or stripes match?

_____Are there generous seam allowances that are smooth and well pressed?

_____Are there enough stitches per inch (8-14)? If not, you will see space between the stitches when the fabric is pulled on either side of the seam, and the garment won't wear as well.

_____Are the hems unpuckered and stitched invisibly?

_____Are the buttonhole stitches close together without loose threads in the cutting space?

_____Are buttons sewn on securely? There should be a shank between the button and the fabric. Did the manufacturer include extra buttons?

_____Is the fabric easy-care? Read the care label. If you don't have the time to hand wash and line dry, or dry cleaning is too costly, don't buy it.

_____Will the fabric pill? Pilling is what happens when a fabric that starts off smooth gets little balls in high-wear areas. Fibers to stay away from are inexpensive acrylic and acrylic blends.

_____Will the garment shrink? Fabrics that are 100% cotton or silk will shrink unless they are labeled "Prewashed" or "Sand-washed." If you buy cotton slacks that you plan to machine wash and dry, do so before shortening them or they may end up too short. If you don't want shrinkage, hand wash them in cold water, or dry clean them.

_____Will the fabric wrinkle? If you don't like to iron and want a wrinkle-free appearance without the fuss, choose fabrics that are blended with synthetic fibers such as polyester, nylon, or spandex. Synthetic-blend knits are good for traveling because they generally wrinkle less than wovens. However, as long as a garment is well pressed to begin with, wrinkles should fall out when steamed.

_____Will the fabric stretch out of shape? Fabrics that are 100% cotton, linen, silk, or wool often will stretch when worn. So will rayon, acrylic, and most knits. Evaluate how the garment fits, how it will be worn, the fiber content, and the fabric structure. For example, because wool trousers are generally cut fuller than a pair of tight-fitting 100% cotton jeans, they may not stretch as much in high-wear areas. Wool trousers are often lined with a synthetic fabric, which would also help prevent stretching.

_____Could I sew it in less time than I can shop for it?

_____Is this a classic style that will stay in fashion more than one season?

_____Can I wear this fabric most of the year?

_____Will the color and style go with other things in my wardrobe?

_____Does this garment fit or will it need major alterations?

Look Better with Less

"I need more suggestions on garments that mix and match or how to make simple changes to extend the use of a garment or garments. One of our profs has a black-and-white collection and she can change it so many ways."

Rosalie Warrick
College professor, Adrian College
Adrian, MI

Have you looked in your closet and said, "I don't have a thing to wear"? Then it's time to clean it out and begin with a core wardrobe. The following are guidelines for clothing that will take you almost anywhere.

Figure 9.6 Here's a core wardrobe for someone who works or volunteers outside the home.

Your Core Wardrobe

If you work or volunteer outside the home, you need (Fig. 9.6):

2 suits in your best and/or neutral colors

1 pair of slacks to coordinate with suit jackets

1 print or check skirt to coordinate with jackets

3 blouses—1 long-sleeved print; 2 solid-colored silkies

1 dress (or a matching skirt and blouse)

1 coat

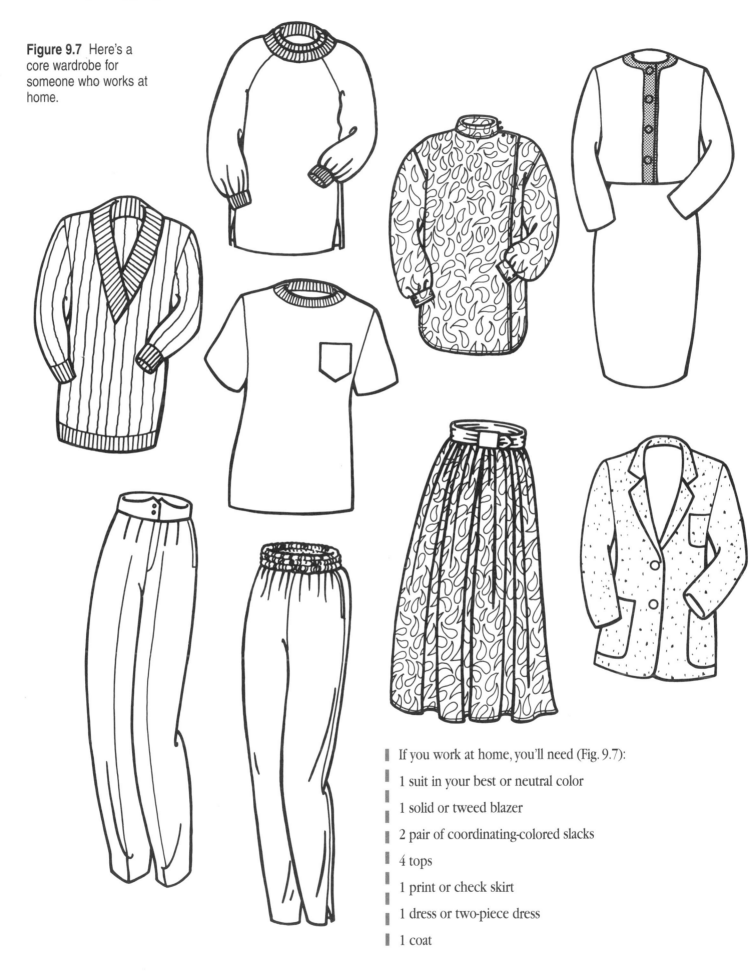

Figure 9.7 Here's a core wardrobe for someone who works at home.

If you work at home, you'll need (Fig. 9.7):

1 suit in your best or neutral color

1 solid or tweed blazer

2 pair of coordinating-colored slacks

4 tops

1 print or check skirt

1 dress or two-piece dress

1 coat

Your "core" is just the beginning. Add other pieces and accessories to pick up the color scheme and add interest. If you are not sure of your ideal colors or the best silhouette for your body type and lifestyle, seek the help of a professional image consultant. Here are some other suggestions.

Are Your Clothes Having a Midlife Crisis?

"I want to know how to change my style to go with my 'changing body' after 65. My clothes are still in style but as one becomes older, we like the higher necklines to cover our 'chicken skin-looking' necks, and a flattering sleeve style to go with the sagging arms. We need help to work with our expanding figure and still feel that we are keeping up with the current styles. I haven't gained that much weight, but the figure has changed from my perfect size 10 of yesteryear."

Evelyn Moser
Retired
Dalton, OH

"Many garments are 'collarless' and cut low on the back of the neck, which reveals and accents a curved spine, or a rounded or heavy shoulder. To solve, either combine blouses with a jacket that has a collar and shoulder pads or add a scarf. If you also have a fuller face, short neck, or double chin, tie the scarf halfway between the base of your neck and the fullest part of your bust. If you have wide hips, tie the scarf low, turn it, and secure it to the shoulder seam by placing a loop of tape under the knot. Drape the folds under the face and create a V, thus flattering your shoulders and face and balancing your hips with one accessory (Fig. 9.8)."

Jan Larkey
Author, *Flatter Your Figure* (Prentice-Hall, 1991)
Pittsburgh, PA

Quick-Fix Travel Tip

Upon arrival, remove and hang clothing on the shower curtain rod. Turn on the water, setting it on the hottest setting (do not turn on the shower, it may get everything wet). Close the bathroom door until the steam has penetrated the clothing. Wrinkles hang out immediately.

"I like mixing pieces of ready-to-wear with things I've made. With my time constraints, I buy hard—sew easy."

Jane Schenck
Manager, education and fashion services
Pellon Division, Freudenberg Nonwovens
Chelmsford, MA

"Although many alterations can be made to ready-to-wear garments, I would, as a custom dressmaker/tailor, suggest comparing the cost of major alterations with the cost of a custom-fitting by a dressmaker."

Marla Kazell
Professional Dressmaker; Custom tailor
Tigard, OR

"Since I can't sew, any improvements I make are limited to wardrobe extension ideas. One trick I used years ago when traveling was to get double use out of a lightweight silk shirtwaist dress. I bought a dressier, longer, fuller-patterned skirt and put it over the dress, which then became a blouse and a 'slip'."

Jo Ellen Helmlinger
Communications consultant
Columbus, OH

Figure 9.8 Drape the fold under the face and create a V, thus flattering your shoulders and face and balancing your hips.

Figure 9.9 Shopping for kids can present unique challenges.

"Yes, construction can be improved (in ready-to-wear), but if you want great fabric, good construction, good design...either shop designer wear or make it yourself if you have the skill. If not, find a good dressmaker."

Kathleen Spike
Author; Fashion consultant; Dressmaker; Founder of
PACC (Professional Association of Custom Clothiers)
Gresham, OR

Shopping for Kids

Save money, time, and your sanity by getting your kids involved with their clothing choices.

- Help your kids research what they like by looking at mail-order catalogs and fashion magazines. I find even my 6-year-old has his own opinions on color and style.

- Buy a few basic and classic core garments for back to school, then wait a few weeks before adding more. Prices will come down, and your kids will know what is "in" before you waste your money on what may be "out."

- Stick with three to four colors that coordinate with what is already in their closet.

- If you expect a growth spurt, don't buy a lot of the same thing in one size.

- Buy separates, and don't go overboard on what is trendy.

- Buy big.

- If you are buying stonewashed garments, be sure they have a guarantee to hold together for longer than 30 days.

- Remember accessories. A new belt, leggings, or tights will give a whole new look to last year's basic.

- For infants, toddlers, and young children, shop children's resale stores. If you inspect the clothing well, looking for quality, you can get broken-in clothing at bargain prices.

Working with a Dressmaker

If you understand and shop for quality but are disappointed with what you find off the rack, consider working with a professional dressmaker. Don't expect to save money over ready-to-wear; do expect a quality investment and a garment that fits.

The following guidelines should help you find a qualified dressmaker in your community.

- Ask for the names of reliable dressmakers from friends, fabric stores, dry cleaners, and fashion design schools. Also look in the Yellow Pages.

- Does the dressmaker have a specialty? One who is experienced in bridal gowns may not have the skills or desire to tackle your alterations.

- Ask to see examples of his or her work.

- Ask for and call references. Is the work done on a timely basis?

- What is the lead time if this is for a special event?

- Can the dressmaker work off a photograph or drawing found in a fashion magazine or mail-order catalog? Is there an extra charge to draft a pattern?

- After you both have discussed the fabric and pattern, ask for a price range and have the dressmaker write it on the pattern envelope. This eliminates a misunderstanding later.

- How is the dressmaker paid? By the hour? By the garment? By the number of pattern pieces in a garment? Is a deposit taken up front?

- Will the dressmaker assist you in your pattern and fabric choices?

- Is there a consulting fee? If so, does it come off the price of the garment if the dressmaker makes it for you?

- If you are buying the pattern and fabric, are you to supply the thread, interfacing, zipper, and buttons?

- Does he or she prefer using particular brands of thread, interfacing, and so on?

- Are two or more fittings included in the price of the garment? If you need extra fittings, what is the cost?

- Because custom-made garments are a good investment, use the best fabric you can afford.

- Be specific in describing what you are looking for, but trust the dressmaker's professional opinion; give the dressmaker the freedom to do what he or she feels is best.

"Where do I find a good seamstress to do alterations at a reasonable price?"
Karen Bennett
Director of consumer affairs, Big Bear Stores Co.
Columbus, OH

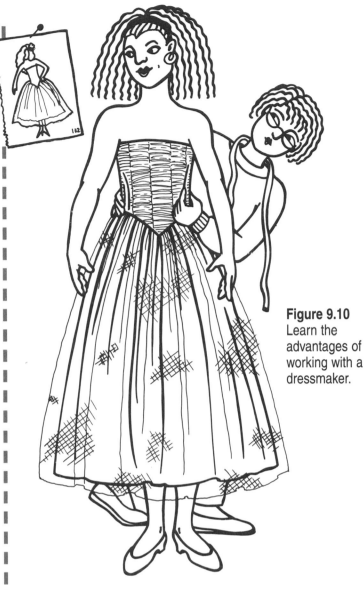

Figure 9.10
Learn the advantages of working with a dressmaker.

"I need to do something to almost every ready-to-wear garment I buy. Usually it is hem-related. I never enjoyed alterations, and now I don't have the time so I have a dressmaker I take my things to. A tuck here and there or repositioning buttons can really make the difference."
Cynthia Weir
Area manager, Columbia Gas of Ohio, Inc.
Logan, OH

Again, ask friends, the dry cleaners, and fabric shops, and look in the Yellow Pages. Most department stores also have alteration departments but will not alter anything that did not come from the store within a certain amount of time. If you are having alterations done, ask for a price list and compare it with others in your area.

Part III

Jan's Quick-Fix Sewing and Serging Guide

When Ted and I were first married, he was more impressed with my sewing ability than my cooking skills (which wouldn't be saying much, but when motivated, I'm a pretty good cook). No more trips to the tailor during rush hour, then waiting a week or two. These alterations take hardly any time (although I don't tell him that), and now he thinks of them as free gifts. For a most appreciated present, why not give your significant other free repairs and alterations? To make your job easier, I have compiled my favorite no-sewing, speed sewing, and serging shortcuts and have included them in Part III. Some of them you may already know. Many may be new; so think of this as a sewing smorgasbord—read what you like and discard the rest.

If you've never threaded a needle, I recommend you learn the basics in chapter 10, "On Your Mark, Get Set, Sew." If you already do some sewing, use chapter 10 as a handy reference. Chapter 11, "All About Hems," provides helpful information on this garment essential. These two chapters, along with the Reference Charts at the back of the book, will give you the keys to sewing and serging success.

On Your Mark, Get Set, Sew!

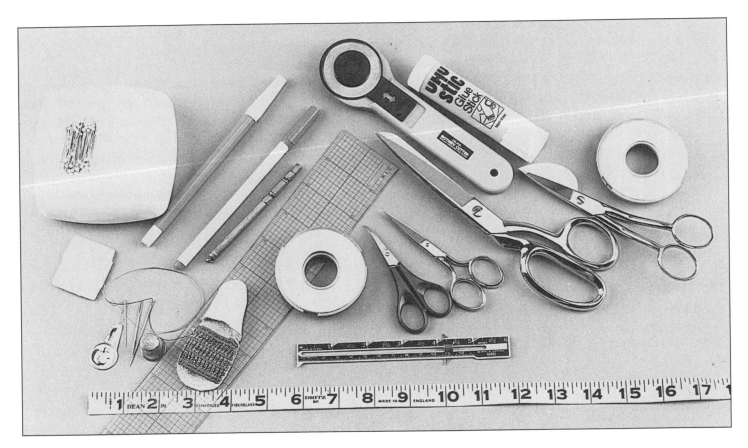

Figure 10.1 Sewing, measuring, and marking tools.(Reprinted with permission from *A Step-by-Step Guide to Your New Home Sewing Machine* by Jan Saunders [Radnor, PA: Chilton, 1992].)

Only about 10% of the population fits into a perfect size, so it's no wonder that the alterations business is booming. Those who aren't having their clothing altered or doing it themselves, look like it. You know—sleeves that are too long, pants that ride up in the back, blouses with "gaposis."

Now that you've learned the many ways sewing and serging can help these wardrobe woes, you're probably eager to start Quick-Fixing. Yet you're not quite sure where to begin. You may want to start right here, with a quick course on common sewing tools, notions, and techniques that you'll use when Quick-Fixing. It never hurts to review, so on your mark...

Pertinent Preparations

Before starting any project, whether altering ready-to-wear or making something from scratch, you need to take two steps: collecting your tools and assessing your fabric.

Collect Your Tools

Many of the small repairs such as replacing buttons; restitching a small split seam; or reattaching an appliqué, trim, or patch can be accomplished without a sewing machine, but for larger repairs and alterations you will need a sewing machine. If you don't have one, there are always used machines available through your local sewing machine dealers. New quality low- to midpriced machines are available, too. Although you can find used machines through the newspaper, you will not get the service or instruction that you would by buying from a sewing machine dealer, so always check there first.

Once you have your machine and have accomplished some of what you read in this book, you may have an interest

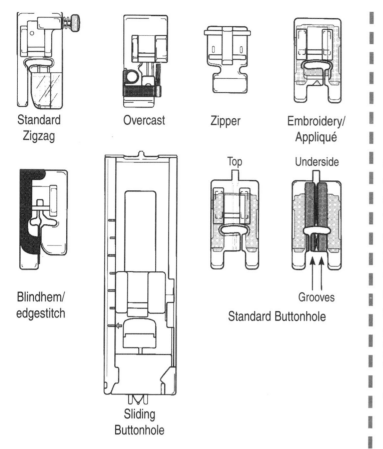

Standard Zigzag · Overcast · Zipper · Embroidery/Appliqué · Blindhem/edgestitch · Top · Underside · Grooves · Standard Buttonhole · Sliding Buttonhole

Figure 10.2 Basic presser feet: standard zigzag, overcast, zipper, embroidery/appliqué, blindhem/edgestitch, sliding buttonhole, or standard buttonhole. (Reprinted with permission from *A Step-by-Step Guide to Your New Home Sewing Machine* by Jan Saunders [Radnor, PA: Chilton, 1992].)

in learning more about your sewing machine. My Teach Yourself to Sew Better series, available in the generic *A Step-By-Step Guide to Your Sewing Machine*, or brand-specific versions (*A Step-By-Step Guide to Your ...Bernina, ...New Home,*) walks you through a self-study course to help you learn hundreds of time-saving shortcuts utilizing your stitches, presser feet, and other helpful features so that the time you spend sewing is more productive.

When you become hooked on the sewing machine, you may want to subscribe to a sewing machine enthusiasts' newsletter called *The Creative Machine*. This beautifully produced quarterly newsletter introduces you to new books, notions, and sewing techniques, while creating a dialogue between sewing machine owners and the home sewing industry. I just love it! For subscription information, write or call:

The Creative Machine Newsletter
Open Chain Publishing
3475 N. Edison Way
Menlo Park, CA 94025
(415) 366-4440
fax (415) 366-4455

Throughout this book you will also see instructions for serging. In case you're unfamiliar with this term, *serging* is overlocking stitching done by a machine for home use called a serger. This machine sews the seam, overcasts the raw edges together, and then cuts off the excess seam allowance, all simultaneously. It has revolutionized home sewing just as the microwave oven did for cooking. While the serger is not necessary for the majority of techniques discussed in this book, often it can perform tasks faster and with more professional results than the sewing machine. Since many of my readers own sergers, I feel it is important to include this information. If you don't have a serger, simply disregard the Serge-Easy Tips. Now on to the tools.

TOOLS FOR SEWING

Sewing machine with the standard accessory feet shown in Figure 10.2. (Most machines come with these feet, so look in your accessory box and compare. If you don't have them, then check with your dealer. If you aren't near a dealer, write or call one of the mail-order sources found in the back of this book.)

Good-quality pins (preferably not those you have removed from men's shirts or the dressing room floor). I like fine glass-head quilting pins. They are sharp, longer than regular pins, and if I accidentally press over them, the heads won't melt.

Pincushion, pin box, or magnetic pincushion

Fine hand needle (for hand hemming) and a thimble

New sewing machine needles from sizes 70/10–90/14 and 4.0/80 stretch twin needles (for most jobs, see Reference Charts B and C for specialty needles and other suggestions)

All-purpose threads (cotton-wrapped polyester) one shade darker than the fabric

Clipping scissors

Appliqué scissors*

Elastic thread

Narrow elastic and/or clear plastic elastic

Tear-away stabilizer, used to stabilize fabric and to minimize puckering* (look for Stitch 'N Tear, Tear-Away, or Easy-Stitch brands)

Paper-backed fusible web, which is a stabilizer and adhesive used in appliquéing. It is also used as a sewing Band-Aid for "Quick-Fix Repairs" (chapter 6) and "Embellishments in an Evening Or Less" (chapter 7). Look for Wonder-Under, Hem-N-Trim, Trans-Web, and Thermo-Web brands.*

Transparent tape for taping on a button, or appliqué, etc.

Straight-Tape for zipper repair

TOOLS FOR MEASURING

Yardstick and thin rubber band (good)

Hem marker (better)—this tool clamps the fabric between a marker arm and stationary rule; a pin slips through the slot for accurate pin marking

TOOLS FOR MARKING

Pins (see "Tools for sewing")

Soap sliver (Ivory brand is good to mark dark fabrics; don't press over soap mark, as it may leave a grease spot; always test on a seam allowance)

Disappearing dressmaker's chalk (better to mark dark fabrics because it will not spot the fabric—disappears in 4-5 days or iron it away immediately without a trace)

Water-erasable or air-soluble marking pens (better to mark light-colored fabrics)

TOOLS FOR PRESSING AND IRONING

Steam iron

Press cloth (for placing on the right side of a garment to prevent the iron from creating shine)

Tailor's ham

Seam roll*

EZY brand hem gauge*

*Not required but nice to have.

Assess Your Fabric

Look at the care labels and other tags stitched inside the garment. This will tell you the recommended cleaning method

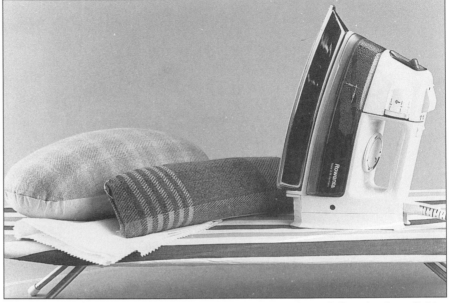

Figure 10.3 Pressing tools. (Reprinted with permission from *A Step-by-Step Guide to Your New Home Sewing Machine* by Jan Saunders [Radnor, PA: Chilton, 1992].)

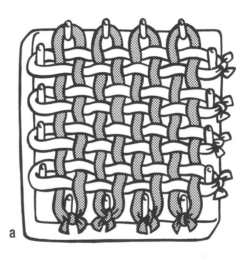
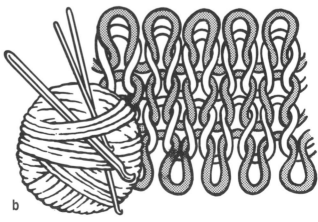

Figure 10.4 Woven and knit fabric construction.

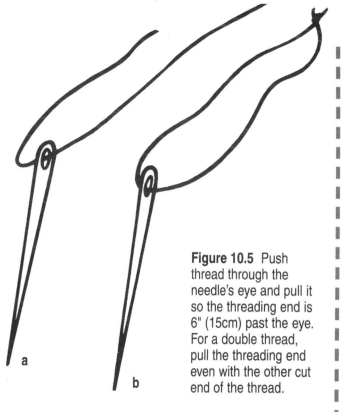

Figure 10.5 Push thread through the needle's eye and pull it so the threading end is 6" (15cm) past the eye. For a double thread, pull the threading end even with the other cut end of the thread.

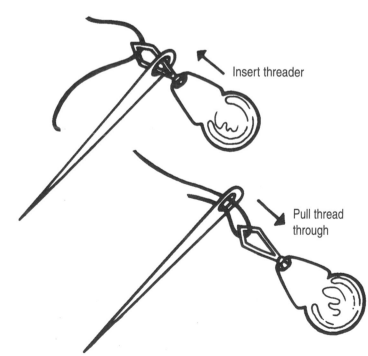

Insert threader

Pull thread through

Figure 10.6 For easy threading, use a needle threader. Push the wire through the eye of the needle, place the thread into the wire, then pull the wire back through the needle's eye, simultaneously pulling the thread through.

and the fiber content (for more information on fiber content, see pages 108–109). You may even learn what iron temperature to use, which will help prevent you from ruining the garment with incorrect care or a too-hot iron.

Is your project a woven or a knit? Woven fabrics are created on a loom and have threads or fibers running lengthwise and crosswise (Fig. 10.4a). Because wovens have stability in both directions, most do not have a lot of stretch and can tolerate a variety of stitching techniques for hemming and other general construction methods.

Knits, on the other hand, are created by continuous loops made on knitting machines. To understand this in simpler terms, you may have seen someone knit or crochet by creating interlocking loops with one continuous strand of yarn used to make a sweater or scarf (Fig. 10.4b). This looped quality generally allows the knit to stretch, which sometimes makes for challenging alterations. Alterations for knits must be durable enough to stretch with the fabric, without pushing the fabric out of shape in the process.

Before getting into specific techniques, look at Reference Charts A through D at the back of the book. If you do a lot of sewing and alterations, you may want to photocopy or paper clip one or more of these helpful references and post them in your sewing area. I refer to them throughout the book, so know where they are and refer to them often.

The Basics: Sewing On a Button and Beyond

If you are a non- or occasional sew-er, here are instructions on the basics—needle threading, knotting, and how to begin and end a stitch.

Thread the Needle

For hemming, or any other fine handwork where you don't necessarily need the stitch for strength, thread the needle with one strand of thread. Pull a length of thread 12-14" (30.5-35.5cm) long; then, for easy threading, cut at an angle with sharp scissors (Fig. 10.5a). If you use a longer length, it tangles and is difficult to work with. For sewing on a button, a skirt hook, or a large snap, use a doubled strand of thread cut 24-28" (61-71cm) long (Fig. 10.5b).

Instead of moistening the end of the thread, lick the eye-end of the hand needle. The moisture attracts the thread for easy threading. Push thread through the eye and pull it so the threading end is about 6" (15cm) past the eye. For a double thread, pull the threading end even with the other end of the thread.

Tie a Knot and Take a Stitch

1 Starting at the end cut from the spool, hold the thread between your thumb and index finger and wrap a loop around your finger (Fig. 10.7, #1).

2 Holding the thread taut, roll the loop between your finger and against your thumb so the loop twists (Fig. 10.7, #2).

3 Continue sliding your finger back while rolling the thread until the loop is almost off your finger (Fig. 10.7, #3).

4 Bring your middle finger to the twisted end of the loop, remove your index finger, and pull on the thread to close the loop and form a knot (Fig. 10.7, #4). Once you have knotted the thread, push the needle through the fabric from the wrong side and pull it until the knot stops the thread from pulling through the fabric.

Finish a Stitch

After you have finished stitching, make a small backstitch. Then sew another backstitch over the first, leaving a small loop. Bring the needle and thread through the loop, and then pull the thread taut. Repeat this if the stitch is in a high-stress area (Fig. 10.8).

Sew On a Button (Learn the Best Way)

1 Mark button placement with a pin. Using a doubled thread and from the right side, push the needle through the fabric so the knot is pulled taut against the fabric. Push the needle up through the wrong side of the fabric a short distance from the first stitch, again pulling the thread taut (Fig. 10.9).

2 Dab the back of a flat button with a spot of glue from a glue stick. With the glue side down, thread the button onto the needle, then push the button down to the right side of the fabric. Position the button on the fabric as desired. The glue should prevent it from scooting around while sewing.

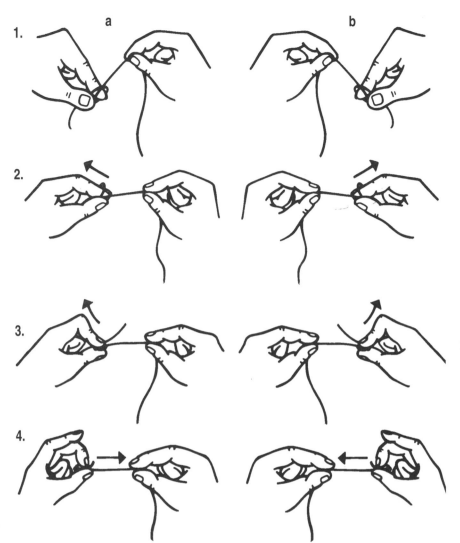

Figure 10.7 Here are the basics for tying a knot, whether you tie left-handed *(a)*, or right handed *(b)*. *(1)* Hold thread between your thumb and index finger and wrap a loop. *(2)* Roll the loop between your finger and against your thumb so the loop twists. *(3)* Slide your finger back while rolling the thread until the loop is almost off your finger. *(4)* Bring your middle finger to the twisted end of the loop, remove your index finger, and pull on the thread to close the loop and form a knot.

"A quick change of buttons can do wonders for ready-to-wear.

• Style lines can be accented with wonderful and exciting buttons. Create vertical lines by adding rows of buttons down the front of a chemise. Remember to keep rows close together. Widely spaced vertical lines will actually widen the body.

• A classy button can change a ho-hum garment into a much more expensive-looking outfit."

Jan Larkey
Author, *Flatter Your Figure* (Prentice-Hall, 1991)
Pittsburgh, PA

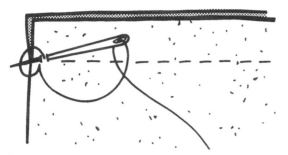

Figure 10.8 To sew a knot, make a backstitch, then sew another backstitch over the first, leaving a small loop. Bring the needle and thread through the loop, and pull thread taut.

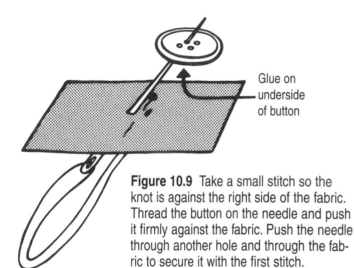

Glue on underside of button

Figure 10.9 Take a small stitch so the knot is against the right side of the fabric. Thread the button on the needle and push it firmly against the fabric. Push the needle through another hole and through the fabric to secure it with the first stitch.

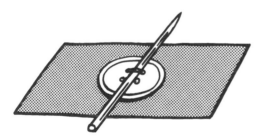

Figure 10.10 To create a shank, slip a toothpick, matchstick, or heavier tapestry needle between the holes and under the stitch as a spacer.

"Anything from coats to evening wear looks much better with upgraded buttons. But remember to take your clothing with you when purchasing. Sizes vary greatly and you need to make sure the buttons fit through your buttonholes."

Virginia Stringi
Friend; Mother of two
Mt. Lebanon, PA

3 Push the needle through another hole in the button and through the fabric to secure it with the first stitch.

Sew How: *To create a shank (a length of thread between the button and the fabric so that there is room to button it through the buttonhole), slip a toothpick, matchstick, or heavier tapestry needle on top of the button between the holes and under the stitch as a spacer (Fig. 10.10).*

4 Repeat stitching up and down through the holes several times until the button is secured. Remove the spacer. To create a thread shank, push the needle between the button and fabric; then wrap the thread around the shank threads several times. Push the needle through to the inside of the garment and secure the stitches (see Fig. 10.8).

Note—*You can also sew on buttons with your sewing machine, using a zigzag stitch and a button-sewing foot (see page 50, and your Operating Manual).*

"Since I sew everything, I rarely buy anything except sweaters, but when I do I always add terrific buttons to make the item special. This lets me put my personal stamp on it."

Sandra Betzina
Designer; Author, *Power Sewing* books and videos
San Francisco, CA

OTHER BUTTON-SEWING TIPS AND TRICKS

• Try one of these creative ways to sew on a four-hole button (Fig. 10.11): parallel stitches, crossed or boxed stitches, an arrow, or a stem and leaves with French knots through one hole, creating a flower.

• To reinforce a coat button, sew a button backing (Fig. 10.12).

• To secure a button that is under strain at the bottom of a coat, stitch it on by hand using elastic thread through your needle (Fig. 10.13).

• To prevent a metal shank button from wearing away the thread, hold it on with the loop end of a hook and eye for extra strength. Stitch the loop, not the button shank (Fig. 10.14).

BUTTON SOURCES

"I would like a source for special buttons. I have found a marvelous store in Chicago, but I am sure there are others."

Carol McGuire
Publisher, *American Fastener Journal*
Columbus, OH

Two outstanding button shops in Chicago are listed here. Both have a mail-order business and can help you select appropriate buttons if they have a swatch and description of the garment.

Renaissance Buttons
(vintage buttons)
826 W. Armitage
Chicago, IL 60614
(312) 883-9508

Tender Buttons
143 E. 62nd Street
New York, NY 10021
(212) 758-7004
and
946 Rush Street
Chicago, IL 60611
(312) 337-7003

Also look in the 16-page source list in the back of *The Button Lover's Book,* by Marilyn Green (Chilton, 1991). The author lists everything from button museums to button shops and includes domestic and international mail-order button sources. You can also call these toll-free mail-order sources that have personal shoppers:

Baer Fabrics
Fashion Mail Order
515 East Market Street
Louisville, KY 40202
1-800-769-7776fax
fax (502) 582-2331

G Street Fabrics
11854 Rockville Pike
Rockville, MD 20852
1-800-333-9191
(301) 231-9155
fax (301) 231-9155

As Ye Sew, So Shall Ye Rip, or How to Un-Sew

Occasionally you need to rip out or "un-sew" a few stitches for the repair. To do this, use either the point of your seam ripper or embroidery scissors to loosen the thread, then lift up the stitch and cut the thread. Pull the two pieces of fabric apart at the cut stitch until the stitches no longer unravel; then cut another stitch. Or, once a stitch has been cut and loosened, pull the thread tail hard and toward the line of stitching you want to rip out. This will break 5 to 7 stitches. Turn the fabric over and pull the other thread tail as before. Repeat this until the area has been un-sewn the desired amount.

Figure 10.11 In a four-hole button, sew parallel stitches, crossed or boxed stitches, an arrow, or a stem and leaves with French knots in one hole to create a flower.

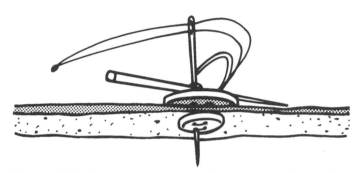

Figure 10.12 Reinforce a coat button by sewing another button on the back side of the fabric, creating a button backing.

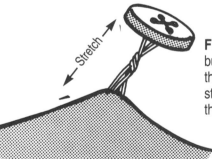

Figure 10.13 For a button under strain at the bottom of a coat, stitch it on with elastic thread.

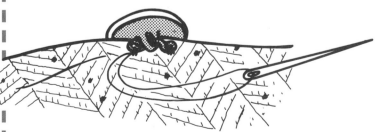

Figure 10.14
To prevent a metal shank button from wearing away the thread, hold it on with the loop end of a hook and eye for extra strength.

All About 11 Hems

Hemming How-To's

The most common alteration is either letting down or taking up a hem. The edge turned to the inside can fray, so it must be finished somehow. Hems are turned up, faced (usually with bias tape), or enclosed or bound off with braid or trim (Fig. 11.1). Within those categories are variations. Here are some general guidelines.

The hemming technique you choose largely depends on the fabric and garment style. Regardless of the technique, when hemmed, the garment should hang evenly, there should be no lumpiness in the hem allowance, and, unless the hem is designed to be decorative, it should be inconspicuous.

Straighten a Crooked Hem

"I want to know the easiest way to straighten a crooked hem."

Cheryl Leiss
Owner, X Cel Forms
Columbus, OH

Occasionally in ready-to-wear, hemlines are not even because the fabric stretches out of shape after the garment is made, shipped to the store and hung on a rack; or because your figure is slightly less than perfect. Try on the garment. Is the hemline even all the way around? If not, remove the hemming stitches and mark the finished hemline (see pages 130–131).

> **Sew-Easy Tip:** *Remove ready-to-wear hemming stitches by pulling a thread in the chain-stitched hem. This is a trial-and-error process, so if by pulling one thread in the chain, the thread does not release the hem, try another. After a few attempts in one direction, try pulling threads out of the chain in the other. I love when a hem unravels on the first try.*

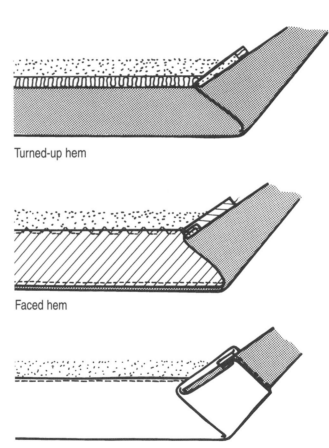

Turned-up hem

Faced hem

Encased or bound hem

Figure 11.1 Hem types: turned up, faced (usually with bias), or enclosed (with braid or trim).

> **Sew How:** *After making a dress or skirt, you are eager to hem it, but give it 24 hours "hang time" so that the fabric can relax and settle into a shape that will remain after wearing.*

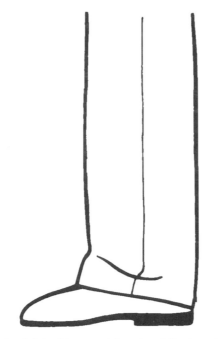

Figure 11.2 Pin up the finished hem so it breaks at the top of the shoe and drops lower at the heel.

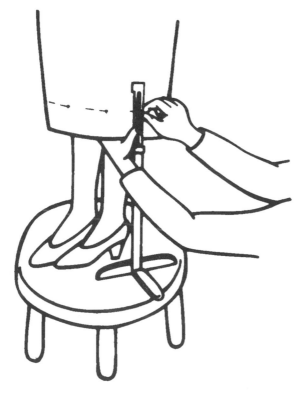

Figure 11.3 Move around the one who is having the hem measured for an even hem.

Measure and Mark the Hem

Although there are devices that will allow you to measure and mark a hem by yourself, it is difficult and time-consuming. Ask someone to help you. Refer to page 123 for marking supplies.

WHEN SOMEONE ELSE IS MARKING YOUR HEM

1 Wear the garment with the same underwear and shoes you will be wearing with it after it is hemmed.

2 Stand on a hard surface (carpet can distort measurements somewhat).

3 Stand up straight with your hands down at your sides. Do not lock your knees (I did once and passed out) and take frequent breaks.

WHEN YOU'RE MARKING SOMEONE ELSE'S HEM

1 For a skirt or dress, temporarily pin up the hem a few inches and decide on a pleasing length. Measure the distance from the floor to the finished hem length, and mark it on the yardstick or hem marker. For slacks, pin up the finished hem so the crease breaks when it touches the top of the shoe (Fig. 11.2). The amount of the break is a personal preference, so compare a pair of slacks you like with those you are altering. You may even want to drop the hem lower at the heel. To do this, refer to instructions on page 4.

2 If you are using a yardstick, mark the finished hem length by tightly wrapping a thin rubber band around the stick, the proper distance from the floor. If you are using a hem marker, adjust the marker arm so that pins slip into the fabric at the finished hem length (Fig. 11.3).

> **Sew How:** *When hemming a skirt or dress that goes under a jacket, remember the basics of good proportion. The most pleasing proportion is divided into thirds. For example, one-third jacket, two-thirds skirt and vice versa (see "The Golden Mean," page 55).*

3 Remove the pins from the hemline and let the fabric hang free. Mark the hemline, placing pins or marks horizontal to the floor and about every 2-3" (5-7.5cm). Mark a few inches (cm), then continue to move around and pin the hemline until it is marked all the way around. By moving around the one who is having the hem marked, rather than the other way around, you ensure that the hem is even (see Fig. 11.3).

Determine the Hem Depth

Once you have measured and marked the hemline, decide on the hem depth or hem allowance—that is, the distance between the fold and the finished edge (Fig. 11.4). Here are some guidelines for creating a hem that is not too bulky or too skimpy.

Standard hem depths are from 1/4-3" (6mm-7.5cm), depending on the garment. The Hem Depth Chart provides specific measurements for a variety of garments. Mark the appropriate hem depth, and even the hem edge by cutting it off and finishing the raw edge. This can be done by attaching hem tape or by stitch-finishing. If the hem allowance is not deep enough, then you will have to face the hem (see page 16).

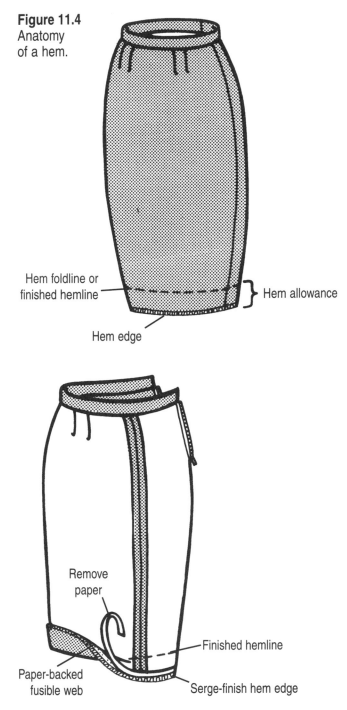

Figure 11.4
Anatomy of a hem.

Hem foldline or finished hemline

Hem allowance

Hem edge

Remove paper

Finished hemline

Paper-backed fusible web

Serge-finish hem edge

Figure 11.5 No-sew hem; fuse on narrow paper-backed fusible web following manufacturer's instructions. Let the fabric cool, then peel off the paper and press up the hem.

Table 11.1

Hem Depth Chart

Garment to Be Hemmed	Hem Depth
T-shirts, sleeves	5/8 to 1 1/4" (1.5-3cm)
Shorts, slacks	1 1/4 to 1 1/2" (3-4cm)
Jackets	1 1/2 to 2" (4-5cm)
Flared skirts, flared coats	1/4" rolled hem to 2" conventional hem (6mm-5cm)
Straight skirts, straight coats	2 to 3" (5-7.5cm)

Penny-Saver Tip: *I prefer not using hem tape or lace because they add bulk to the finish. It's also one less notion I need to keep on hand. Instead, I finish the raw hem edge with one of the overlocking or overcasting stitches on my conventional sewing machine, or by serge-finishing (see Reference Chart A).*

Hem Options

No-Sew Hems

For a quick, permanent hem, prepare the hem by measuring and marking it and determining its depth, as described earlier in this chapter. Then, instead of stitching it, fuse it up using a paper-backed fusible web (Trans-Web, Thermo-Web, Hem-N-Trim, or Wonder-Under).

1 Using the paper side up, lay fusible web strip on the hem edge and fuse, following the manufacturer's instructions. Let the paper cool; then use scalloping

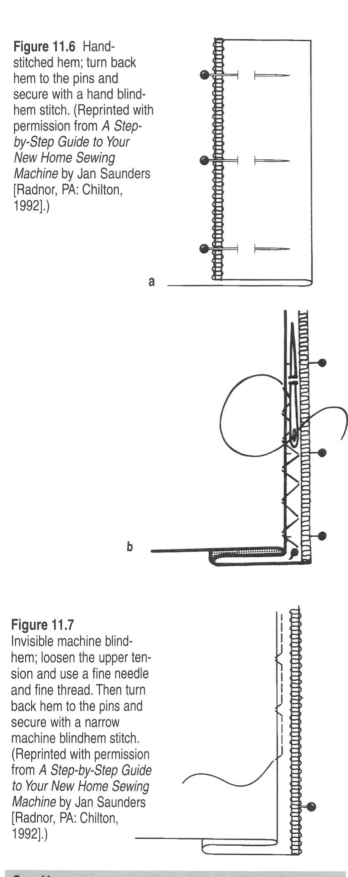

Figure 11.6 Hand-stitched hem; turn back hem to the pins and secure with a hand blind-hem stitch. (Reprinted with permission from *A Step-by-Step Guide to Your New Home Sewing Machine* by Jan Saunders [Radnor, PA: Chilton, 1992].)

a

b

Figure 11.7 Invisible machine blind-hem; loosen the upper tension and use a fine needle and fine thread. Then turn back hem to the pins and secure with a narrow machine blindhem stitch. (Reprinted with permission from *A Step-by-Step Guide to Your New Home Sewing Machine* by Jan Saunders [Radnor, PA: Chilton, 1992].)

Sew How: *Keep a roll of paper-backed fusible web near your ironing board for quick fixes such as fusing loose facings, hems, or edges.*

or pinking shears and pink the hem edge. Remove the release paper.

2 Turn the hem up the desired amount and press, again following the manufacturer's instructions (Fig. 11.5). If this finish is on an edge that occasionally blows open, the scalloping shows, while the hem edge is firmly secured.

Hand-Stitched Hems

Using a fine hand needle and thread one shade darker than the fabric, turn the hem edge back where the pins enter the fabric and secure it by hand with a blindhemming stitch (Fig. 11.6).

Almost Invisible Machine Blindhems

Woven fabrics fray if they are not cut on the bias so be sure to finish the hem edge by using hem tape or lace, or by finishing with an overcasting stitch (see Reference Chart A). To ensure almost invisible blindhems on both wovens and knits, use a fine needle and thread.

Machine Readiness Checklist

stitch: straight blindhem (wovens); stretch blindhem (knits)
foot: blindhem
stitch length: 2-3 (9-13 stitches per inch)
stitch width: 1.5-2 (narrow enough to pick up a thread)
needle: size 60/8 or 70/10 universal
thread: 50-weight machine-embroidery (needle and bobbin)

1 Use the appropriate blindhem stitch for your fabric (see Reference Chart A). Loosen the top tension to prevent the stitch from pulling in a dimple on the right side of the fabric.

NOTE——*If after testing you still see a dimple, bypass the bobbin tension by threading the bobbin through the bypass hole or by omitting the bobbin tension altogether (see your Operating Manual).*

2 Using the blindhem foot designed for your machine, set the stitch just wide enough to catch a thread of the fabric, snug the guide in the foot against the fold, and then stitch (Fig. 11.7). If the stitch is too wide, it will show when you open out the hem.

Terrific Topstitching

TOPSTITCHING BASICS

You may want to topstitch a hem. Here are basic guidelines to follow.

- Use a medium to long 3.5–4 stitch length (6 stitches per inch) for midweight to heavy fabrics

- Be consistent with the topstitching on other parts of the garment (i.e., if you use a 3 length on the collar, do so on the cuffs and front tab)

- Use two threads through the same needle or heavier topstitching thread through a size 90/14 universal or topstitching needle (see Reference Charts B and C)

JEANS HEMS IN A JIFFY

Sometimes the hem is the focal point because it is top-stitched—jeans are a good example of this, as well as other sporty attire. But do you like to rehem jeans? If not, try this. You will need 1¼" (3cm) hem allowance to do a doubled jean hem.

Machine Readiness Checklist

stitch: straight
foot: standard, Teflon, or roller
stitch length: 3–4 (6–9 stitches per inch)
stitch width: 0
needle: size 90/14 HJ jeans
thread: two strands of all-purpose or heavier topstitching through the needle
accessories: Jean-A-Ma-Jig, Hump Jumper, or button reed

1 Turn up a doubled ½" (1.3cm) hem and press.

> **Serge-Easy Tip:** *For easier topstitching, with less bulk, serge-finish the hem edge ⅝" (1.5cm) from the hemline fold. Turn up the hem once and topstitch.*

2 To prevent the foot from stalling on the way up and coasting on the way down a flat-felled seam or other uneven thickness, use a wedge under the heel of the foot as you approach a thickness (Fig. 11.8). Stitch across the thickness until the toes begin to tip down. Stop with the needle in the fabric, lift the foot, and slip the wedge under the toes as you come off the thickness (see Fig. 11.8). The wedge levels the foot for even feeding and even, better stitching.

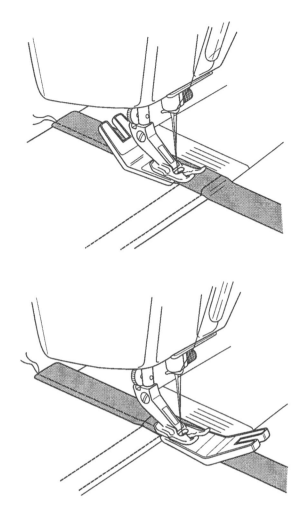

Figure 11.8 Use a wedge to sew up and over flat-felled seams without breaking a needle or skipping stitches.

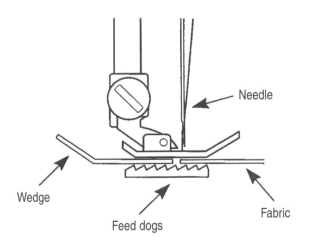

Figure 11.9 Use a wedge to start on the edge of a thick seam. Remember to put the pressure foot down for perfect stitch formation.

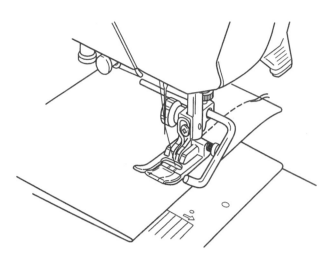

Figure 11.10 Place the edge of the fold so it guides against the quilting bar or guide. (Reprinted with permission from *A Step-by-Step Guide to Your New Home Sewing Machine* by Jan Saunders [Radnor, PA: Chilton, 1992].)

Figure 11.11 For skirts, dresses, or robes that will be on a group of people standing together, sew each hem an equal distance from the floor.

> **Sew-Easy Tip:** *Use this same technique when starting at the edge of a thickness. Put the needle into the edge of the fabric, butt the end of the wedge up to the end of the fabric, then lower the presser foot (Fig. 11.9).*

Straightest Edgestitching

Edgestitching is a line of stitching ⅛" (3mm) or less from the finished edge and is generally stitched with thread matching the fabric. In addition to hems, edgestitch altered collars, front tabs, cuffs, belts, and waistbands using a blindhem or edgestitch foot.

Machine Readiness Checklist

stitch: straight
foot: blindhem or edgestitch
stitch length: 2–2.5 (10–12 stitches per inch)
stitch width: 0
needle: appropriate for fabric
(see Reference Charts B and C)
thread: all-purpose

1 Press the edge to be edgestitched. Place the edge of fold so it is snug up against the guide in the foot (Fig. 11.10).

2 Set your needle position so the needle is the desired distance from the edge and stitch, using a 2 to 2.5 length (10-12 stitches per inch) straight stitch. The foot enables you to edgestitch uniformly from the edge of the fabric.

Sew How: When hemming skirts, dresses, or robes that will be on a group of people standing together—bridesmaids and choral groups come to mind—measure, mark, and sew each hem an equal distance from the floor so when the group is standing together they look uniform (Fig. 11.11).

Ready-in-a-Minute Rolled Hems

Although you can stitch a rolled hem by hand, it is faster to stitch by machine, using a rolled-hem foot to duplicate the rolled hem commonly found on shirttails, scarves, and ruffle edges. The foot has a scroll that turns the fabric before the needle reaches it for stitching. It takes a little practice, but once mastered, the rolled-hem foot is a great help with repairs and alterations.

BASIC ROLLED HEM

The width of the groove on the underside of the rolled-hem foot determines the finished hem width (i.e., 4mm hemmer = 4mm finished hem). The foot can also be used with a zigzag stitch.

Machine Readiness Checklist

stitch: straight
foot: rolled hem
stitch length: 2-3 (9-13 stitches per inch)
stitch width: 0
needle: size 70 or 80 H universal
thread: all-purpose
accessories: tear-away stabilizer

1 Roll and press a couple of inches of the hem to get started. Work with the underside of the fabric up.

Sew How: To start stitching a rolled hem on the edge of the fabric, overlap a 2" (5cm) square of tear-away stabilizer and stitch it to the raw edge of the fabric at the starting edge of the hem. Start rolling the stabilizer into the hemmer by "sawing" it back and forth into the scroll. You will remove the tear-away after stitching (Fig. 11.12).

2 With the needle in center position, feed the stabilizer into the scroll and begin sewing. With your right hand, hold the fabric up and slightly to the left of center, curling the edge of the fabric before it enters

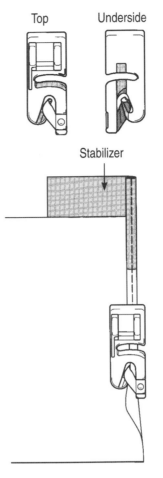

Top   Underside

Stabilizer

Figure 11.12 Starting with tear-away stabilizer on the edge, move the needle position and stitch a narrow hem, guiding the fold to the inside edge of the scroll. (Reprinted with permission from *A Step-by-Step Guide to Your New Home Sewing Machine* by Jan Saunders [Radnor, PA: Chilton, 1992].)

Sew-Easy Tip
On tricot, use the rolled-hem foot and a wide 2 to 3 length (10-12 stitches per inch) zigzag to roll and shell tuck an edge at the same time. Use the scroll to guide cord, yarn, pearl cotton, or narrow trim for a corded edge finish.

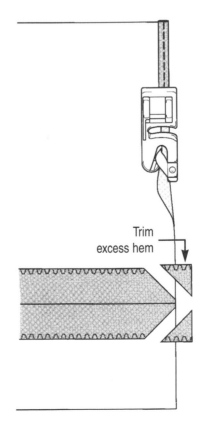

Trim excess hem

Figure 11.13 Press the curved hem. Turn the fold into the scroll and stitch the curve. Trim away excess hem allowance. (Reprinted with permission from *A Step-by-Step Guide to Your New Home Sewing Machine* by Jan Saunders [Radnor, PA: Chilton, 1992].)

Topside   Underside

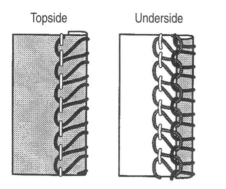

Figure 11.14 Narrow rolled hem.

Serge-Easy Tip: Finish an edge with a narrow rolled hem. For the best results, use Woolly Nylon in the upper looper and all-purpose serger thread in the lower looper and needle. Tighten the upper looper tension and use a short satin length stitch (Fig. 11.14; see also Reference Chart A).

Figure 11.15
Clip the seam allowance at the hem edge to remove the unnecessary bulk. (Reprinted with permission from *A Step-by-Step Guide to Your New Home Sewing Machine* by Jan Saunders [Radnor, PA: Chilton, 1992].)

Trim excess hem allowance

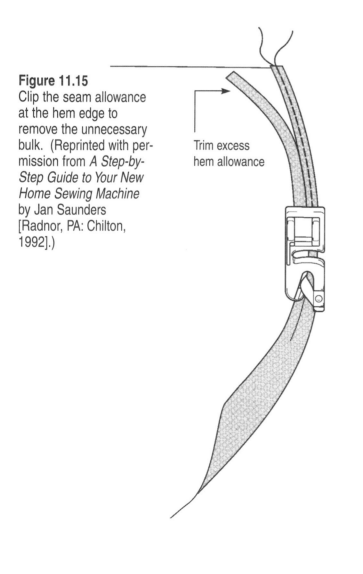

the scroll. Watch that the curl on the left does not exceed the "ditch" in the foot or the hem will have extra fabric in it. Also watch that extra fabric on the right does not get caught under the foot.

3 To roll the hems over a seam allowance, clip the seam allowance at the hem edge as shown in Figure 11.13. This will remove unnecessary bulk so that the seam allowance rolls into the scroll smoothly. If the seam allowance section is too bulky, skip over it and return to it later with a regular foot.

4 If you need to turn corners on a rolled hem (for the vents on a tunic top or the corners of a scarf, for example), stitch the rolled hem as described in Steps 1-3, all the way to the corner. Stop and remove the fabric. Stitch a small piece of tear-away stabilizer under the corner, then roll it into the scroll of the foot. Begin stitching on the stabilizer, then into the fabric. This way your stitching starts right at the corner. Pull thread ends to the underside of the fabric and tie them off. Remove stabilizer.

CURVED ROLLED HEM

If you are going to rehem a circular skirt made of light-weight fabric such as chiffon or georgette, use your rolled-hem foot. If the hem needs to be straightened after stitching, it is easy to rip a few stitches, even the hem, and then restitch before trimming (Fig. 11.15).

1 Press a 1/2-3/4" (1.3-2cm) hem all the way around the curved hemline.

2 On the wrong side, turn the fold into the scroll of the hemmer and stitch. The hem will turn only once this way.

3 When you get back to where you started, remove the hem edge from the scroll for the last inch (2.5cm), and stitch it so that the stitches meet where you began.

4 Try on the garment to be sure the hem is even. If it is even, trim excess fabric away from the hem close to the roll.

Knit Knack

Although these hemming techniques can be used on knits, some knits, such as wool jersey, T-shirt knits, velour, and stretch terry, are extremely stretchy and need more durable seams and hems than the more-stable double knits. Most knits are commercially seamed using a 1/4" (6mm) seam allowance for durability (also because 5/8" [1.5cm] seams won't stay pressed open). To simulate this 1/4" (6mm) seam finish on your sewing machine, stitch the seams using use a tiny zigzag (1 width, 1 length [24 stitches per inch]). To the right of the seam, stitch the seam allowances together with a three-step zigzag (4-6 width and about a 1 length [24 stitches per inch]) as shown in Figure 11.16.

Twin-Needle Hems

A quick and professional method of hemming knits is to use a 4.0/75 stretch twin needle. This means that the needles are 4mm apart and are a size 75/11 stretch—appropriate for most knits. Because the bobbin thread must share itself between the two top threads, the zigzag stitch created on the underside stretches with the fabric without breaking. Use this technique on stretchy knits such as sweater knits, stretch terry, and velours.

Note—*Because the needles sit in the machine with the flat side to the back, twin needles can be used only by those machines with a top- or front-loading bobbin.*

Machine Readiness Checklist

stitch: straight
foot: transparent embroidery or satin stitch
stitch length: 3.5-5 (4-8 stitches per inch)
stitch width: 0
needle: 4.0 11/75 HS stretch twin
thread: two spools of all-purpose through needles to match the fabric, all-purpose on bobbin

Note—*You may want to lighten up the presser foot pressure and loosen the upper tension slightly. To prevent threads from tangling through the upper tension, place one spool so the thread pulls from the front of the spool; place the other spool so the thread pulls from the back of the spool.*

1 Fold hem up the desired amount and press.

2 With the garment right side up, place the fabric under the foot the width of the hem so the foot is resting on a double layer of fabric. Stitch.

Sew How: *If the fabric puckers, shorten the stitch. If the fabric waves out of shape, lengthen the stitch.*

3 Trim excess fabric from the underside using a pair of pelican-shaped appliqué scissors to prevent cutting a hole where you don't want one. To do this, position the rounded blade between the hem allowance and the wrong side of the garment, then cut (Fig. 11.18).

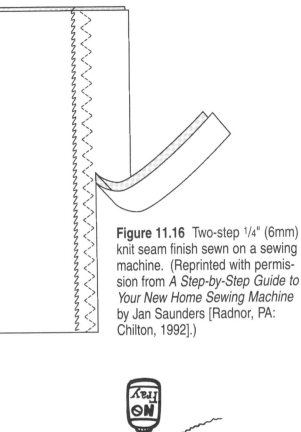

Figure 11.16 Two-step 1/4" (6mm) knit seam finish sewn on a sewing machine. (Reprinted with permission from *A Step-by-Step Guide to Your New Home Sewing Machine* by Jan Saunders [Radnor, PA: Chilton, 1992].)

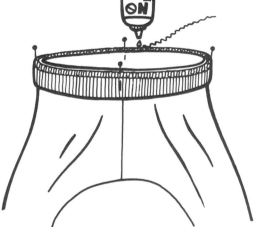

Figure 11.17
Repair a split seam by serging on and off the seam. Dot threads with seam sealant (Fray Check, No-Fray, or Stop Fraying), let dry, then clip the thread chain close to the seam.

Serge-Easy Tip: *To repair a serged seam that has come out, use a balanced 3- or 4-thread overlock. Carefully serge on, then off leaving about a 4" (10cm) tail at either end of the repair. Unravel the straightest thread in the chain of the tail and tie off the threads. To prevent the original serged stitching from coming unraveled where the repair begins and ends, dot threads with a liquid seam sealant such as Fray Check, Stop Fraying, or No-Fray (Fig. 11.17).*

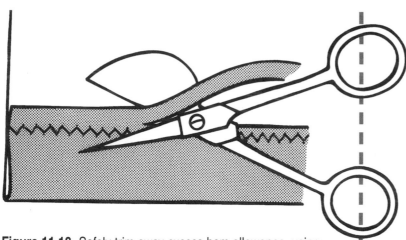

Figure 11.18 Safely trim away excess hem allowance, using pelican-shaped appliqué scissors.

Single-Needle Hems with a Memory

Hem or topstitch knits with a single needle using all-purpose thread through the needle and elastic thread in the bobbin. You get the look you want and the resiliency you need with this quick-to-stitch technique.

Machine Readiness Checklist

stitch: straight
foot: transparent embroidery or satin stitch
stitch length: 3-5 (5-9 stitches per inch)
stitch width: 0
needle: appropriate for the fabric (see Reference Charts B and C)
thread: all-purpose through needle
bobbin: threaded with elastic thread; bobbin tension loosened enough or bypassed with only slight drag on the thread (see your Operating Manual)

1 Wind a bobbin with elastic thread by putting the bobbin on the bobbin winder and slowly guiding the thread on the bobbin without stretching it.

NOTE—*If you have a self-winding bobbin, wind elastic thread on your bobbin by hand, without stretching it.*

2 Fold up the hem and press. Place the presser foot on the right side of the hem as for topstitching so the foot is resting on a double layer of fabric. Stitch around the hem, then trim away the excess fabric with appliqué scissors (see Fig. 11.18).

A Word to My Readers

Whether you have read through this book page by page, or have just looked at a few of the ideas, I hope *Wardrobe Quick-Fixes* has shed some light into your dark closet of potential—given you an "aha!"—so you can get more mileage out of your clothing investment. I also hope you enjoyed the comments, questions, and suggestions from my family, friends, and colleagues.

If you are interested in adding to these ideas, I want to hear from you. If I didn't cover a subject as thoroughly as you'd like, I want to hear from you. If you found a better way to do something, I want to hear from you. So please write me c/o *The Creative Machine Newsletter*, P. O. Box 2634-B, Menlo Park, CA 94026-2634.

Happy creating,

J. S.

Reference Charts

Reference Chart A – Stitch Technique Reference Guide

Fabric Type	Fabric Weight	Technique	Sewing Machine – Conventional Stitch	Stitch Length	Stitch Width	Foot	Needle size / type	Pressure	Stabilizer	Serger Stitch	Length	Width	Needles	Differential Feed
Woven	Light	seam	straight stitch	2 - 2.5	0	standard zigzag	70/10 universal; 60/8 - 70/10 sharp for microfibers	100%	no	3-thread overlock	med	narrow to med	one	no
		overcast	3-step zigzag	0.5 - 1	4 - 5	standard zigzag								
		seam/overcast	overlock	4 - 7	4 - 5	overcast								
		shell hem	shell hem	1.5 - 2	4 - 5	standard zigzag					med	narrow		
		hem	straight stitch	2 - 2.5	0	standard zigzag				rolled hem	short	narrow		
		buttonhole	sheer buttonhole	0.5 - 0.8	3 - 5	buttonhole			yes	n/a	n/a	n/a	n/a	n/a
	Mid-Weight	seam	straight stitch	2 - 2.5	0	standard zigzag	80/12 universal or sharp for microfibers	100%	no	3 -, 3/4 -, or 4 -thread mock safety; 5 - thread safety	medium	med to wide	one or two	no
		overcast	3-step zigzag	1.5	4 - 5	overcast								
		seam/overcast	overlock	2.5 - 6	4 - 5	overcast								
		blind hem	blind hem	1 - 2.5	2 - 3	blind hem				blind stitch	long	narrow	one	
		topstitch	straight stitch	3 - 3.5	0	standard zigzag				flatlock	short to med	wide		
		buttonhole	buttonhole	0.5 - 0.75	4 - 5	buttonhole			yes	n/a	n/a	n/a	n/a	n/a
	Heavy	seam	straight stitch	3 - 3.5	0	embroidery	80/12 universal or sharp for microfibers	100%	no	3 -, 3/4 -, or 4 - thread mock safety; 5 - thread safety	medium to long	wide	one or two	no
		overcast	3-step zigzag	1.5 - 2	6	overcast								
		seam/overcast	double overlock	3 - 5	5 - 6	embroidery								
		blind hem	blind hem	0.8 - 2	2 - 3	blind hem				blind stitch	long	narrow	one	
		topstitch	straight stitch	3 - 4	0	standard zigzag or embroidery	90/14 topstitch			flatlock	medium	wide		
		buttonhole	corded buttonhole	0.5 - 0.75	4 - 5	buttonhole	80/12 universal		yes	n/a	n/a	n/a	n/a	n/a
Knit	Light	seam	tiny zigzag	2 - 2.5	1 - 2	standard zigzag	75/11 stretch	75%	no	2-thread or 3-thread overlock	medium	narrow to med	one	yes
		overcast	3-step zigzag	0.5 - 1	3 - 5	overcast								
		seam/overcast	interlock	0.75 - 2.5	4 - 5	overcast								
		rolled hem	straight stitch	2 - 3	4 - 5	rolled hem								
		hem	straight stitch	2	0	standard zigzag	3.0/80 twin			rolled	short	narrow		
		buttonhole	sheer buttonhole; stretch buttonhole	0.5 - 0.8	3.5 - 4	buttonhole	75/11 stretch		yes	n/a	n/a	n/a	n/a	n/a
	Mid-Weight	seam	3-step zigzag	2 - 2.5	1 - 2	standard zigzag	75/11 stretch	60 - 75%	no	3/4 thread overlock, or 4 - thread mock safety	medium	med to wide	one or two	no
		overcast	3-step zigzag	1.5 - 2	4 - 5	overcast								
		seam/overcast	double overlock	3 - 5	5 - 6	embroidery								
		blind hem	blind hem	0.8 - 2	2 - 3	blind hem	60/8 universal			blind stitch	med to long	narrow to med	one	
		hem	straight stitch	3	0	embroidery	3.0/80 twin			flatlock	short to med	wide		
		buttonhole	stretch buttonhole	0.8 - 1	3 - 4	buttonhole	75/11 stretch		yes	n/a	n/a	n/a	n/a	n/a

(n/a) - Technique not appropriate for fabric or technique.

(n/r) - Technique not recommended for fabric type.

Note that the above stitch settings are GENERAL guidelines; check your operating manual for brand-specific information.

This chart is from the book Jan Saunders' Wardrobe Quick-Fixes.

Stitch Key / Conventional Sewing Machines

- straight stitch
- zigzag
- tiny zigzag
- 3-step zigzag
- seam and overcast
- overlock
- double overlock
- interlock
- blind hem
- stretch blind hem
- picot, pin stitch
- buttonhole
- stretch buttonhole
- sheer buttonhole
- corded buttonhole
- corded stretch buttonhole

Reference Chart A – Stitch Technique Reference Guide (continued)

Fabric Type	Fabric Weight	Technique	Sewing Machine: Conventional Stitch	Stitch Length	Stitch Width	Foot	Needle size / type	Pressure	Stabilizer	Serger: Serger Stitch	Length	Width	Needles	Differential Feed
Knit (cont.)	Heavy	seam	^^^^^^	2.5 - 3	1 - 2	embroidery	75/11 - 90/14 stretch	50 - 60%	no	3 -, 3/4 -, or 4 - thread mock safety; 5 - thread safety	med to long	wide	one or two	yes
		overcast	/\/\/\	1.2 - 1.5	5 - 6	overcast								
		seam/overcast	//_//_//	3 - 5	5 - 6	embroidery								
		blind hem	V^^^^V^^^^	0.8 - 2	2 - 4	blind hem				blind stitch		narrow to med	one	
		hem	— — — —	3 - 4	0	embroidery	4.0/75 twin stretch			flatlock		wide		
		buttonhole		0.8 - 1	5 - 6	buttonhole	75/11 - 90/14 stretch			n/a	n/a	n/a	n/a	
Leather, Suede and Faux Suede		seam	— — — —	3	0	Teflon or roller	75/11 stretch or 90/14 leather	80%	no	flatlock	med to long	wide	one	no
		topstitch	— — — —	3 - 4	0 - 4									
		seam/overcast (n/r)	n/a	n/a	n/a					n/a	n/a	n/a	n/a	n/a
		blind hem (n/r)												
		hem	— — — —	3 - 4	0					dec. 3-thread	short	wide	one	no
		buttonhole	— — — —	3	0				yes	n/a	n/a	n/a	n/a	n/a
Vinyl		seam	— — — —	3	0	Teflon or roller	80/12 universal or 90/14 leather	100%	no	flatlock	short	wide	one	no
		topstitch	^^^^^^ or — — —	2	0 - 4									
		seam/overcast (n/r)	n/a	n/a	n/a									
		blind hem (n/r)								n/a	n/a	n/a	n/a	n/a
		hem	— — — —	3	0					decorative 3 - thread	short	wide	one	no
		buttonhole	— — — —	0.5 - 1	0					n/a	n/a	n/a	n/a	n/a
Furs and Faux Furs		seam	— — — —	3 - 4	0	embroidery	80/12 sharp	50 - 60%	no	n/a	n/a	n/a	n/a	n/a
		overcast (n/r)	n/a	n/a	n/a	n/a								
		seam/overcast (n/r)								flatlock	med to long	wide	one	no
		blind hem	‾V‾‾‾V‾	1.5 - 2.5	2 - 3	blind hem				n/r	n/a	n/a	n/a	n/a
		hem	— — — —	3 - 5	0	roller								
		buttonhole (n/r)	sew on fur hooks	n/a	n/a	n/a	n/a	n/a	n/a					

Basic serged seams:

- Needle thread
- Upper looper
- Lower looper
- Chain stitch needle
- Chain looper
- Chain looper for 5-thread safety

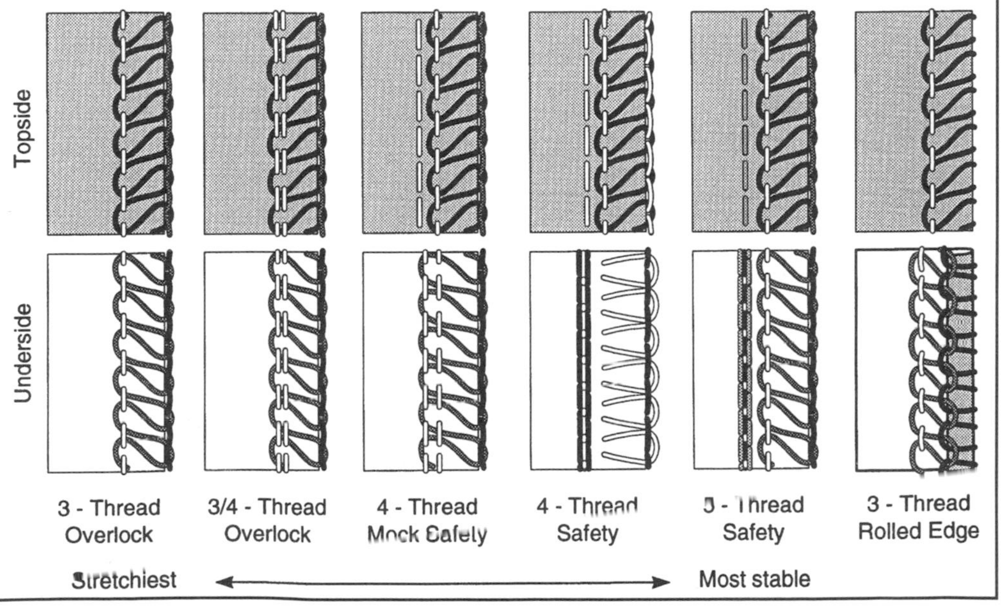

Topside
Underside
3 - Thread Overlock
3/4 - Thread Overlock
4 - Thread Mock Safety
4 - Thread Safety
5 - Thread Safety
3 - Thread Rolled Edge
Stretchiest
Most stable

Stitch Length Guide

Setting in mm	Stitches per inch (spi)
0.5	60
1	24
2	13
3	9
4	6
5	5
6	4

Reference Chart B–American and European Equivalent Needle Sizes

American	European	Suggested Fabrics
8	60	Silk chiffon, organza, sheers, fine cottons, and microfibers
9	65	Tissue faille, voile, georgette, blouse-weight silks, and microfibers
10	70	Blouse and lightweight dress fabric
11	75	Knit interlock, Lyrca activewear, knit sheers, Ultrasuede and other synthetic suedes and leathers, midweight microfibers
12	80	Suitweight silks, linens, and wools
14	90	Denim, topstitching with topstitching thread, heavy duck cloth, midweight real leather and suede
16	100	Very heavy duck cloth, some upholstery fabrics, upholstery vinyl
18	110	Some decorative hemstitching; use if the size 16/100 breaks
–	120	Decorative hemstitching; use if the size 18/110 breaks

This chart is from the book *Jan Saunders' Wardrobe Quick-Fixes*, Chilton, 1995.

Reference Chart C–Needle Point Types

Classification	Type
General Purpose Sewing Machine Needles	
15 × 1H 130/705H	**Universal:** Cross between a sharp point and a ballpoint tip used on most knits and wovens. This needle is most widely available and sews beautifully on the majority of fabrics. Twin-needle sizes available in 1.6 12/80, 2.0 12/80, 2.5 12/80, 3.0 12/80, 3.0 14/90, 4.0 12/80, 4.0 14/90, 6.0 16/100; triple needles available in 2.5 12/80 and 3.0 12/80.
15 × 1SP 130/705 SUK	**Ballpoint:** A round-tipped needle designed for use on heavy knits such as power net. The ball point slips easily between the loops in the knit fabric without skipping stitches or snagging. Not as widely available as the universal but available in sizes 10/70–16/100.
Blue Tip 130/705HS 130/705HPS (Pfaff) Sears "Q" Singer 2045	**Stretch:** Has a sharper point than a universal needle, with a deeper scarf, which aids in stitch formation to prevent skipped stitches. Recommended for swimwear knits, Lycra, synthetic suede, free-machine embroidery, and some microfibers. Often has a blue tip or shaft for easy identification. Twin-needle sizes available in 2.5 11/75 and 4.0 12/80.

Classification	Type

General Purpose Sewing Machine Needles (continued)

15 × 1DE 130/705HJ	**Denim or Jeans:** Sharp point to penetrate closely woven fabrics easily, without breaking. Recommended for denim, corduroy, and upholstery fabric. Single needles available in sizes 10/70-18/110. Twin needle sizes available in 4.0 16/100.
15 × 1 or 705B (B for Bernina) 130/705 HM Singer 2020 Microtex	**Sharp or Pierce Point:** A sharp needle used for sewing woven silks and microfibers. The small sizes (from 8/60-14/90) produce a very straight line of stitching. Also recommended for French hand sewing by machine on fine cottons and linen. Often has a violet shaft for easy identification. Bernina owners, read inside the hook cover to see if this needle is recommended for your machine.

Specialty Sewing Machine Needles

130/705 HM Metafil	**Embroidery:** Designed for use with metallic, novelty, and machine embroidery threads; available in sizes 11/75 and 14/90. This needle has larger eye and groove dimensions to prevent threads from splitting and shredding. It also has a deeper scarf for better stitch formation and to prevent skipped stitches. The sharp point avoids damage to the fabric and other threads when embroidering. Often has a red shaft or band for easy identification. Twin-needle sizes available in 2.0 11/75 and 3.0 11/75.
705 Handicap	**Handicap:** *Sharp* point with a self-threading eye available in sizes 12/80 and 14/90.
130/705 HQ	**Quilting:** Durable tapered point for sewing the many seams required for piecing without damaging the fabric. Currently available in sizes 75 and 90. Often has a green shaft or band for easy identification.
130/705H 130/705HS SPRING	**Spring:** Available in universal sizes 10/70-14/90, stretch 11/75 or 14/90, and denim 16/100, they have darning springs around them. Used for free-machine embroidery, darning, and quilting for better visibility. When using this needle, you don't need a darning foot.
15 × 1ST 130/705N	**Topstitch:** The eye and front groove of the needle are twice the size of a normal 11/75 or 14/90 needle to accommodate heavy topstitching thread. Some topstitching needles have sharp tips to produce the straightest topstitch.
15 × 1LL 130/705HLL 130/705NTW	**Wedge Point or Leather:** Available in sizes 10/70-18/110, this large-eye needle has a wedge point to penetrate leather. The point slices into the leather rather than perforating it.
130/705 H WING	**Wing:** The needle has wings running the length of the shaft to poke a large hole when hemstitching. The stitch goes in and out of the same hole, binding it open after stitching. Twin wing is available in size 16/100.

This chart is from the book *Jan Saunders' Wardrobe Quick-Fixes*, Chilton, 1995.

Reference Chart D – Measurement and Ease Chart

WOMEN		Your Measurement	Ease to be Added	Tissue Paper Measurement to Seam Line*
Bodice	High bust		3-5"	
	Bust		3-5"	
	Center front bodice length		1/2"	
	Length center back, neck to waist		3/4"	
	Back shoulder width		1/2"	
Sleeves	Upper arm circumference		2-3"	
	Arm length, shoulder to elbow		—	
	Arm length, shoulder to wrist		—	
	Wrist circumference		3/4"	
Skirt	Waistline		3/4"	
	High hip, 3" below waist		3/4"	
	Hips at fullest part, parallel to floor		2-3"	
	Waist to fullest part of hips		—	
	Thighs, parallel to floor		2-3"	
	Shirt length, waist to desired length		—	
Pants	Waistline		3/4"	
	Thigh circumference		2"+	
	Calf circumference		2"+	
	Inseam		—	
	Crotch depth (sitting)		1"	
	Crotch depth (standing)		1"	
MEN				
Upper body	Neck		1/2"	
	Chest		3-5"	
	Center front waist length		1/2"	
	Center back waist length		1/2"	
	Back width		1"	
	Shoulder width		—	
Sleeves	Shirt sleeve length		—	
	Upper arm circumference		2-3"	
	Arm length		—	
	Wrist circumference		3/4"	
Lower body	Waist		3/4"	
	Waist to fullest part of hips		—	
	Hips (seat)		1-2"	
	Thigh		1-2"	
	Trouser outseam (side length)		—	
	Trouser inseam		—	
	Waist to knee length		—	
	Crotch depth (sitting)		3/4"	
	Crotch depth (standing)		2-3"	

* Beginning sewers need take only the measurements found on the pattern envelope.

Reprinted with permission from *A Step-by-Step Guide to Your New Home Sewing Machine* by Jan Saunders (Radnor, PA: Chilton, 1992).

Quick-Fix Glossary

Basting

A row of long hand or machine stitches that temporarily holds one piece of fabric to another to check for fit and correct fabric position. Basting stitches are generally removed after permanent stitching is complete.

Basting (speed)

A long, wide zigzag stitch, and a loosened upper sewing machine tension used to baste a stretchy knit together. These stitches stretch with the fabric without breaking. To quickly remove the basting stitches, pull the bobbin thread.

Bias

On a woven piece of fabric, any line drawn or cut on a 45-degree or smaller angle from the lengthwise or cross grain.

Bobbin

A narrow spool that holds the lower thread in a sewing machine.

Clip

A short snip made through both layers of the seam allowance starting from the edge of the fabric and stopping just short of the seamline. A clip is made *after* the seam is sewn to help the seam lie flat after the garment is turned or pressed.

Crossgrain

The fabric grain perpendicular to the selvage edges, knit ribs, or lengthwise grain. Crosswise threads in a woven fabric are weaker than lengthwise threads; knits generally stretch the most on the crossgrain.

Dart

A wedge-shaped tuck taken in on a flat piece of fabric to give shape to a garment. Common places for darts are at the bust and waist.

Disappearing dressmaker's chalk

Chalk used to mark hems or button position that disappears after a period of time, usually 3 to 4 days. To make the marks disappear sooner, steam over them or remove them with water.

Double needle (twin needle)

A sewing machine needle with one shank that fits into the needle bar of the sewing machine, and a cross bar that holds two needles. Used to create pin tucks, decorative stitching, topstitching, or double- or twin-needle hems on knits (see page 137).

Ease (fitting)

The amount of room between a garment and your body so that you can sit and move with comfort.

Ease (style)

The amount of room between a garment and your body that the designer builds into a garment, which can be more or less than fitting ease.

Ease stitch plus

A way to ease more fabric into a smaller opening or space; for example, easing a circular hem edge to fit into the shape of a skirt (see pages 10–11).

Edgestitch

Topstitching sewn 1/8" (3mm) or less from the edge of a collar, cuff, front placket, and so on.

Finger-press

Pressure applied to an area of a garment using your fingers or fingernails, such as pressing a crease in a ribbon or belt loop, or to start a narrow hem.

Fusible web (or paper-backed fusible web)

Heat-sensitive adhesive that can be applied to the wrong side of the fabric to make it fusible. If the web does not have a paper backing, then a Teflon pressing sheet must be used between the web and the iron. If the web is paper backed, the paper acts as the pressing sheet and is removed after the web has been applied and the fabric has cooled.

Gathering

A row of excess fullness pulled into a seamline.

Hand catch-stitches

Loose, hand stiches that catch a little of the garment fabric, then stitch into the lining or back of another fabric to attach a trim or embellishment—attaching the lining of a faux fur collar to a coat, for example.

Hong Kong finished seam

A beautiful, quality seam finish suitable for most fabrics, but especially good for bulky fabrics, such as velvet or satin. A strip of lightweight fabric cut on the bias binds the raw edge, and a ⅝" (1.5cm) seam allowance is sewn, then pressed open. To create this look with a serger, thread the upper looper with a 2-ply knitting machine yarn, shorten the stitch, and finish the fabric edge by serging with the right side of the fabric up. Then sew a ⅝" (1.5cm) seam and press the seam open.

Hook-and-loop tape

The most common trade name for this closure is Velcro. One side has fine loops that grab on to the softer loop side.

Inseam

The seam that runs from the crotch to the hem on the inside of a pant leg.

Interfacing

A third layer of fabric used to stabilize an area such as a collar, cuff, facings, or front plackets.

Looper(s)

One, two, or three fingers, each with an eyelet that holds thread, that are used to form a stitch on a serger.

Notions

Helpful sewing aids used in many aspects of clothing construction and repair. You'll usually find them along one wall in your favorite fabric store. Sewing notions are also available through mail-order sources (see pages 62–63 and 148–149).

Nylon monofilament thread

Clear thread often used by clothing manufacturers for seaming and hemming. Available through local fabric stores and mail-order sources, nylon monofilament thread can also be used for appliquéing, hemming, and other invisible applications.

Outseam

The seam that runs from the waistline to the hem on the outside of a pant leg.

Overcast

Stitches either stitched by hand, by the sewing machine, or by the serger that finish or encase the raw edge of a piece of fabric (see Reference Chart A).

Press cloth

A piece of fabric (usually cotton) placed on the right side of a garment when top pressing to eliminate shine.

Presser foot

The foot or sole positioned under the needle of a sewing machine or serger. Several presser feet come with your sewing machine and serger, each having its own purpose (i.e., the button sewing foot for button sewing, the zipper foot for sewing on zippers, the rolled hem foot for rolled hems, etc.).

Quarter-mark

When sewing or serging a neckband or cuff into an opening, the technique of marking the band and opening into four equal parts, matching the two sets of quarter-marks, and then stitching.

Right side

The top side, outside, or correct side of the fabric or garment.

Rolled hem

A hem that is rolled rather than turned under to finish. Rolled hems done on a sewing machine include those found on shirttail hems and silk scarves. A serged rolled hem is often found around napkin edges.

Seamline

Where two pieces of fabric are sewn together.

Seam allowance

The distance between the cut edge and the seamline, usually ⅝" (1.5cm) or ¼" (6mm).

Selvage

The finished edge of fabric yardage that is parallel to the lengthwise grain.

Serged seam

A seam stitched by a serger.

Serger

A compact sewing machine that sews the seam, overcasts the edge, and trims off the excess fabric in the process.

Shank

A length of thread, or the metal loop on the underside of a button used as a spacer between the button and the fabric to allow the fabric to lie smoothly over a buttoned button.

Shell-tuck

An edge-finish made on a sewing machine using a reverse blindhem stitch. This scalloped-looking edge-finish is commonly found on lingerie hems, sleeves, and necklines, and on the sleeves of children's clothing.

Stabilizer

A tear-away substance similar to paper or a water-soluble

film used to keep a piece of fabric flat and smooth for stitching. Stabilizers are used for appliqué and machine embroidery work, and for starting rolled hems; they are removed after stitching.

Stitch in-the-ditch

A row of stitching sewn from the right side of the garment through all layers so that the stitches fall almost invisibly in the crack of the seam. You can tack facings and cuffs and attach the back side of waistbands by stitching in-the-ditch.

Stitch length

The length of the stitch from top to bottom, which is measured metrically or imperially. The following chart shows you what stitch length really means:

Setting in Millimeters	Stitches per Inch
0.5	60 (fine)
1	24 (fine)
2	13
3	9
4	6
5	5
6	4

Stitch width

The width of a stitch from one side to the other is measured in millimeters. A 1 stitch width is 1mm wide, a 2 stitch width is 2mm wide, and so on. At publication, many sewing machines and sergers have the capability of a 7–9mm stitch width.

Stretch stitches

Special stitches, available on many conventional sewing machines, that sew the seam and overcast the edge at the same time. If the fabric travels through the machine, feeding forward and backward simultaneously, the stitch will stretch with the fabric, then return to its original shape—a real advantage when working with stretchy knit fabrics.

Tape-baste

Using transparent, masking, or other type of sticky tape to temporarily hold something in place before gluing, fusing, or stitching.

Topstitch

Stitches on a garment, usually on a collar, cuff, front placket, tuck, or pocket, that are on top of the fabric.

Tuck

A narrow column of fabric that has been pinched in and stitched down for a decorative or fitting purpose.

Water-erasable or air-soluble marker

Marking tools used to mark fabric for button placement, for example. Water-erasable marks disappear when washed; air-soluble marks disappear automatically after 24 to 48 hours.

Wrong side

The inside or back side of a piece of fabric or a garment.

Quick-Fix Source List

If you are looking for an item listed in this book, please check your local sources first. You'll discover that once you develop a special relationship with your local sewing machine dealers and fabric and craft retailers, they'll become a convenient source for advice and inspiration. You'll also have the added benefit of purchasing and using the item immediately. However, if something I mention is not available locally and your retailer cannot get it for you, these mail-order sources are a viable option. While I have tried to be accurate and complete, addresses change, businesses move or die, and I make regrettable omissions by mistake (advance apologies to anyone I left out). Please send any corrections to me at Open Chain Publishing, P.O. Box 2634-B, Menlo Park, CA 94026-2634.

Buttons

Baer Fabrics
Fashion Mail Order
515 East Market Street
Louisville, KY 40202
1-800-769-7776
fax: (502) 582-2331

G Street Fabrics
11854 Rockville Pike
Rockville, MD 20852
1-800-333-9191
fax: (301) 231-9155

Renaissance Buttons
826 W. Armitage
Chicago, IL 60614
(312) 883-9508
vintage buttons

Tender Buttons
143 East 62nd Street
New York, NY 10021
(212) 758-7004
and
946 North Rush Street
Chicago, IL 60611
(312) 337-7033

Sewing Notions
(write or call for a catalog)

Aardvark Adventures
P. O. Box 2449
Livermore, CA 94551
(415) 443-2687
beads, buttons, bangles, an assortment of decorative threads and related products, and books

Clotilde, Inc.
2 Sew Smart Way
B 8031
Stevens Point, WI 54481-8031
1-800-772-2891
Res-Q Tape, Res-Q Tabs, Emergency Shirt Buttons, It Stays adhesive, Drawstring Restringer, Zipper Safety Hook, Clo-Chalk disappearing dressmakers chalk, pattern transfer material, Zipper Pull Repair Kit, and hundreds of other Quick-Fix sewing and crafting notions, and books

The Green Pepper, Inc.
3918 West First Avenue
Eugene, OR 97402
(503) 345-6665
active and outerwear patterns and fabric: replacement separating and sport zippers; specializing in nylon/Lycra and poly-propylene/Lycra knits, water-repellent fabrics, and insulating battings

Nancy's Notions, Ltd.
P. O. Box 683
Beaver Dam, WI 53916
1-800-833-0690
Rainbow Thread Braid, elastic thread, bodkins and elastic guides, Stitch 'n Stretch elastic treatment, Color It Gone Stain Removal Kit, Straight-Tape, Do-Sew, Fly Front Zipper Guide, and hundreds of other Quick-Fix sewing and crafting notions and books

Oregon Tailor Supply
2123 Division Street
P. O. Box 42284
Portland, OR 97242
1-800-678-2457
replacement zippers, plastic dry cleaner bags, hangers,
buttons, and tailoring supplies

The Paris Connection
4314 Irene Drive
Erie, PA 16510
sewing machine feet and accessories, as well as old
sewing machine manuals; send pre-addressed stamped
envelope for more information

Sewing Emporium
3918 W First Avenue
Chula Vista, CA 91910
(619) 420-3490
hard-to-find sewing notions, sewing machine
and serger furniture, and books

Sew/Fit Co.
P. O. Box 565
La Grange, IL 60525
1-800-547-4739
sewing notions and accessories; modular tables
for serger/sewing machine set up; books

Treadle Art Magazine
25834 Narbonne Avenue
Lomita, CA 90717
1-800-327-4222
books, specialty threads, creative inspiration

Sewing Machine Companies
(write or call for the dealer nearest you)
Allyn International
1075 Santa Fe Drive
Denver, CO 80204
1-800-525-9987
Necchi brand

Baby Lock U.S.A. (a.k.a. Tacony)
P. O. Box 730
Fenton, MO 63026
(314) 349-3000
Baby Lock and Esante sewing machines and sergers

Bernina of America, Inc.
3500 Thayer Court
Aurora, IL 60504-6182
(708) 978-2500
Bernina and Bernette brands

**Brother International
Corporation**
8 Corporate Place
Piscataway, NJ 08854
(201) 981-0300

Elna, Inc.
7642 Washington Avenue South
Eden Prairie, MN 55344
(612) 941-5519
Elna, Elnita, and ElnaLock brands

J.C. Penney (catalog)
Lincoln Center #3
5430 LBJ Freeway
Dallas, TX 75240-2650
Penney's brand

Juki Industries of America, Inc.
421 North Midland Avenue
Saddle Brook, NJ 07662
(201) 633-7200
Juki Lock brand

Juki (West Coast)
3555 Lomita Boulevard, Suite H
Torrance, CA 90505
Juki Lock brand

New Home Sewing Machine Company
100 Hollister Road
Teterboro, NJ 07608
(201) 440-8080
MyLock, New Home, and Combi models

Pfaff American Sales Corp.
610 Winters Avenue
Paramus, NJ 07653
(201) 262-7211
Pfaff and Hobbylock brands

Riccar America
14281 Franklin Avenue
Tustin, CA 92680
(714) 669-1760
Riccar brand

Sears Roebuck Company
Sears Tower
Chicago, IL 60684
Kenmore brand

Simplicity Sewing Machines
P. O. Box 56
Carlstadt, NJ 07072
Simplicity brand

Singer Sewing Machine Company
200 Metroplex Drive
P. O. Box 1909
Edison, NJ 08818-1909
(908) 287-0707
Singer brand

Viking Sewing Machines
11760 Berea Road
Cleveland, OH 44111
(216) 252-3300
Viking and Huskylock brands

White Sewing Machine Co.
11760 Berea Road
Cleveland, OH 44111
(216) 252-3300
White and Superlock brands

Look for these products and brand names available through your local fabric and craft retailers

CM Offray & Son, Inc.
P. O. Box 601
Chester, NJ 07930
Offray ribbons and woven braid

Coats & Clark
30 Patewood Drive, Suite 351
Greenville, SC 29615
Transparent Nylon Monofilament thread and other quality all-purpose threads; bias tape and hem facing tapes for sewing and crafting

Dritz Corp.
P.O. Box 5028
Spartanburg, SC 29304
Stitch Witchery and Hem-N-Trim paper-backed fusible web, Disappearing Ink Marking Pen, Fray Check, covered buttons, fine interfacings such as Knit Fuze, and hundreds of other sewing and crafting supplies

Handler Textile Corp.
24 Empire Boulevard
Moonachie, NJ 07074
Trans-Web paper-backed fusible web, other fine woven, non-woven, sew-in and fusible interfacings, and fabric stabilizers such as Easy-Stitch

Jones Tones, Inc.
68-743 Perez Road, D-16
Cathedral City, CA 92234
stretchable fabric paint, polyester glitter, iron-on transfers, and other great products for fabric painting and garment embellishment

Pellon Division
Freudenberg Nonwovens
1040 Avenue of the Americas
New York, NY 10018
Wonder Under paper-backed fusible web, Easy-Knit fusible knit interfacing, Stitch 'N Tear fabric stabilizer, and a host of other fusible and sew-in interfacings, and crafting products

Tulip Paints
Polymerics, Inc.
24 Prime Parkway, 4th Floor
Natick, MA 01760
fabric paints and other crafting products

Periodicals

The Creative Machine
Open Chain Publishing, Inc.
P.O. Box 2634-NL
Menlo Park, CA 94026
(415) 366-4440
quarterly, two-color, 48-page newsletter for the sewing machine enthusiast

Creative Needle
1 Apollo Road
Lookout Mountain, GA 30750
(706) 820-2600 or 1-800-443-3127
bimonthly, four-color magazine on heirloom sewing, smocking, and other fine sewing techniques

Serger Update
PJS Publications
News Plaza, Box 1790
Peoria, IL 61656-1790
(309) 682-6626
monthly, two-color, eight-page newsletter for the serging enthusiast

Sew Beautiful
518 Madison St.
Huntsville, AL 35801-4286
(205) 533-9586
quarterly, four-color magazine on heirloom sewing, smocking, and other fine sewing techniques

Sew News
PJS Publications
News Plaza, Box 1790
Peoria, IL 61656-1790
(309) 682-6626
monthly, four-color magazine for the fashion sew-er

Sewing Decor
PJS Publications
News Plaza, Box 1790
Peoria, IL 61656-1790
(309) 682-6626
bimonthly, four-color magazine on home decorating

Sewing Update
PJS Publications
News Plaza, Box 1790
Peoria, IL 61656-1790
(309) 682-6626
quarterly, two-color, eight-page newsletter for the sewing enthusiast

Threads Magazine
The Taunton Press, Inc.
63 S. Main St.
P.O. Box 5506
Newtown, CT 06470-5506
(203) 426-8171
bimonthly, four-color magazine on fine sewing, knitting, weaving, crocheting, and other fiber arts

Subject Index

Skill-Level Index

Serging Techniques (Easy to Advanced)

Sewing Techniques (Moderate to Advanced)

About the Author

After her guest experience at the New York Fashion Institute of Technology in New York City, Jan Saunders graduated with a B.A. in home economics, secondary education, and business from Adrian College, Adrian, Michigan. Saunders has spent the past 21 years sharing her flair for fashion and love for sewing with home sew-ers nationwide.

Formerly the education director of both a major sewing machine company and the largest fabric chain in the United States, this Swiss-trained specialist has handled company public relations, developed marketing plans and educational materials, written teaching curriculums, conducted sales training, and written company newsletters.

In 1980, her first book, *Speed Sewing*, became a Book-of-the-Month selection. Since then she has written the best-selling *Sew, Serge, Press* (Chilton, 1989) and the *Teach Yourself To Sew Better* (Chilton, 1990–1993) four-book series. Look for her regular contributions to *Serger Update, Sewing Update, The Creative Machine Newsletter, Sew News,* and *Threads Magazine*.

Saunders has co-authored two books with Jackie Dodson and they are now writing a *Sew & Serge* series for Chilton. The first two books, called *Pillows, Pillows, Pillows* and *Terrific Textures*, are due out in 1995.

In her spare time, she enjoys sewing for pleasure, sailing, cross-country and downhill skiing, classical music, and spending time with her husband Ted and son Todd.